THE POWER SURGE

THE POWER SURGE

ENERGY, OPPORTUNITY, AND THE
BATTLE FOR AMERICA'S FUTURE

MICHAEL LEVI

A Council on Foreign Relations Book

OXFORD
UNIVERSITY PRESS

OXFORD
UNIVERSITY PRESS

Oxford University Press is a department of the University of Oxford.
It furthers the University's objective of excellence in research, scholarship,
and education by publishing worldwide.

Oxford   New York

Auckland   Cape Town   Dar es Salaam   Hong Kong   Karachi
Kuala Lumpur   Madrid   Melbourne   Mexico City   Nairobi
New Delhi   Shanghai   Taipei   Toronto

With offices in

Argentina   Austria   Brazil   Chile   Czech Republic   France   Greece
Guatemala   Hungary   Italy   Japan   Poland   Portugal   Singapore
South Korea   Switzerland   Thailand   Turkey   Ukraine   Vietnam

Oxford is a registered trademark of Oxford University Press
in the UK and certain other countries.

Published in the United States of America by
Oxford University Press
198 Madison Avenue, New York, NY 10016

Library of Congress Cataloging-in-Publication Data
Levi, Michael A.
The power surge : energy, opportunity, and the battle for America's future / Michael Levi.
pages cm
Includes bibliographical references and index.
ISBN 978–0–19–998616–3 (hardback : alk. paper)   1. Renewable energy—United States.
2. Energy industries—United States.
I. Title.
TJ807.9.U6L48 2013
333.790973—dc23
2012043264

3 5 7 9 8 6 4 2
Printed in the United States of America
on acid-free paper

CONTENTS

1

THE BATTLE FOR THE FUTURE OF AMERICAN ENERGY 1

2

"THE BARBARIANS ARE AT THE DOOR" 20

3

ENERGY INDEPENDENCE ON THE HORIZON 50

4

"GAME OVER" 81

5

THE CAR OF THE FUTURE 109

6

"WIN, WIN, WIN, WIN" 143

7

WILD CARDS 179

8

THE ENERGY OPPORTUNITY 195

Acknowledgments 211

Glossary 213

Notes 217

Index 249

THE BATTLE FOR THE FUTURE
OF AMERICAN ENERGY

"Are you with the pipeline company?"

The question was undoubtedly a recent addition to the young trooper's arsenal. A year earlier, had you asked the officer patrolling State Route 43 outside Carrollton, Ohio, whether people would be crisscrossing his territory in search of oil and gas, he probably would have laughed. The state had its smattering of wells, most left over from booms turned to busts decades earlier, but fossil fuels, like much else in rural Ohio, had long been in decline. The area had briefly become famous the previous October when eighteen tigers, along with a menagerie of other exotic animals, escaped a zoo about seventy miles away and rampaged over the surrounding countryside.[1] Back then, the prospect of an earth-shaking oil boom would have been less plausible than a highway encounter with a cheetah.

Yet change had come fast, which helped explain why the officer, his squad car lights flashing, now found himself suspecting that I was involved in the oil business as he questioned me by the side of the road, having pulled me over for an ill-timed pass. Earlier that afternoon,

I'd donned steel-toed boots, a light blue fire-retardant coat, and plastic safety glasses as I walked toward Neider 10-14-5 5H, a well being drilled by Chesapeake Energy a few miles northeast of Carrollton. The mercury read eighty-nine degrees, but with diesel generators firing and the drill rig operating at full force, it felt like well over a hundred. I'd been given a pair of fluorescent green earplugs to protect myself from the hundred-decibel fury of the operation (think good seats at an intense rock concert), but I pocketed them; I wanted the full sensory experience.

The rig, more than ten stories tall, held a drill that had already bored several thousand feet underground. Now the drill was turning. Slowly, with the operator at a panel of electronic controls and another hefty man who introduced himself as Tar Baby ("first name Tar, last name Baby") watching over his shoulder, the giant machine fed slightly curved pipe down the well. Deep underground, the borehole was beginning to bend, and over the next few days, it would finish a full ninety-degree twist, ending up parallel to the earth's surface but more than six thousand feet down in the heart of the Utica shale. By the time drilling was complete, the well would extend sideways another five thousand feet. Then the rig would move, and a procession of trucks would come in. The well would be pumped full of water, sand, and a proprietary mix of chemicals, and fracked.

If Chesapeake was lucky, the well would spit back much of the water and then start gushing a mix of natural gas and liquids that were similar to oil. John Neider, at fifty-three, would hit the jackpot, too: having leased his farmland to the gas company, he'd be in line for a big royalty check, just like the one he collected when the company successfully drilled its first well on his property barely a year before.[2]

That well was just the third in Ohio to produce natural gas and valuable oil-like liquids from the deep shale. The first had started producing on June 14, 2011, a year to the week before my visit. It initially pumped out 9.5 million cubic feet of natural gas and 1,425 barrels of oil and other liquid fuels every day.[3] Neider's wells didn't quite measure up, but by most industry yardsticks they still scored as a smashing success. So did properties as far away as Texas, Oklahoma, North Dakota, and, just next door, Pennsylvania, all of which were being transformed by an oil and gas revolution that seemed to be sweeping the land.

For decades, most analysts on Wall Street and in Washington (not to mention Houston and Dallas) had been resigned to a long, slow decline for American-produced oil and gas. Now the gush of fossil fuels, not just from shale but from the deep waters of the Gulf Coast, and, beyond the U.S. border, the wilds of northern Canada, was bringing with it ever more excited predictions: billions of dollars in revenues, millions of new jobs, and, because natural gas was replacing coal in power plants across the nation, plummeting emissions of carbon dioxide, which drives climate change. In Youngstown, forty miles north of Carrollton, mills were humming as they churned out steel pipe and machined equipment for wells not only in Ohio but also across the Pennsylvania border to the east. Carrollton itself, like countless other towns across new oil patches now spanning the country, was being buoyed by an influx of drillers who had moved to follow the new jobs. Perhaps the most tantalizing prospect, though, was the one captured in two-foot-tall letters on a Chesapeake billboard by the side of the highway. For forty years, Americans had dreamed of freeing themselves from the shackles imposed by the need to import oil from volatile regions and distasteful dictators. Now, with domestic supplies surging, many were convinced that the goal was within reach. The billboard described the oil and gas boom simply: "The Answer to Foreign Oil."

Not everyone, though, was convinced. Indeed, many were down-right hostile to the developments. Two days before I visited the rig near Carrollton, I'd joined some of the most passionate opponents in Columbus, the state capital, at what its organizers billed as the biggest antifracking gathering ever. Andrew Sidesinger, a thirtysomething soft-ware engineer, brought his three young children; it was how he wanted to spend Father's Day. Warren Huff, a seventy-four-year-old geology professor from the University of Cincinnati, spent the drive down tutoring his van mates on the finer details of energy in general and shale in particular. They were among nearly a thousand people who traveled from every corner of the state, and well beyond its borders, to send a clear message: oil and gas were not the answer to the nation's problems. Indeed, oil and gas only promised to make those problems worse.

Shortly after eleven o'clock in the morning, the group gathered in Arch Park, a narrow strip of green framed by the Nationwide Arena on one end and dominated by the massive office tower of AEP, the largest coal-burning utility in the United States, on the other. As a light rain threatened, volunteers handed out pale blue "Don't Frack Ohio" bandannas. Hand-painted signs revealed a litany of concerns. One read "Drinking H_2O Should Make You Glow But not in the Dark," a nod to worries that fracking was contaminating drinking water. Another, "Eliminate Halliburton Loophole," took aim at a rule that let drillers avoid mandatory disclosure of the fluids they pumped into wells. A third, "This Is Our Land, Not Gas Land," spoke to how the oil and gas boom pitted neighbor against neighbor, tearing communities apart. Interspersed among these expressions of local concern were placards emblazoned with the figure "350," which had become a rallying cry for many who were concerned about climate change; exploiting new oil and gas discoveries, they feared, would make planetary safety impossible.

Josh Fox, a New York filmmaker who made his name with a controversial documentary titled *Gasland*, starkly summed up the stakes, as he saw them, for the crowd: "There's a horizontal wellbore, going down, from somewhere in the gas industry, snaking underneath the Capitol, and injecting money, up through the chamber." The assembled group roared. Drilling across the country for new oil and gas seemed so patently foolish to them—so transparently insane—that only special favors and borderline corruption could explain why anyone would allow it to advance.

But their message wasn't all doom and gloom. After the rally in Arch Park wrapped up, the group marched through the streets of Columbus, eventually gathering inside the rotunda of the Ohio Statehouse. As the thunderous chanting subsided, a series of speakers stood in the center and told their stories. One after another spoke of woes inflicted by oil and gas development, but nearly everyone also spoke of a different future. Jamie Frederick, a Youngstown resident who became painfully ill soon after a well had been drilled on a neighbor's property, begged the crowd to take action: "It's a real shame that we have to come here, in the year 2012, with all the technology for clean, renewable energy that's available, and defend our need for clean air and water." Others evoked similar themes. "I want to expedite the renewable energy future of our country," intoned Stephanie Spear, an energy entrepreneur and organizer, to sustained applause.

One needn't venture far from Columbus to see what that future might look like. Just off State Route 83, a few days later, I found myself passing by an AltraBiofuels ethanol plant; its owners aspired to turn crop waste into fuel. To the west, wind turbines were being built at a record pace: in 2011, capacity in Ohio increased tenfold.[4] Two hundred miles to the east, on the outskirts of Pittsburgh, new manufacturing plants were bending high-end mirrors for massive solar power installations across California and the Southwest. Meanwhile, a similar distance to the north, outside Detroit, the big automakers were steadily introducing ever more efficient cars for American roads. Indeed, as I'd confirm a week later on a closed track at Ford's R&D facilities in Dearborn, Michigan, although electric cars weren't quite ready for a mass market, they were making striking progress. They were also already rather fun to drive.

This pattern wasn't confined to the Midwest. In 2011, while many Americans were transfixed by the boom in oil and gas production, U.S. companies invested nearly as much in new energy technologies such as wind and solar as they did in drilling for fossil fuels. That same year, new power generation from renewable energy surpassed additions from fossil fuels. Meanwhile gains of nearly two hundred thousand barrels a day in U.S. crude production were eclipsed by even bigger declines in U.S. oil consumption—and both trends would intensify in the following year. (At the time, the United States consumed about twenty million barrels of oil every day, and produced slightly over five million.) Money was pouring into clean-energy startups in Silicon Valley, and prices for alternative technologies continued to fall. Here, said opponents of oil and natural gas, was the real way to deliver the jobs, prosperity, environmental protection, and energy security that Americans desired.

Oil and gas enthusiasts, by and large, were as enamored of this vision as those who had rallied in Columbus were about one of plentiful fossil fuels. "Let's be realistic," Rex Tillerson, the CEO of ExxonMobil, warned a room of experts and officials back in 2009.[5]

Clean energy was too new, too expensive, and too unreliable to power the United States, let alone the planet. Someday, perhaps—it was tough to find anyone opposed to that—but the day was a long way off.

The following years did little to shake skeptics' beliefs that new energy technologies weren't ready for prime time; indeed, in many quarters, that view had strengthened. Clean-energy enthusiasts celebrated falling prices, which seemed to be a powerful response to claims that the technologies were too expensive. But the same low prices had helped bankrupt a string of high-profile renewable energy firms, some backed by the federal government, sending a clear message to would-be skeptics that something in the entire business was unsound. The AltraBiofuels facility in Coshocton, Ohio, declared bankruptcy the same day I visited it; the solar manufacturing plant outside Pittsburgh remained only half used. David Kreutzer, an analyst at the Heritage Foundation in Washington, D.C., compared claims that clean energy could create jobs to assertions that bank robbers might stimulate economic growth.[6] In any case, said the skeptics, clean energy remained too expensive. Chevron CEO John Watson, speaking to a Washington audience in late 2011, laid down his bottom line bluntly: "On a per-unit basis, stripped of subsidies, wind, solar and biofuels are simply not cost-competitive with fossil fuels."[7] "Our energy policy is rife with contradictions," he warned.[8] Government efforts to aggressively push clean energy were bound to make little sense—especially when America was blessed with abundant fossil fuels.

Everything we once knew about American energy seems to be changing. Oil imports have fallen for the first time in decades. Natural gas supplies, long in continuous decline, are on the rise. Cars and trucks are delivering extraordinary and often unanticipated gains in fuel efficiency. Wind, solar, and other alternative technologies have seen costs plummet and deployment accelerate like never before. Every one of these trends has the potential to play out not just in the coming years but over the next decade and beyond, and all are being propelled by a mix of technological developments, market dynamics, and political forces that barely registered a decade ago.

Across the nation, people are picking sides. Some are enthusiastic about booming oil and gas production, and deeply skeptical of alternative fuels. Others see renewable energy and advanced cars as the key to the future of U.S. energy and argue that expanded oil and gas production is taking the country down precisely the wrong road. There are, of course, some people, like the CEO of an electric-car battery manufacturer who bragged to me about his new natural gas-fueled vehicle, who see merits in both sides. But among the most passionately engaged, that sort of ambivalence is unusual. Sometimes this is because the two sides disagree about priorities, but more frequently their goals largely coincide: they want economic prosperity, national security, and a cleaner environment for their kids. They just disagree, often vehemently, about what matters most and the best way to deliver it.

These fundamentals of the fight over the future of American energy aren't new. Many of the details are novel, but the roots of the basic conflicts stretch back to the first modern oil crisis, which rocked the world in the autumn of 1973, and its aftermath. It is no exaggeration to claim that most of the battle lines defining today's clashes were first drawn decades ago.

The oil shock that struck on October 16, 1973, came at a time of enormous change and uncertainty for the United States. The Paris Peace Accords, signed in January of that year, had begun to end the Vietnam War, but Americans remained torn by the conflict. The Watergate scandal, which would eventually end Richard Nixon's presidency, was slowly coming to light. In 1971, the United States had abandoned the gold standard, ending the system of global controls on money and investment that had marked the decades since the end of World War II. The economy had already been through recession once that decade, and even before the oil crisis struck, inflation was running at a staggering 11 percent a year.[9] Halfway around the world, a showdown between Israel and its Arab neighbors quickly escalated. Now the Arab oil cartel, unsuccessful five years earlier in cutting the West off from its crude supplies, jacked up prices and slashed shipments to the United States and its allies around the world.

And so another crack had emerged in the foundations of what seemed to be an increasingly unpredictable and dangerous world. Soon Americans found themselves waiting in long lines at gas stations; when they reached the pumps, their reward was record prices for fuel. The economy quickly tipped into recession; it remained in the doldrums for a decade. This was a searing moment for most Americans. There was something deeply wrong with what was going on with oil.

People immediately looked for someone to blame. Western oil companies and the federal government saw the brunt of the opprobrium, but no one, from Saudi sheiks to California environmentalists, escaped the public wrath.[10] President Nixon, desperate to appear in control, announced a bold endeavor: by the end of the decade, the United States would achieve self-sufficiency through a mix of conservation, increased production, and domestic alternatives to oil.

Today that pronouncement is usually recounted as an example of either flimflam or hubris; by 1980, the United States was importing far more oil than in 1973. But despite falling short of Nixon's lofty goals, the system actually did respond. Two lasting changes that would help the United States over the next decade eventually emerged, though neither was without controversy.[11]

The first was the opening of the Trans-Alaskan Pipeline, a ten-billion-dollar, two-million-barrel-a-day behemoth running from Prudhoe Bay on the North Slope of Alaska to the Pacific port of Valdez. The pipeline had been on the table before the energy crisis but stalled in the face of hostility to its construction from environmental and Native American groups. The oil shock quickly broke down the opposition, and on November 16, 1973, Nixon signed broadly supported legislation moving the pipeline forward. By the end of the 1970s, it would allow previously landlocked oil to flow to the lower forty-eight states, reversing the earlier decline in U.S. crude production. American output bottomed out in 1976, and U.S. production would remain above its 1976 level until 1989.

The second battle came a year after the pipeline went into service. American oil consumption was soaring, and legislators were determined to stop that through the first-ever fuel economy standards for cars and light trucks. Automobile companies and their workers were staunchly opposed.[12] Too much conservation, they warned, would saddle Americans with ugly, dangerous vehicles, make U.S. manufacturers uncompetitive, and put legions of people out of jobs. One Ford executive explained to Congress that new standards would "result in a Ford product line consisting either of all sub-Pinto-sized vehicles or some mix of vehicles ranging from sub-sub-compact to perhaps a Maverick," another pint-sized Ford offering.[13] Yet proponents of new standards prevailed. Passed by Congress in 1975, the new rules demanded that new vehicles double their efficiency over the following decade. Together with rising prices for gasoline, these new standards would cause U.S. gasoline consumption to fall beginning in 1978. This trend would eventually reverse, but it would take until 1993 for U.S. gasoline use to reach its previous peak again.

Amid these tactical developments, a more fundamental fight over the future of American energy emerged. It began among experts and officials. "The contention," wrote Allen Hammond in the New York Times, "is not just over specific elements of technology. The two sides differ over whether energy salvation lies in conservation or expanded production; in renewable or depletable energy resources; and in small-scale, decentralized energy sources or in large, centralized systems."[14]

The apparent tension was crystallized in a 1976 essay that, as the Atlantic Monthly later observed, would "become something of a focal point for the debate over national energy plans."[15] Its author was Amory Lovins, then a twenty-nine-year-old staffer at the environmental group Friends of the Earth, and his article, published in the journal Foreign Affairs, was titled "Energy Strategy: The Road Not Taken?"[16] Lovins laid out two options. The "hard energy path," on which he argued that the United States was embarking, featured ever-rising energy consumption, drawn particularly from coal and nuclear power, along with no meaningful role for alternative fuels. The "soft energy path," in contrast, would see U.S. energy consumption deliberately peak and then decline, with "soft technologies"—solar power, biofuels, wind energy, and the like—delivering an increasing share of the remaining needs. The result, he argued, would be benefits to the U.S. economy, national security, and the environment; the opposite course would risk disaster on all fronts.

Lovins and his acolytes did not just claim that the soft energy path was better than the hard one; they insisted that the United States faced a stark choice. Introducing a concept that would later become a touchpoint for advocates of another energy transformation, Lovins warned of lock-in: "Because commitment to the [hard path] may foreclose the [soft path], we must soon choose one or the other." The country, the *Atlantic Monthly* explained, "lacks the material and spiritual resources to follow both."

On this point, his critics were largely in agreement. Those firms responsible for the bulk of the existing energy system warned that rapid transformation was unrealistic. In one ad in the *New York Times*, Mobil cautioned against pushing too hard and fast on alternative energy: "You can't make a baby in a month," they explained, "by making nine women pregnant."[17] Exxon, then as now the largest oil company in the country, took out ads in the *New York Times*, *Newsweek*, and elsewhere: "EXXON ANSWERS QUESTIONS ABOUT ONE OF THE NEWEST ENERGY SOURCES UNDER THE SUN—THE SUN!" read one headline.[18] Many people didn't like the ads' answers. Senator Gary Hart and Representative Richard Ottinger would write to Exxon, asserting that it had "misinformed the public" with advertisements "riddled with inaccurate statistics and pessimistic projections about solar power." The oil company, which had invested substantially in solar itself, naturally disagreed.[19]

The two sides in the battle—one favoring traditional fossil fuels (often along with nuclear), the other emphasizing conservation and alternatives—were not the only elements having parallels today. Much about the world in which the energy debates were unfolding was similar, too. Then as now, Americans were searching simultaneously for footings on multiple fronts. A changing economy—the 1970s saw the first real wave of postwar globalization—forced Americans to rethink how they would live. A shifting security landscape—then, Vietnam and the apparent resurgence of the Soviet Union; today, terrorism, instability in the Middle East, and the rise of China—made them question their role in the world. New environmental threats also figured prominently: a massive oil spill off the coast of Santa Barbara galvanized the environmental movement in 1969, and the 1972 book *The Limits to Growth*, which would sell millions of copies, warned that the world would quickly run out of natural resources unless something changed. It would have been tough enough to cope with a rapidly shifting energy scene. Doing it amidst such sweeping change and uncertainty made the task far more difficult.

The battle reached its peak in the 1980 presidential race between Jimmy Carter and Ronald Reagan. Hans Landsberg, writing for the *New York Times* less than a month before the election, captured what was happening. "For the last few years," he wrote, "this country ostensibly has debated energy policy but in reality has been engaged in a fierce, prolonged bout of soul-searching." Energy was no longer being discussed on its own merits but was now symbolic: "It can be argued that energy was tailor-made to become the arena for the clash of opinions that, to be sure, are related to energy but for which energy is at best a proxy."[20]

Landsberg, then an economist at a think tank named Resources for the Future, was trying to play the straight man in this debate. But its most strident participants were nowhere close to being ready to agree with each other. David Stockman, who would become the budget director responsible for ushering in Reagan's supply-side revolution (before turning apostate in the face of staggering budget deficits), wrote the energy plank of the Republican platform that year. In his memoir, he spared few words. The energy plan, he wrote, was the part of Reagan's platform "that most clearly manifested an anti-statist breakthrough." "The Carter Soviet-like 'Gosplan,'" he continued, "was then reaching its final absurdity":[21]

> The "moral equivalent of war" [a term that Carter had used to describe the energy crisis] and its attendant issues was really a front for state control of resources and the economy.... The current glut of oil on the world market [Stockman was writing in 1986] is eloquent refutation of how idiotic their position was, but at the time they were prosecuting their views with a determination befitting the smallness of their minds. The New Deal had given birth to the statist impulse; during the Great Society it had gathered momentum; with the "Era of Limits" it had become an imperative.[22]

Reagan himself would put it more pithily: "Our problem isn't a shortage of fuel," he explained. "It's a surplus of government."[23] Sliding the energy fight into his broader appeal to the American people, he observed that "Mr. Carter has led us to believe that there is an acute shortage of energy resources in this country," explaining that "the truth is, America has an abundance of energy."[24] Perhaps this was based on a detailed assessment of U.S. resources (the campaign regularly cited statistics for U.S. reserves of oil, gas, and coal), though Reagan's frequent claim—firmly detached from reality—that Alaska held more oil than Saudi Arabia suggested something else was at work, too. The Gipper had no plans to don a sweater and turn down his thermostat. Four years before "Morning in America," the intended contrast between optimism and pessimism was clear.

Some of Reagan's description of his opponents was caricature, but much of it was on target, particularly when it came to the left wing of the Democratic party, which did not trust markets much. Ted Kennedy, the liberal standard bearer in the 1980 Democratic primary, "proposed an energy program based on massive conservation, renewable resources, limited synthetic fuel production and Federal funds for [switching oil-fired power plants to run on coal]."[25] He called for "new controls on oil prices…to protect the poor and average income consumer," "gasoline rationing," and "a moritorium [sic] on the construction and operation of nuclear power plants."[26] Behind this, in part, was an argument about equity: the Carter administration, a Kennedy pamphlet charged, had "created a scale of unequal sacrifice based on unfair prices that would bring hardship to ordinary people."[27] The Kennedy plan also had roots in distrust of big business, something most Americans shared, at least when oil companies were concerned. And, across the left, there remained confidence in the ability of government to solve problems. As the election returns ultimately showed, in the decade of Watergate and stagflation, this was not a popular view.

Here the basic ingredients of the present fight over the future of American energy were already in place. Some saw salvation in abundant supplies of fossil fuels; others feared scarcity, and barring that, environmental destruction if plentiful resources were developed. Those who were suspicious of fossil fuels threw in their lot with alternative energy; those who saw vast potential in oil, gas, and coal saw little need or market for novel sources of power. Permeating this apparent fight over fuels was a second, more fundamental, battle over the relationship between Americans and their government. Some saw salvation in getting Washington out of the energy business and counting mostly on markets to deliver. Others insisted just as ardently that confronting massive economic, security, and environmental challenges meant the federal government would need to play a far more central role. A national survey in 1977 asked Americans whether they wanted some government involvement in boosting energy production and curbing energy consumption or whether the task should be left to private companies and individuals. The split was sharp: "Half of [Americans] favored a government program, while 41 percent felt things should be left to private companies and the public."[28]

The 1980 election was a landslide: Reagan won, carrying forty-four of fifty states. Following his inauguration in January 1981, energy quickly receded from view. As Reagan was being sworn in, the leaders of the Iranian revolution released the fifty-two American hostages they'd held for 444 days. The price of imported oil, which had nearly tripled over the previous two years, would soon peak and begin a steady fall.[29] Meanwhile, the new president quickly set to work on a far broader agenda, targeting the federal tax code, the size and scope of government, and the American role in the world.

The two decades that followed were largely ones of relative calm in the American energy world. Oil prices crashed in 1986 and then flattened; with the exception of the months surrounding the first Gulf War in 1991, they held fairly steady at levels not much higher than they had been before the 1973 crisis. Natural gas, coal, and electricity followed similarly benign paths. OPEC, the geopolitical power behind the first energy crisis, fell into disarray, unable to sort out its internal squabbles and thus incapable of threatening the world. Public attention to energy waned, and with it so did the pitched battles of the 1970s. In 1985, when the first round of fuel economy standards ended, Washington chose not to push farther. Around the same time, saddled with low crude prices and declining reserves, U.S. oil production began an apparently interminable decline. Meanwhile, U.S. energy consumption rose, and with it so did the demand for fossil fuels. The Reagan administration, skeptical of government meddling in the economy, shut down or starved alternative energy programs that had begun the decade before. There was no official energy policy, since this would mean state involvement in markets.[30]

In 1986, Secretary of Energy John S. Herrington concluded in a *New York Times* op-ed that the market-focused energy policy approach of the administration had succeeded. "If the energy story of the last five years tells us anything," he wrote, "it is that market-oriented energy policies are the answer to our nation's energy-security needs."[31] Many critics would later argue that this laissez-faire attitude had led to future economic and security crises, not thwarted them. But, at least at the time, these opponents seemed to have little to stand on: the country appeared not to suffer from its hands-off approach to energy.

Environmental advocates spent the decade focused elsewhere. Rather than fight over abstract and long-term energy issues, green groups focused on the most visible challenge at the time: pollution and its damaging effects on public health. Efforts to stem water pollution, halt toxic waste dumping, and regulate substances that damaged the ozone layer all began during the 1980s. Government controls on pollution had become so accepted by the 1988 presidential election that George H. W. Bush ran an attack ad against Michael Dukakis charging that the Massachusetts governor had not done enough to clean up Boston Harbor.[32] When Bush took office, he appointed William Reilly, then head of the World Wildlife Fund, to run the Environmental Protection Agency.

Then, on August 2, 1990, Saddam Hussein began marching troops into Kuwait. By October, with the Iraqi president threatening the oil-fields of neighboring Saudi Arabia, crude prices had doubled. The United States began to mobilize an international response. Suddenly energy was back at the center of American life. But the Gulf War, fought between January 17 and February 28, 1991, ended in a rout for the United States. Oil prices quickly returned to prior lows and mostly remained there for the rest of the decade. Little happened to U.S. energy strategy. Both sides in the old energy fights offered warmed-over versions of their previous platforms—stricter fuel economy rules and alternative fuels on the left, new drilling in Alaska on the right—and both largely failed.[33] The best-known legacy of the Energy Policy Act of 1992 may have been its mandate for low-flush toilets, much to the chagrin of those energy experts who remember it for introducing renewable energy tax credits.

The next year, global warming rose to major public prominence, as the United States signed up to the first big international climate agreement at the Earth Summit in Rio de Janeiro, Brazil. Yet little came of that thin convention during the next decade. During the eight years of the Clinton administration, energy remained a third-tier issue. In 1993, the president attempted to pass a "BTU tax" that would have taxed consumption of fossil fuels. He lost in a bloodbath—the experience was credited with a big role in the Democrats' drubbing at the polls the next November—and after that he shied away from major confrontation on energy. With energy cheap, the economy humming, and local pollution on the decline, Americans and their political leaders had other things they preferred to focus on.

The two decades following the intense energy battles of the 1970s revealed both sides as better at tearing down their adversaries than at boosting their own positive agendas. Skeptics of mandated conservation and efficiency tasted victory in 1985 when new fuel economy standards for cars and trucks, deemed expensive, unnecessary, and dangerous, were shelved. Opponents of nuclear power successfully mobilized public fear following the Three Mile Island meltdown in 1979, which, together with rising costs, put the U.S. nuclear industry largely out of business. Adversaries of offshore oil drilling, buoyed by the *Exxon Valdez* disaster in 1989, sought and delivered a ban on new exploration and production off U.S. coasts. Supporters of small government and skeptics of alternative fuels nearly dismantled the Department of Energy and succeeded in starving it of cash. During the 1990s, climate change rose to join the pantheon of previously contested energy issues, yet once again opponents of action—this time by an overwhelming ninety-five to zero vote in Congress that preemptively rejected the Kyoto Protocol and, more importantly, set the tone for domestic U.S. climate policy—made sure that little if anything would be done.

The first years of the twenty-first century would challenge the stasis quickly. National security was the first concern to thrust energy back into the spotlight. On September 11, 2001, two airplanes struck the

World Trade Center, another smashed into the Pentagon, and a fourth crashed into a Pennsylvania field on its way to the White House. The most destructive terrorist attacks in history prompted many Americans to turn their minds to energy. Fifteen of the nineteen attackers were Saudi Arabian nationals, and Riyadh remained the world capital of oil. Washington and the nation began talking in earnest about the continuing dangers of dependence on oil.

Four years later, environmental concerns vaulted to the core of the energy agenda. On the morning of August 29, 2005, Hurricane Katrina struck land over southeast Louisiana. Later the same day, the levees that were supposed to shield New Orleans from the ocean broke, devastating the city, forcing more than a million residents to evacuate, and killing well over a thousand residents. People were quick to draw connections to climate change: scientists couldn't say that global warming had caused the hurricane, but with mounting emissions of carbon dioxide from the burning of coal, oil, and natural gas, uglier weather appeared to be in store.

Then, in 2008, those concerns were joined by economic ones. When the world celebrated the beginning of a new millennium on December 31, 1999, a barrel of oil cost barely more than twenty-five dollars. Beginning in 2002, though, crude prices began a steady march upward, ultimately breaching $145 on July 14, 2008. Markets would eventually crash in September of that year, when Lehman Brothers declared bankruptcy, ushering in the worst of the Great Recession. But the U.S. economy had already begun to contract in late 2007. The housing market was front and center in the explanation, but many people, including some prominent economists, blamed the rapidly rising cost of oil.

Energy was back at center stage. So was the classic trio of concerns—economics, security, and environment—and the old debates and divisions over what to do. Yet the world has changed dramatically since the battle lines were set in the 1970s. The U.S. economy is now twice as large as it was four decades ago, yet improved efficiency means the average American uses less energy than she did then.[34] The Cold War is over: no longer must the United States worry that the Soviet Union might invade the Persian Gulf, dominating global oil resources and denying them to the free world. Climate change was barely a blip on scientists' radars in the 1970s; today, with the accumulation of four decades of evidence, it has become a top-tier concern in much of the world. Meanwhile, the balance of global economic power, once firmly anchored in the West, is steadily shifting to the East as billions emerge from poverty to modern life. China endured much of the 1970s in the isolation of the Cultural Revolution, which began to genuinely subside only following the death of Mao Zedong in 1976; indeed, wholesale reform of the Chinese system did not commence until 1979. Chinese GDP never exceeded 1 percent of the global economy during that decade. Today, its share is ten times as large, a figure that only continues to rise.

By the time the financial crisis hit in 2008, the energy world had also changed enormously. Oil was a major source of electricity in 1973, but by 2008 its share had fallen below 1 percent. Coal-fired power steadily declined from 1956 through the early 1970s, but in the wake of the oil crisis the trend reversed. By 1980, coal yielded more than half of U.S. electricity supplies; it would stay above that threshold through 2004. Nuclear power, a fringe source of U.S. electricity in 1970, topped 20 percent by 1992 and retained its share afterward.

Renewable energy, once at the fringe, would also grow steadily if not as strongly, even before its steep ascent over the past few years. Power from wind and solar in the 1970s was so minuscule that the U.S. government did not start reporting statistics of their use until 1984. That year, the two would combine to deliver less than 0.0005 percent of the U.S. electricity supply. By 2008, though, their contribution would rise by a factor of nearly three thousand, breaking the 1 percent threshold for the first time. Ethanol, relegated to the sidelines ever since Henry Ford decided to go with more abundant gasoline for his Model T, began to crawl back out of obscurity in the late 1970s. At first, it was adopted as a replacement for lead, promising to improve engine performance with no damaging consequences for public health. Eventually, farmers and policymakers seized on it as a potential replacement for oil, and the U.S. government started to subsidize its growth. Output would ultimately rise nearly fortyfold between 1980 and 2007.[35]

The U.S. oil scene did not stand still either. In 1973, when the first oil crisis hit, the United States was importing barely more than three million barrels of oil a day. By 2004, U.S. imports topped ten million daily barrels, and Canada and Mexico had emerged as major suppliers. Beginning in 1975, the United States developed Strategic Petroleum Reserves, massive stockpiles of oil designed to help the country ride out any supply cutoff, and flexible global markets had emerged in the place of previously rigid systems for allocating crude. The U.S. automobile sector made big leaps, too: efficient cars, once purely the province of Japanese and European manufacturers, were increasingly being built in Detroit.

❉ ❉ ❉

Yet the political battle lines barely shifted. They remain the same today and consistently lead the same outcome: a battle between enthusiasts for promoting traditional fuels and supporters of a new energy path— and, often, a more fundamental accompanying fight over the right role for government in American society. Just as they did in the 1970s, Americans appear to face a stark choice. Though proponents of each path agree on little else, they largely concur that the nation must now decide firmly one way or the other.

This view is mistaken. The world has changed fundamentally since the battle lines in the fight over American energy were first set. It is no doubt possible to push too hard on any particular energy source: to expand oil and gas production so blindly and rapidly that it entails massive environmental damage outweighing any economic, security, or (for natural gas) climate gains, or to push so quickly into new cars and trucks and alternative energy that the economic costs overwhelm any economic, security, or climate benefits. But the fact that there are wrong ways to pursue each energy source does not mean there aren't opportunities to gain from all of them. The United States can strengthen its economy, improve its national security, and confront climate change if it intelligently embraces the historic gains unfolding all across the energy landscape.

To see why and how, we need to dive deep into the transformations sweeping American energy. It's useful to keep three questions in mind as we do so. Does each energy source that has recently thrived offer important opportunities to improve the U.S. economy, strengthen national security, or mitigate climate change while not causing intolerable damage on any of those fronts? Is it possible to seize those opportunities simultaneously—or would pursuing some of them severely undermine the others? And can the United States take advantage of these opportunities without fundamentally altering the role of government in American society?

If the answer to any of these questions is no, then there is indeed a fundamental choice between the two unfolding energy revolutions, and Americans should commit decisively to one or the other. But if the answer to all of the questions is yes, then the United States should be wisely embracing energy opportunities across the board.

Either way, big changes are in store. Massive shifts in everything from clean energy to oil and gas are leading to far-reaching consequences for the U.S. economy, the environment, and America's role in the world. There's no better way to start seeing how than by returning to the fight over fracking in Ohio.

"THE BARBARIANS ARE AT THE DOOR"

I'd been watching Warren Taylor and Bill Dix have at it for nearly an hour when the rain started to come down. But that didn't stop either of them. Dix, in his sixties with a tanned face weathered by decades on the land, wore dirty jeans, a Red Bull t-shirt, and a muddy green cap over his balding hair. He sipped on a grapefruit soda and spit chew as we talked. Or, more precisely, as I listened. Dix was on a roll, and when that happened, you didn't get in his way.

Twenty years had passed since Bill Dix and his wife, Stacy, started raising Jersey heifers to make milk on this patch of southern Ohio land. Recently, though, the sleepy community had woken up. The rumors started in earnest the past autumn when landmen from out of state swooped into Athens County and started offering cash in exchange for the right to drill for oil and gas. A few years earlier, another natural gas rush had grazed this patch of southern Ohio. In neighboring Pennsylvania, drillers had tapped into the Marcellus shale, bringing forth billions of cubic feet of fuel. A few unsuccessful wells were drilled on the Ohio side of the border too. Just north of town, beside the highway, a sign offering financial planning to people with new gas wealth remained.

This time was different. Hopes and fears were both higher. The target was the Utica shale, a layer of deep underground rock formed some hundred million years before the Marcellus. By now Athens residents had already seen the intense battles break out across the border to their east. Many Pennsylvanians embraced the drillers as their economic salvation in a tough time. Others cursed them for tearing apart communities and, they said, for bringing environmental ruin.

Dix was all for letting the drillers in. Many opponents, he had concluded, were hypocrites, happy to profit when their pension funds invested in ExxonMobil and Chesapeake but unwilling to accept gas development in their own backyard. But it wasn't just what he saw as a double standard from those worried about the local environment that rankled; it was what he thought natural gas could do for the community. "They're worried about the Athens way of life, when the barbarians are at the door," he excitedly warned with a hint of a smile on his face. "The rural men aren't workin'. The kids don't have fathers. There's heroin. The barbarians are at the fuckin' gate. And you're worryin' about havin' to see fuckin' oil rigs when you're takin' your fuckin' Sunday night drive?" The rhythm in his voice was almost hypnotic. "Excuse me," he added.

Half an hour earlier, I'd been talking to Warren Taylor, a sixty-one-year-old man with more energy than most people half his age, when Dix drove up and joined the conversation. Taylor, wire-thin with close-cropped hair, sported a long-sleeved white t-shirt; he would have fit right in in Northern California, where he had lived a good part of his life. Today he was the proprietor of Snowville Creamery, a four-year-old operation that promised "milk the way it used to be" and was one of the more vocal area opponents of natural gas development. Dix, who had lived around Athens his whole life, rented Snowville its property and sold the creamery its milk. The two friends, who shared a stretch of land not far from the West Virginia border, were clearly used to sparring.

Their disagreement didn't fit into neat lines. "I'm a far leftist, is where I'm coming from," explained Dix, whose views on everything from capitalism to Karl Marx confirmed that. Then he launched into a spirited defense of private property rights, particularly his right to lease his land

to gas drillers. Nor was Taylor, whom I had first seen the previous day
sermonizing at the rally in Columbus, a Luddite who just wanted technology to go away. A few minutes spent listening to him extol the virtues
of the latest milk-processing equipment and marveling at his cutting-
edge creamery were enough to dispel that suspicion.

"My parents bought woodland property down here in the early
1960s," Taylor recalled. "Beautiful, not a virgin forest, but a damaged
World War II vet had moved onto it in 1945 and hadn't allowed any
logging since. So by the 1960s, unlike most places around here, where
they're constantly being logged for a little pittance, this was a beautiful
woods." Later, after living in California, Taylor moved back to the area.
"The farm adjacent to the property my parents bought, I bought a year
after I moved here, and its corn bottom had won a blue ribbon at the
Meigs County Fair as the finest corn bottom in the county. Two years
later the neighbor strip-mined his place, and the runoff from those high
walls destroyed that corn bottom that was the basis of the profitability
of a six-hundred-and-forty-acre farm." Taylor could barely contain his
emotion. "After we moved here and bought the place, a guy did a PhD
in geology from Ohio State University examining that exact place and
concluded that it would be a thousand years before it would return to
being what it had been. Now you do the economic analysis for me on
a thousand years of corn versus one year of coal." He recounted one
more tale of pollution for which no one had been punished. "Now,"
Taylor said, his face red with anger and not far away from mine, "do
you understand my perspective about fracking?"

Shale gas came fast, transforming communities that had long been
set in their ways. Only a few years earlier, high and volatile natural gas
prices seemed inevitable.[1] People speak about natural gas in terms of
thousands of cubic feet: the United States uses about seventy million
thousand cubic feet each day, and the typical household uses about seventy thousand cubic feet each year.[2] After averaging about two dollars
for a thousand cubic feet of natural gas during the 1990s, prices began
an upward climb. The first peak, in early 2001, reached nine dollars;
after quickly crashing, prices started heading up again, reaching a staggering fourteen dollars in late 2005. Then the cycle repeated, with prices
sliced in half a few months later before bouncing back close to their

historic highs by June 2008. In one year, Americans might collectively be spending forty billion dollars on natural gas; the next, their total bill could easily come to five times that.

But then something happened that surprised most market watchers: after prices fell sharply through late 2009—a development people anticipated, given the deep recession that had hit the country—they never recovered. Analysts repeatedly revised their projections downward. First they predicted five dollar natural gas; then, by 2010, they were forecasting prices of four dollars for a thousand cubic feet. By late 2011, even those projections seemed dated, with natural gas below three dollars an apparent reality. Something fundamental had changed.

Natural gas production in the United States was booming.[3] Flat for about a decade through 2006, output suddenly took off in 2007, rising 14 percent by 2010. The United States hadn't witnessed growth like that since the 1960s, which marked the tail end of a twenty-year boom following World War II sparked by the introduction of inexpensive long-distance natural gas pipelines. And this didn't seem like a flash in the pan: by early 2012, U.S. government analysts were projecting steady increases in natural gas production, and relatively low prices, for decades to come.[4]

Most of the U.S. natural gas industry had evolved pretty much as expected.[5] Traditional onshore production from simple vertical wells had been in decline for decades, and offshore output peaked around the turn of the century. Production from coalbed methane, in which drillers extracted natural gas from seams in underground coal deposits, remained small and pretty much flat. Something called tight gas—natural gas trapped in dense formations that made it difficult for the gas to flow—had been on the rise a few years back, but production leveled off. There was only one source that could explain what was happening: natural gas from shale.

The breakthrough had come about ten years earlier. It combined two well-worn techniques. The first was horizontal drilling, which allowed developers to drill down before turning ninety degrees and then drilling a mile or more sideways. That was particularly valuable for getting at shale gas, which is found deep underground in thin layers; by drilling horizontally, a well could be placed through a big slice of gas. Horizontal drilling had been around since 1929 but didn't really take off until the 1980s, when the French firm Elf Aquitaine demonstrated its commercial promise in southwest France and off the Mediterranean shores of Italy.[6] The second technology, hydraulic fracturing, was introduced into commercial practice by Stanolind Oil and Gas in 1947 at the Hugoton field in Grant County, Kansas.[7] Similar techniques were used in the early days of oil—back in the 1860s, drillers used liquid nitroglycerin to coax oil out of rock from New York to Kentucky—but that approach was dangerous and never became particularly widespread. By 1949, Stanolind had a patent (and Halliburton secured an exclusive license) on the new process that shot water, chemicals, and other materials deep underground to break apart rock and help oil and gas flow.[8]

Geologists had long known that there was a massive amount of natural gas trapped in shale rock formations. It took a stroke of innovative genius, though, to tap into it. In the 1980s, George Mitchell, a Texas entrepreneur, began to experiment with combinations of horizontal drilling to span the deep shale with hydraulic fracturing to release natural gas within it; by the late 1990s, his engineers had made the essential commercial breakthroughs. Yet as recently as 2009, you couldn't even find the words "shale gas" in the annual U.S. government energy outlook.[9] By 2012, the document was reporting that nearly a quarter of U.S. natural gas production had come from shale in 2010, a number it projected would jump to half of U.S. production by 2035.[10] Prices would rise moderately over that period—government forecasters figured five or six dollars for a thousand cubic feet of natural gas by 2020 seemed reasonable, and most Wall Street analysts pretty much agreed—but natural gas appeared destined to be abundant and relatively cheap.

The sudden change set off debates across the country. "What's happening with unconventional natural gas," said John Deutch in 2011, "is the biggest energy story that's happened in the 40-plus years that I've been watching energy development in this country."[11] That was a big statement from someone who had watched from some pretty high places, including as deputy defense secretary, undersecretary of energy, and head of the CIA. Many pundits soon began speaking of natural gas as the country's economic savior and about geopolitical consequences that would reverberate throughout the world.

Not everyone, though, was enthused. Geologists fought over how much natural gas could really be extracted from the ground. Neighbors argued over whether the jobs and money that industry brought were outweighed by the environmental risks and community disruption that happened when gas drillers started moving their trucks into town and when some people got rich quick while others didn't. Economists debated precisely how transformative gas might be for the national economy, while strategists sparred over exactly what the boom in gas production might mean for U.S. national security. Others warned that cheap gas would kill renewable power, and along with it any hope of confronting climate change. One thing was for certain: shale gas challenged almost every assumption that had been made only a few years before. As Bill Dix put it, recalling the iconic 1980s TV show, "It's Dallas!" He was enjoying the change of pace. "I've been milking cows for twenty years, man. I'm bored!"

❦ ❦ ❦

Shale gas was shaking up the U.S. economy. It's usually difficult to figure out how much credit to give any particular development for a big gain in jobs. Most economists would say that when the economy is working properly, it doesn't even make much sense to try. They call this "full employment," and it means that, most of the time, the unemployment rate in the country is basically fixed. The number is a consequence of basic factors including how many people are able and want to work, how flexible they are when it comes to switching jobs, and what the Federal Reserve in Washington does with interest rates; add a job in one industry, theory says, and you'll ultimately find someone out of work in another.[12] But when the economy is in the dumps, and the unemployment rate is abnormally high, the usual rules don't apply: new jobs are much more of an unalloyed good, and jobs added in one part of the economy don't clearly come at the expense of others. When the shale gas boom took off, around 2009, there was no question that the U.S. economy was in awfully poor health.

The shale boom had another feature that made it relatively easy to pin down its impact: it came out of nowhere. People studying the problem knew that employment in the sector would have been nonexistent without the boom. Most anything they saw, then, counted as new employment.

In 2011, researchers at the respected consultancy IHS Global Insight used those fundamentals to estimate how many people had gotten jobs because of the shale boom.[13] They looked at how many wells were drilled and how many people were needed for each well. Putting the pieces together, they found that nearly 150,000 people were employed in the industry in 2010. They estimated that the number could climb to 250,000 by 2020 as production from shale gas rose.

But the economic consequences went further. In Youngstown, Ohio, I met Becky Dearing, a co-owner of the Dearing Compressor & Pump Company. Dearing was in her late forties with shoulder-length brown hair. Her desk was littered with papers, including an application from someone looking for a job; on the other side of the room, two big maps of the area's shale deposits hung on the wall. The company had been around since 1945, which meant it had seen its share of booms and busts. Coal came first, then steel, then the oil boom of the 1970s followed by the 1980s bust. Now Dearing was riding the shale gas wave. The company supplied equipment that the drilling companies used to produce gas and to move gas through the pipeline system to customers. Its clients had drilled some of the first test wells in Pennsylvania in 2008. Now a combination of good timing, luck, and a willingness to bet on shale gas was paying off. While its neighbors were shuttering during the worst economic crisis since the Great Depression, Dearing built an entire new manufacturing plant on the back of shale-related demand. "We went from 60 to 160 [people] in a year and a half," said Dearing; three years before that, they'd employed only 30.

The IHS people figured into their calculations the fact that people were getting jobs supplying the shale gas industry. It's called indirect employment, and it includes everything from steel makers to drillsite caterers to companies producing the chemicals that go down the wells. The analysts estimated that another 190,000 jobs of this sort had been created by 2010 and that the number might rise to 370,000 by 2020.[14] They also included another category, called induced employment, which counts up all the jobs that are marginally related to the gas industry, from hoteliers who rent rooms to drillers to retailers who sell them their boots. Counting such jobs is particularly controversial. Some undoubtedly are new—there are hotels opening up where none existed before—but some surely would exist without fracking, even if people remained unemployed. (People who don't have jobs need to eat and occasionally buy shoes too.) In any case, when the IHS people added jobs of this kind into the mix, they came out with a staggering number: shale gas had already added six hundred thousand jobs to the economy by 2010. A month later, President Barack Obama cited that figure in his State of the Union address. The number, IHS estimated, could grow to more than a million by the end of the decade.[15]

The analysts also figured that, whatever shale gas did for jobs, development would add to American wealth. This was far less controversial than the estimates about jobs. Finding gold underground makes people rich, and so does finding natural gas. The trick is to take into account the cost of extracting the resource: little money can be made drawing natural gas out of the ground unless the gas can be sold for more than it costs to produce. Factoring this into their estimates, the IHS analysts came out with a big number: by 2020, shale gas could add $150 billion to U.S. GDP, about 1 percent of the U.S. economy, which totals about $15 trillion.

For shale gas enthusiasts, though, this was far from the end of the story. Americans wouldn't just make money extracting natural gas; they'd also profit from using it. Fifty miles east of Carrollton, where I visited the Chesapeake drill site, Shell had announced plans to build an ethane cracker. Shale gas is a mix of chemicals. The most abundant one, methane, is the bulk of what gets burned in power plants and in stoves and heaters at home. But natural gas comes up with a host of slightly heavier molecules, known collectively as natural gas liquids (NGLs); ethane, propane, and butane are the most common. Ethane is particularly useful to petrochemical producers. They send it through multibillion-dollar plants called crackers to make a chemical called ethylene, a core building block for everything from plastic bowls to fleece sweaters to car doors. The only other way to make ethylene—the method that Europeans and Asians depend on—is to use naphtha, which is produced when oil is processed in a petroleum refinery. With oil prices far exceeding those for natural gas, U.S. producers grabbed a massive cost advantage, and it looked as if it wouldn't disappear any time soon.

How big of an edge could this deliver? The American Chemistry Council, which lobbies for the chemicals industry, claimed in 2011 that a sustained natural gas boom could support more than four hundred thousand jobs in the chemicals industry and its suppliers, $32.8 billion in new chemicals sales, and $132 billion in boosted U.S. GDP.[16] Numbers of this kind are over the top; they include not only the ethylene made from ethane but also the plastic bowls and fleece sweaters where the ethylene ultimately ends up. (There's no reason to believe that U.S. production of such final products will change much.) Indeed the entire global ethylene market totals somewhere just around two hundred billion dollars—and a handful of other producers, most prominently Qatar and Saudi Arabia, still have far lower costs than the United States, because their natural gas remains cheaper to produce.[17] The bottom line, though, remains: the U.S. chemicals industry is poised for big gains.

Other industries using a lot of energy have also become targets of speculation about potential expansion. Steel production, cement manufacturing, and aluminum and glass making consume massive amounts of fuel; cheaper natural gas means companies can cut their costs, and perhaps undercut their overseas competition. But it's tricky to figure out how much these areas are actually gaining from low natural gas prices. Steel and cement makers benefit because gas producers buy a lot of their products—about a fifth of the material used to build a well is steel, and about a tenth is cement—and the fact that shale gas helps them probably has more to do with this boost in demand than with any decline in their costs.[18] Cheap gas could help slow the decline in some of these U.S. industries—low-cost natural gas makes it easier to continue to operate existing plants—but substantial growth due to low fuel prices is unlikely.[19]

Low natural gas prices have also helped consumers, many of whom were strapped for cash in the wake of a recession. This in turn helped the economy (and will continue to help it so long as the economy is weak). Figuring out the extent of this impact is tricky, since it requires making guesses about how high natural gas prices would have been without the shale gas boom, and about whether gas distribution companies and electric power producers pass on natural gas cost savings to consumers. Crude estimates, though, suggest that Americans may be saving between twenty and forty billion dollars a year on natural gas.[20] When they spend those savings, the economic impact is multiplied, perhaps totaling north of fifty billion dollars every year.

All the contributions from natural gas could collectively add up to hundreds of billions of dollars annually without much of a stretch. Those are big numbers, but, topping out at a percentage point or two of the U.S. economy, they're not revolutionary. People who claim that natural gas will spark a broad-based U.S. economic renaissance, if only pesky environmentalists and other concerned citizens lay off, are exaggerating the benefits of the shale gas bonanza. But one needn't exaggerate on this front to conclude that shale gas is a big deal. Indeed, the potential consequences go well beyond economics.

❧ ❧ ❧

On January 1, 2009, revelers in Europe woke up to a rude surprise. For weeks, Russia and Ukraine had been locked in an esoteric fight over the price of natural gas. Most of the world lacks true markets for the fuel, which makes negotiations over contracts to buy and sell natural gas an inevitably complicated process. In the case of Russian sales to Ukraine, the discussions also took on an intense political cast: the former Soviet satellite had long enjoyed cut-rate prices from Moscow and good relations with its former imperial master. Both, though, appeared to be a thing of the past. With negotiations going nowhere, Russia decided it was time to use a trump card. It cut off Ukraine's supplies of natural gas.[21]

Within days the crisis spread to Europe. Much of the continent depended on Russia for its gas, and a substantial portion could be delivered only through pipelines that crossed Ukraine. Soon Bulgaria, Hungary, Poland, and Romania were reporting shortfalls in their gas supplies; Greece, Italy, Macedonia, and Turkey would follow.[22] On January 7, Russia ordered a halt to all European gas that flowed through Ukraine. As gas supplies ebbed, an Arctic front swept the continent from the north, sending temperatures plunging just as Europeans were losing their heat.[23]

For policymakers in Washington, the outlook was grim, but it was still far better than in Brussels. The United States was deeply engaged in helping to defuse the crisis, but when it came to physical supplies of natural gas, North America was isolated. Canada, Mexico, and the United States collectively produced roughly as much natural gas as they consumed, trading among themselves but buying little natural gas from overseas. Americans were used to foreign energy crises spreading quickly to the home front, but those crises had been about oil. Oil was cheap and easy to ship across long distances, which meant that problems in one place were quickly felt in others. (If one region ran short of crude, bidders there could buy it away from others, which spread the pain.) Natural gas, to Americans' good fortune, was different. Shipping it from one place to another was expensive, and it required multibillion-dollar facilities that were built only after firm long-term deals to buy and sell gas were in place. Crisis-stricken Europeans couldn't just buy fuel in the U.S. market and ship it home to make up for the supplies that Russia had cut off. The mechanics of the natural gas trade made North America an island during crises.

But this fortunate isolation was poised to change soon. In September 2008, the U.S. government published its annual outlook for international energy.[24] The message was the same as it had been for years: the nation would not be independent much longer. "U.S. gross imports of LNG [liquefied natural gas] are expected to grow rapidly," the authors warned. In fact, the report claimed, they were set to nearly quadruple: by 2015 the United States would import nearly a tenth of the natural gas it consumed. That, strategists feared, meant the next Eurasian crisis might not be so benign for the United States.[25] With America becoming deeply dependent on a global natural gas market, Russian-style blackmail seemed to be only a short way off.

Then, almost overnight, those fears vanished. The boom in U.S. shale gas production quickly led analysts to revise their predictions, and all of a sudden large-scale LNG imports weren't in the cards. On December 19, 2008, the same forecasters who were recently projecting import dependence published a preview of their next big study.[26] The new message was dramatically different: not only would imports not rise in the coming decades, they would fall sharply, with shale making up the difference. The United States, already facing more global risks that it could handle, would have one less to worry about. Rarely had the prognosis regarding a key energy source changed so fast.

Not everyone, though, was welcoming the news. In the Middle East, the tiny state of Qatar had been building up capacity to produce and ship natural gas to an import-dependent United States. Now, the owner of the third-largest gas reserves in the world and by far the biggest exporter of LNG was left without a critical customer. It quickly turned to Europe (and later to Asia) to sell its surplus supplies. (The turn to Europe may also have been part of a deliberate strategy to undermine Russia, a major Qatari rival in the global LNG trade.) In 2008, Qatar sold a bit less than three hundred billion cubic feet of liquefied natural gas to the Continent.[27] By 2011, the number had skyrocketed to 1.6 trillion.[28] European purchases from Russia, meanwhile, nudged down.

Only a few years earlier, Russia had plunged Europe into the dark, sending a clear message that continental policymakers needed to keep Moscow's wishes in mind. Now the power was shifting. Europeans had options, and they would barely hesitate to use them to alter the relationship.

In the opaque and esoteric world of the global natural gas trade, power is often manifested through price. Stronger countries extract steep prices for the fuel, and weaker ones pay them. Liquefied natural gas has long been sold on multiyear contracts where prices are set on the basis of formulas that derive the price of natural gas from the price of oil and related products. In recent years, as the price of oil skyrocketed, that arrangement was a great deal for producers but a raw one for consumers. In the United States, which has long been isolated from the world natural gas market, a barrel of oil cost north of a hundred dollars for much of 2012, but a shipment of natural gas containing the same amount of energy often sold for less than twenty. Meanwhile buyers in Europe were paying more than twice the U.S. price for natural gas, and Asian buyers were paying five times that sum or more.

This was a sign that power still rested with the natural gas producers. In 2012, though, under pressure from a glut of U.S. natural gas, the relationship between Europe and Russia began to visibly shift. E.ON, a German company that is the world's largest investor-owned electric utility and the world's biggest buyer of Russian gas, found itself locked in a fight over prices with Gazprom, the Russian natural gas monopoly. This commercial relationship is inseparable from politics. (Evidence? Gerhard Schroeder, the German chancellor for seven years, took a post on the board of a Gazprom-controlled pipeline company only months after leaving office.) As the dispute dragged on, both sides stuck to their guns. Gazprom insisted on lucrative contracts that tied the price of gas to the high price of oil. E.ON was adamant that much more of its gas be bought at considerably lower free-floating prices determined by what other buyers were willing to pay for natural gas and what other producers, such as Qatar, were willing to sell for. In the end, on July 3, Gazprom blinked. The new arrangement would save Europeans billions of dollars.[29] Only three years after the New Year's showdown, the balance of power between Europe and Russia was being rewritten by American natural gas.

For many shale gas enthusiasts, though, this was only the beginning. There are no physical principles that prevent technology and techniques developed in the United States from being applied around the world, further breaking down the concentrated and politically charged gas market. In 2011, the Department of Energy released the first estimates of shale gas resources around the world.[30] The United States wasn't even number one; that honor went to China, with an estimated 1,300 trillion cubic feet of "technically recoverable" shale gas, compared to about 900 trillion cubic feet in the United States (a number revised downward by about a third the next year). Close behind were Argentina (800 trillion), Mexico (700 trillion), and South Africa (500 trillion); another seven countries spanning five continents came in at over 100 trillion cubic feet each.[31] (The United States uses about 20 trillion cubic feet of natural gas every year.)

Some of these developments could, in principle, turn geopolitics on its head. Poland, long under the thumb of Russia (not just because of energy dependence), is estimated to have more than three hundred times as much natural gas as it consumes every year.[32] Estimated Chinese resources add up to more than four hundred times its annual consumption; if even a modest fraction of those could be brought to production, China might be able to forgo fraught gas trading relationships with Russia or with troubled countries, like Iran, in the Middle East.[33]

For all the promise, though, it's far too early to count on a shale gas boom beyond U.S. borders. Opposition to drilling is even more intense in Western Europe than it is in southern Ohio or upstate New York— and France appears to have more shale gas than all but eleven other countries in the world. Environmental protests have also met efforts to drill for shale gas in the Karoo region of South Africa.[34]

Perhaps even more important, though, the U.S. shale gas boom has been facilitated by a particularly attractive investment environment. Private natural gas producers, rather than the government, make investment decisions, while open markets let entrepreneurs easily sell shale gas to the highest bidder—both conditions that are distinctly missing in China and (in the latter case), to a good extent, in Europe.[35] Well-developed financial markets let producers sell their production several years in advance; they can then use those contracts as backing when they go out to finance their projects.[36] Resources are mostly owned by individuals, not governments, keeping politics a step removed from development.

None of these features are present in other places (save Canada) where there's lots of shale. And some of the countries where shale gas might develop don't just lack a positive environment for development; they create a downright negative one. Argentina, for example, keeps domestic gas prices artificially low, which makes a mess of economic incentives for drilling. It also doesn't help that the government periodically makes it impossible to take money out of the country, or expropriates the holdings of foreign oil and gas companies, which scares off all but the most intrepid and risk-hungry investors.

There is another way, though, that many imagine U.S. shale gas could upturn global markets and geopolitics: American exports of LNG. With natural gas prices overseas at levels many times those in the United States, enthusiasm for exports has been strong. In July 2012 Mark Mills, a fellow at the Manhattan Institute, published a study whose title, "Unleashing the North American Energy Colossus," captured a broad slice of sentiment about the potential of American energy exports.[37]

The central message was clear: the United States needed a "pro-export" energy policy if it wanted to succeed.

The push to export LNG has been strong. As of late 2012, more than a dozen companies had applied for permits that would allow them to build terminals to freely export the fuel, and most observers anticipated more. Were all of them to be built, the combined fleet could ship more than a quarter of current U.S. natural gas consumption abroad.[38] So big an export push would indeed turn global markets and politics upside down; it would be equivalent to nearly two-thirds of the world's LNG trade as of 2011.

But exports are unlikely to materialize at that scale. Most analysts expect U.S. prices to stabilize at a higher level than what prevailed in 2011 and 2012. Add to this the cost of liquefying and shipping natural gas—it easily adds five dollars or more to the price of a thousand cubic feet of natural gas by the time it makes its way from the United States to Asia—and the opportunity to profit from exports isn't as massive as it seems. Moreover, when you dump a lot of product on a market, something predictable happens: prices in the market plummet, further eroding (and sometimes eliminating) whatever economic opportunity originally existed. This is why, as of 2012, most U.S. energy analysts were predicting much more modest exports, perhaps adding up to 10 percent of U.S. supplies (and possibly quite a bit less) before the present decade is out. Most applications to export LNG, they concluded, would never turn into real facilities, just as scores of applications to import LNG years earlier had failed to do. The impact on overseas markets and politics wouldn't be negligible— having alternate suppliers with lower costs would give big importers such as Japan and Korea a stronger hand in dealing with producers, just as Europeans have gained in their dealings with Russia—but it might not be as transformative as many have supposed.

And even this modest impact is not foreordained. By 2012, the prospect of exports had stirred up widespread controversy, and opponents of exports held some leverage. Companies had applied for export permits because the United States, by law, does not allow broad LNG exports without one. Opponents brought a range of concerns to the table. Consumer advocates feared higher bills for electricity and home heating. Operators of regulated power plants worried they wouldn't be able to pass on increased gas costs to their customers. Chemical manufacturers, who have benefited from a glut of ethane, were concerned that it will instead be shipped to their competitors overseas; steelmakers, experiencing a boon from cheap gas-fired electricity, didn't want that to change. Nor had it escaped environmental groups and local skeptics of fracking that natural gas exports required natural gas, and that more production meant more risk. Even some national security hawks found the prospect of gas exports perplexing. After all, wouldn't it be better to get off oil by finding a way to put natural gas into American cars and trucks?

But there's also a lot of upside to allowing exports, beyond the potential to shake up global markets. Setting aside the matter of who wins and who loses, there's little question that gas exports would be good for the economy as a whole: far more money would be made producing and selling gas overseas than could be made trapping it in the country to keep prices low.[39] Indeed, although many will claim that gas is better used in manufacturing or power plants than in shipping it overseas, the choice is misleading: the main impact of blocking natural gas exports would likely be to keep the gas in the ground.[40]

The United States also benefits on the whole from reinforcing an open system for world trade, particularly in energy—something it's pursued for decades. And because U.S. gas exports are something that other countries such as Japan and India want, they give the United States special leverage in trade talks that it wouldn't otherwise have. To the extent that gas exports could also help insulate consuming countries in Europe and Asia from political arm twisting by suppliers in Russia and the Middle East, this would be good for U.S. foreign policy, freeing up would-be allies to work with the United States to deal with tough situations, rather than having them hold back for fear of economic retaliation.

The hottest speculation about the geopolitical consequences of the shale gas boom doesn't revolve around exports, though; it focuses on whether it might be possible to use natural gas to power American cars and trucks, and by doing that, decrease U.S. reliance on oil.

Here's a striking set of numbers. The Department of Energy projects that the United States will be producing nearly fourteen trillion cubic feet of shale gas annually within twenty-five years.[41] Basic chemistry says that a thousand cubic feet of natural gas contains almost as much energy as eight gallons of gasoline. Some quick arithmetic tells you that within a quarter century, the United States may be producing shale gas that contains as much energy as a hundred billion gallons of gasoline annually. That's almost as much as Americans consume every year.

Alas, there's more to the world than chemistry. The real question is whether there's a way to use natural gas to power U.S. cars and trucks that ultimately benefits the country as a whole. If you think it's obvious that powering American vehicles with natural gas would be good for the country, think about this: there's more than enough energy in the U.S. food crop to power the country's cars and trucks too, but it's clear that using it all for that purpose wouldn't be wise. Benefits aren't the only thing that matters; costs do too.

One way to use natural gas to power cars and trucks is to use the gas to generate electricity, and then use the electricity to power electric cars. But the big barrier to doing so isn't the price or availability of natural gas. Before the shale gas boom, the biggest hurdle to deploying electric vehicles was the cost of the cars themselves, not the fuel; now that shale gas has taken off, the same barriers remain.

There are two other prospects that are unique to natural gas. On a visit to California, I met Atul Kapadia, the chief executive of Envia Systems, one of the hottest developers of battery technology for electric cars in Silicon Valley. Kapadia, who still carries a light Indian accent despite his decades in the United States, speaks calmly but with the conviction of someone who has succeeded before. Battery CEOs typically brag to you about their new electric vehicles or about how they've had their cars retrofitted to run off electric power. Kapadia, though, had a different boast. "I drive a natural gas car," he told me. It had taken him all of fifteen minutes to make the decision: "There is no compelling reason for me right now to use my own technology. Because I get twice the mileage [by using natural gas], and half the cost. So I'm saving four times the money."

This idea of compressing or liquefying natural gas and using it to power automobiles—Kapadia's car uses the first approach—has been popularized by T. Boone Pickens, the Texas oilman turned alternative energy promoter who has a lot of money riding on the success of natural gas. The Natural Resources Defense Council, a major environmental group, estimates that his "Pickens Plan," which focuses mainly on using government to get compressed natural gas into trucks, "could reduce oil consumption by 4.9 million barrels per day," equivalent to about a quarter of U.S. oil demand.[42]

Cars and trucks that use compressed natural gas (CNG) are relatively rare in the United States—roughly one hundred thousand are in use—but they're more popular in a few pockets elsewhere.[43] One in five Argentinean vehicles runs on natural gas; worldwide, more than ten million are in use. The vehicles use engines similar to those in typical cars and trucks, but because natural gas is far less dense, even when it's compressed, a tank can last only a quarter the distance of that in a normal car.[44]

This is one reason natural gas vehicles aren't flying off dealers' lots. Another is infrastructure. "The airport is on the way [between home and work]," Kapadia told me. "There is a natural gas station on the way." Most people, though, aren't so lucky. "CNG is very inconvenient," he emphasized. "Very inconvenient. You have five filling stations in the entire Silicon Valley." That's actually a high count compared to many parts of the country. As of July 2012, there were fewer than five hundred publicly accessible natural gas filling stations in the country, in contrast with more than a hundred thousand regular gasoline stations.[45] South Dakota, West Virginia, and Maine did not have any natural gas stations; Missouri and Iowa each had only one.[46] Building out infrastructure will be a challenge: without it, people won't buy CNG cars, but unless people are driving CNG cars, building filling stations for them won't be an attractive way to make money.

There are, however, some big niches where range and frequent refueling doesn't matter much. Delivery trucks, urban buses, and garbage trucks all tend to have bad gas mileage, run up lots of miles every year, and frequently return to depots for a variety of reasons, at which point they can also be refueled. Together with fleet vehicles—things like mail delivery trucks and taxis (which might be bad candidates for CNG)—they currently use 1.3 million barrels of oil every day.[47]

But the equation is more complicated for efficient cars and trucks that don't rack up as many miles. A team of scholars at MIT recently did a simple estimate.[48] The typical U.S. vehicle clocks about twelve thousand miles every year. If it costs $10,000 to convert a gasoline-based car to run on natural gas (a representative cost today in the United States) and fueling that car with methane is equivalent to saving $1.50 for every gallon of gasoline, it would take seventeen years of savings to pay back the conversion cost, assuming that the car goes thirty miles on a gallon of gasoline.[49] Even if drivers could save two dollars for every gallon of gasoline they replaced (a likely outcome if oil prices remained around a hundred dollars a barrel), it would take thirteen years to pay back the cost of converting a car.[50] That remains far too long for the typical consumer.

Indeed, even this may overstate how attractive the proposition of converting to CNG would be to buyers. Saving money now is worth more to people than saving the same amount of money later—but most savings from using a natural gas car show up only over time. If you incorporate a rational treatment of that, it would take a staggering twenty years for a CNG car buyer to break even.[51] And real consumers appear to discount future savings far more deeply; the way they see the world, a CNG car would never pay off, even if it were used forever.[52]

A few things could change this equation. One possibility is significantly higher oil prices. Let's say oil reaches two hundred dollars a barrel and stays near there. A consumer will now take only seven years to pay off her up-front costs.[53] Of course, two hundred dollar oil will also spur a move toward more fuel-efficient cars and less driving, which erodes these savings. If the typical car doubles in fuel efficiency in response to higher oil prices, it will take at least eighteen years to pay off the extra cost of switching to natural gas.

A more promising possibility is a drop in the cost of buying a natural gas vehicle in the first place. As of 2012, there were few options if you wanted to buy a new natural gas car in the United States; your best bet was a Honda GX, which cost $7,000 more than the gasoline-powered equivalent. But it's a lot cheaper to buy a natural gas vehicle in Europe;

the natural gas version of the Volkswagen Passat, which can run on both natural gas and normal gasoline, costs only $3,700 more than the pure gasoline version.[54] Researchers aren't sure what explains the disparity, but it makes a stunning difference: if natural gas vehicles in the United States were to cost as little as they do in Europe (something that might happen if U.S. markets for natural gas vehicles grew), a sensible U.S. consumer could expect to break even after only five years.[55] Even more impressive, if oil prices doubled while natural gas prices stayed flat, the payoff time would fall to under three years.

A third big possibility is the potential to liquefy rather than compress the natural gas. Liquefying natural gas, and using the resulting product in a vehicle, is an expensive proposition; for this and other reasons, it doesn't make sense for cars or light trucks. But many industry watchers are becoming convinced that LNG could gain a big share of the market for large long-haul trucks. Because those trucks log lots of miles, lower fuel costs can pay off rapidly. And because many of them travel a fairly small set of long-distance routes, it may be relatively easy to outfit those routes with a network of LNG fueling stations.

The last thing that could tilt the tables is government. Kapadia made the numbers for his car work in part with tax credits from the state of California that covered the extra cost of a CNG car. Without them, the math would have been a lot tougher. He also got a special sticker that let him drive in the HOV (high occupancy vehicle) highway lane even if he was by himself. Governments might also help bring down the cost of CNG vehicles by buying lots of them and creating economies of scale; many suspect that CNG cars are cheaper in Europe than America simply because the market in Europe is bigger. People have battled fiercely over the costs and benefits of government intervention in all these dimensions. Most economists would say that at least some involvement is warranted. Others, ranging from environmentalists to libertarians, would disagree. It's a question we'll return to in Chapter 5 of this book.

The other big prospect for getting natural gas into cars and trucks is converting it into a liquid fuel that could replace gasoline or diesel. In Qatar, where natural gas is dirt-cheap to produce, Shell spent upward of twenty billion to build a massive plant, called Pearl, that could turn

1.6 billion cubic feet of natural gas into 140,000 barrels of petroleum products every day.[56] Qatar provided Shell with the natural gas for free; the project wouldn't have made sense in the United States, where producers actually have to pay for their natural gas.

Despite the costs, a few companies have looked at doing something similar in the United States. There are two ways to attack the problem, both of which are referred to as "gas-to-liquids," or GTL. The first is to put methanol made from natural gas directly into cars and trucks; the second is to make gasoline or a diesel substitute from that methanol and use it instead. The first route is cheaper for fuel producers but requires upgrades to gas tanks and fueling infrastructure; the second one reverses the pattern. The costs to produce gasoline and diesel from natural gas are particularly uncertain, because of the sparse historical track record for the technologies involved.

In 2008, three scholars at Carnegie Mellon University in Pittsburgh estimated that producing liquid fuels (mostly gasoline and diesel) from natural gas would cost $2.30 a gallon if natural gas prices were near $9 per thousand cubic feet.[57] They started by surveying past costs for the sorts of technologies a GTL plant would need. Then they tacked on extra costs by figuring that whoever put up the money to build the plant would expect a 15 percent annual return on their investment. When you add in distribution and marketing costs, as well as taxes, that's barely competitive with gasoline at the oil prices most people expect.

Since 2008, though, assumptions about natural gas prices have been turned upside down. If you redo their estimates with $5 natural gas, the result is a cost of $1.45 a gallon, or about $60 a barrel, to make synthetic fuels. This seems like a great bet to take on.

So why haven't American industrialists thrown themselves enthusiastically into the business? Because it's risky. Assume for a moment that the Carnegie Mellon researchers are right about the costs of building and operating a GTL plant. If natural gas prices were to climb to, say, seven dollars for a thousand cubic feet, and oil prices were to fall to seventy dollars, both of which are eminently possible, GTL producers would lose money (assuming that the researchers' other assumptions are right). Because analysts estimate that it costs a billion dollars or more up front to build a plant that produces the equivalent of fifty thousand barrels of fuel a day, that's a big risk to take.

There's also the danger that construction costs will be higher than expected. Early GTL plants were immensely expensive. In the early 1990s, Shell spent nearly a billion dollars building a plant in Malaysia that could produce only fifteen thousand barrels of fuel a day; this was equivalent to spending three billion dollars on a fifty-thousand-barrel-a-day facility.[58] A 1999 report from the Idaho National Engineering and Environmental Laboratory pegged the cost of a new fifty-thousand-barrel-a-day GTL plant at $1.6 billion (after adjusting for inflation through 2012).[59] In 2005, a University of Houston professor named Michael Economides estimated the capital cost of a similar facility at $1.25 billion.[60] The most recent attempt to actually build a major GTL plant— Shell's Qatar-based Pearl project—came in massively over budget. Only time will tell whether developers can gain enough confidence in GTL, and in oil and natural gas prices, to make GTL a significant contributor to displacing oil. (Several companies have made serious noises about investing in U.S.-based plants, but this hasn't yet translated into anything on the ground.) And, down the road, governments might step in to provide incentives. For now, though, prophesying a revolution in how Americans fuel their cars as a result of the shale gas revolution requires a premature leap of faith.

❦ ❦ ❦

Some analysts would say that even the more modest expectations for shale gas are greatly overblown. History is littered with heralded resource booms that quickly fizzle out. Why should shale gas be different?

A vanguard of critics argues that it won't be. Their claims typically come down to three letters: EUR. Short for estimated ultimate recovery, EUR is one of the most important quantities in determining the economic viability of any given shale gas well and, as a result, in influencing future shale gas production.

When a shale gas well first starts operation, its production tends to be prolific. Industry experts refer to this as a high initial production, or IP, rate. But then production falls—often quickly. Shale gas wells have strikingly high decline rates, the industry term for how quickly production drops. These two quantities—initial production and decline rate—combine to tell you how much gas a given well will produce: its EUR. High EUR means a producer will ultimately have lots of gas to sell, which makes it more likely a well will be attractive enough to drill and maintain in the first place. Low EUR means the opposite, and at some point it makes development and production unattractive and unwise.

Critics of shale gas euphoria argue that the industry, investors, and government analysts are badly overestimating EUR. People have a good idea of how much gas a well will produce in its first few years of operation. But skeptics point out that industry estimates of total EUR include decades of expected production from each well (a typical shale gas well is expected to remain in service for more than twenty years). They charge that industry has exploited the fact that no one has much experience with aging shale gas wells in order to overestimate how much natural gas each well will produce as it gets older.[61] Moreover, they argue that as drillers move beyond "sweet spots" in parts of Texas, Louisiana, and Pennsylvania where production has been prolific into less-attractive areas, initial production will fall too. If we correct the estimates—and critics typically point to analyses of shale gas geology to explain how that should be done—then EURs, and eventually investment and production, should ultimately come down. In that case, only one thing would rise: the price of natural gas.

This debate over geology is unlikely to be fully resolved except through experience, something that will take years if not decades. Even absent that, though, there are big reasons to be suspicious of the skeptics' more extreme arguments. The first few years of production, rather than the subsequent few decades, are typically far more important to the driller's bottom line. Money earned in the first few years after an investment is made is worth a lot more than money earned ten or twenty years later, because early earnings can be reinvested. New knowledge about long-term performance might have smaller consequences than one might instinctively imagine.

Moreover, when skeptics estimate the impact of weaker well performance on shale gas economics, they typically treat drillers' costs as fixed; as a result, slightly lower performance can all too easily destroy the economic prospects of a given well. In practice, one of the biggest costs of production—the cost of leasing gas-rich territory from landowners—isn't fixed at all. If the value of the gas falls because it turns out to be less economical to extract it, lease prices will drop too, blunting the ultimate impact on production. Moreover, as drillers gain experience and innovate, their other costs fall too.

These shock absorbers kick in impressively when you try to simulate what will happen to shale gas if EUR estimates turn out to be badly wrong. The U.S. Department of Energy did just that in 2011 in one of its big annual energy studies.[62] Its "reference case"—the best guess of what will happen unless policies change—predicted 26.32 trillion cubic feet of annual natural gas production by 2035. Then it asked what would happen if the per-well output—the EUR—was slashed in half. The result? Production came in at 22.43 trillion cubic feet, less than in the original case, but not drastically lower. Prices also rose about 30 percent above what they otherwise would be. None of this is trivial, but none of it is a deal killer for shale gas development either.

Most analysts project U.S. natural gas prices settling somewhere between four and six dollars for a thousand cubic feet over the long run. Such prices would be enough to make money for producers and facilitate a wide range of uses in industry, power generation, and beyond. Something truly drastic would need to happen for shale gas economics to fall apart and for prices to consistently clock in higher. Policymakers and the public would be unwise to stick their heads in the sand and assume that nothing could go wrong. If they're worried that shale gas might collapse, though, they would be wiser to turn their attention toward a force potentially more powerful than mere geology: public skepticism of drilling, which can fuel firm opposition to it.

❧ ❧ ❧

None of the potential benefits of shale gas—not the economic gains, not the geopolitical consequences, not the prospect of using less oil—sway Warren Taylor or the people who joined him in Columbus to protest gas development. Their attitudes aren't unusual. For every claim about natural gas riches, Taylor can cite a danger to communities, the environment, and businesses like his that depend on it.

Chuck Sammarone feels the tension quite acutely. The sixty-nine-year-old mayor of Youngstown, Ohio, sporting slicked-back hair and a bold silver tie when we met, won office in 2011, a fortuitous time. Shale-driven business was providing some hope in an area that had been in decline for decades. V&M, a prominent French player in the oil and gas industry, would announce later in the year that it would spend nearly a billion dollars to build a new manufacturing plant in the city to make steel tubes. Sammarone was firmly in favor of fracking. Few in his position wouldn't be.

When the earthquake hit, though, the upside of shale gas was the last thing on his mind. "It was New Year's Eve, three o'clock. I was watching the football game. This loud noise occurred." For more than a year, drillers had been injecting wastewater from their operations into the Northstar 1 well, located just outside of Youngstown. Unbeknownst to the operators, who had received all the permits they needed from the state, the well struck near an underground fault.[63] "When the noise stopped, my house shook. I mean, me and my wife were home, and it shook. Stuff fell off the wall. We heard the dishes in the cabinet. So I told my wife, 'We better go outside.'" Scientists at the Lamont-Doherty Observatory 350 miles away in New York would later analyze recordings at their station and come to an unavoidable conclusion: the fluids pumped into Northstar 1 had sent the nearby fault over the edge, triggering a 4.0 magnitude quake.[64]

At the next city council meeting, Sammarone successfully pushed for a moratorium on injections in the area. He reminded me that, twenty years earlier, he had sponsored legislation to allow drilling. "So I'm not against drilling. Just like I sponsored an ordinance a year ago for a well to be drilled. So I'm not against drilling," he emphasized. "I'm against earthquakes." Jobs were important, but they weren't everything. "You get a pot of gold. But if you got earthquakes, people say, they don't want the pot of gold that's creating the earthquakes. 'Cause if they wanted earthquakes they'd have moved to California. . . . I feel the same way."

Later in 2012, the National Academy of Sciences appointed a panel to study the earthquake issue. It concluded that, with some simple precautions, the big tremors were entirely avoidable.[65] But earthquakes were only the latest in a long litany of ills that were increasingly attributed to the operations surrounding natural gas production from shale.

Worries tended to zero in on two areas. The biggest environmental concern came down to water. Some people worried about possible leaks of toxic fracking fluids and natural gas escaping from wells into water supplies. It didn't help that many companies refused to disclose the full list of the chemicals they used, and even those that did reveal their formulas often insisted such disclosure should not be mandatory. Most in the industry have long insisted that leaks don't happen, arguing that wells are isolated from their surroundings by thick layers of concrete, and that the various contaminants found in peoples' water supplies come from other sources.

The science is still indeterminate on whether any contamination stemming from underground has actually been happening. There's still no compelling evidence that fracking fluids themselves have leaked from wells, and there are good theoretical reasons to believe they won't. (The one case that's often pointed to, which happened in Pavilion, Wyoming, doesn't involve a shale gas well at all.) The trickier question is whether methane itself might have migrated into water wells. There, the evidence is mixed. In the most careful and prominent study to date, four Duke University scholars compared methane levels in drinking water near hydraulic fracturing activities with those elsewhere, and they found that being near drilling made high methane concentrations more likely.[66] The problem is that there are two explanations for this: drilling is contaminating water supplies, or drilling is occurring in areas where there's a lot of methane around. This second explanation isn't implausible, because drillers gravitate to areas with a lot of natural gas, which is mostly methane. More work is undoubtedly needed.

Industry is quick to point out that methane contamination doesn't make water unsafe to drink. But once you need to explain away flaming drinking water, you've already lost much of the battle for public acceptance. It also doesn't help that excessive methane contamination can lead to explosion hazards in people's homes. In any case, drillers know how to avoid methane leaks: they can use better well casing that extends deep underground to seal off wells from their surroundings.[67] The only question is whether companies will do it or whether governments will force them to.

The bigger water problem, though, appears to be not what goes into shale gas wells but what comes out of them. Massive amounts of water are sent down into wells when they're fracked, and millions of gallons come back out, bringing with them toxic salts.[68] These can be disposed of safely, either underground or at appropriately equipped processing facilities; but if they aren't, it can be a big problem. Irresponsible operators have ditched their wastewater in local streams or stored it in poorly constructed ponds that then let the water seep into the soil.[69] The result can be dangerous contamination of surrounding freshwater supplies. Once again, in principle this is an easy problem to fix, if producers are willing to step up; but again, there's no reason to assume they all will.

Supporters of shale gas development have often accused those who favor stricter standards of trying to shut down the industry. In 2011, the International Energy Agency launched a study that would implicitly address this claim.[70] It asked a simple question: How much more would it cost to drill wells that met the highest standards for safety? They tallied up steps drillers would need to take, such as buying more cement and allotting more time for drilling so that they could pause if anything was amiss. Their calculation was striking for its modest result: for a mere seven cents on every dollar that producers were already spending building their wells, all the operations could easily be brought up to snuff.[71]

Instead the toughest challenge surrounding shale gas may not be protecting water or avoiding earthquakes, or anything else that admits to a technical fix. The most vexing problem may be managing how drilling affects the way communities, like Bill Dix's and Warren Taylor's, work. Natural gas development can be an enormously disruptive activity. In places like Pennsylvania and Ohio that lack a large number of properly trained workers, the hordes of young men who move in from out of state to work in the industry can anger local communities; one Keystone State lawmaker went so far as to accuse them of "spreading sexually transmitted disease among the womenfolk."[72] For a couple weeks near each well, trucks drive around twenty-four hours a day, seven days a week, disturbing neighborhoods and sometimes wrecking inadequate roads.[73]

Development can happen remarkably close to where people live. When I visited the Neider well with the men from Chesapeake, there wasn't a house to be seen for miles. But later that day, as I drove through the state, I noticed a small sign on the highway and turned off to another drilling pad. No fewer than six homes stood in its immediate shadow. When the fracking started in earnest, an endless procession of trucks full of water and sand would presumably rumble by, with no end in sight for weeks. Someone there was making a ton of money, but the odds were high that many others were getting little or nothing.

It's the mix of winners and losers that often makes gas development so fraught. You don't need to be employed in the industry or own gas-rich land to cash in on the bonanza; everyone from restaurant owners to dentists in places that are booming have seen payoffs. But for some, like retirees on fixed incomes, the local inflation that accompanies an influx of shale money can be tough. Even more galling to some is the fact that lots of property owners in certain states (particularly in Pennsylvania) don't hold title to the gas under their property. Because shale gas involves horizontal drilling, it's possible for the industry to drill deep under people's homes without paying the homeowners a cent.[74]

This would all be bad enough if industry were doing a good job of managing inevitable frictions. That's sometimes the case, but too often companies have done just the opposite. Many executives, steeled from decades of fights over development, have elected to simply ignore any backlash, only fueling further suspicion that they have something to hide. Chuck Sammarone experienced this during the fight over who was responsible for the tremors that shook his home. Decades before, he was a teacher: "I used to tell the kids: don't bullshit me. If you know the answer, good. If you don't know it, just say 'I don't know it.' Nobody knows everything!" The stonewalling extended to government: "I think the state made a mistake 'cause they tried to give reasons for this earthquake. And all those reasons were everything but the well."

But no one can top Talisman Energy, which until 2011 was probably best known in Pennsylvania for having more citations for safety violations than any other shale gas operator in the state.[75] (In its defense, Talisman had also drilled the most wells, and in 2011 it radically reduced the number of citations.) A couple years before, concerned executives at Talisman headquarters in Calgary, Alberta, dreamed up a way of improving their relations with the communities where they were operating: they would commission a kids' coloring book.[76] The result was twenty-four pages chronicling the exploits of Talisman Terry, the Friendly Frackasaurus, a hardhat-wearing dinosaur who showed kids where shale gas came from (apparently the fossilized remains of Terry's ancestors) and how rainbows appear after fracking. This all went largely unnoticed until Stephen Colbert, the Comedy Central host, caught wind of it. He spun a five-minute segment out of the unintentionally hilarious coloring book; a day later, Talisman Energy put the Friendly Frackasaurus to rest.

For Bill Dix, like so many people who were caught in the middle of the fights over shale gas, the debate over whether development was safe or dangerous seemed to miss the point. What mattered was how it was done and regulated. "This can happen in two really drastically different ways," he told me. "All the environmentalists from Athens go over the hill here to Wetzel County. Wetzel County is over in West Virginia. It is steep. It is up and down. It's big country." The area had long been mined for coal and recently been drilled for gas. "The whole government of West Virginia basically has been in the pocket of the mineral companies forever," he charged. "It's a hell of a mess. It's terrible. I visited there, I came back, I couldn't sleep for days. It is a disaster."

Dix put this in stark contrast with another recent experience. "A group of landowners, we had a connection over in Bradford County, Pennsylvania, which was where the real heart of the whole thing with the dry gas was. We went to Bradford County, and it was meticulously done. Everybody was happy with it. The earthwork, the environmental safety, I mean it was just incredible." Dix chalked up the difference, compared to West Virginia, to how Pennsylvania and Bradford County handled development: "The landowners had some rights, there was a decent lease in place, and the state of Pennsylvania, for all their environmental shortcomings, is night-and-day compared to West Virginia."

The lessons seemed clear. Shale gas has the potential to deliver big (though not revolutionary) economic gains, promises to spare the United States dependence on overseas natural gas suppliers, and could be used to help reduce U.S. consumption of oil. (It also has consequences for climate change and clean energy that we'll see in Chapters 4 and 6.) But even though shale gas development can be done well, it can also be done poorly, not only threatening local communities but also placing promised economic and security gains at risk. And though markets will deliver on many of the opportunities stemming from shale gas regardless of what governments do, fully seizing other opportunities such as using natural gas to cut U.S. oil use will require governments to take a more active role. Whether the country will chart a course that protects communities and exploits the potential of abundant natural gas remains to be seen.

ENERGY INDEPENDENCE ON THE HORIZON

Oil skeptics like to point out that the United States consumes 20 percent of the world's oil but owns only 2 percent of its oil reserves. Such lopsided numbers, they insist, make optimism foolish when it comes to oil and destine the United States to depend on foreign crude unless it slashes its consumption and embraces alternatives.

Howard Jonas would undoubtedly disagree. Jonas is not your typical oilman. In the early 1990s, he developed a simple but ingenious system that let overseas telephone users avoid exorbitant long-distance rates; by age forty, he had sold his company, IDT, and was worth more than a billion dollars. The tall, soft-spoken Bronx native with a slightly corny sense of humor eventually moved on, writing two books (one person who reviewed *On a Roll: From Hot Dog Buns to High-Tech Billions* called him a "genial multimillionaire" hiding "a closet rabbi"), founding a string of other businesses, and, in 2004, moving to Israel to retire.

To hear him tell it, though, his heart has always been in oil. "During the 1973 embargo I was seventeen. I'd just gotten a car, just gotten a girlfriend. Next thing, I've got gas lines." Jonas is holding forth in his spare office, not in a gleaming tower in Dallas or Houston but in a grungy part of downtown Newark, where he now does business as founder and chairman of American Shale Oil. "When I was on those gas lines," he recalls, "people were speaking about the enormous shale resources in Colorado. That was a dream worth pursuing. But it wasn't my time."

Nor, it turned out, was it time for oil shale. Richard Nixon, Gerald Ford, and Jimmy Carter would all make the legendary resource, estimated to match the holdings of Saudi Arabia, central to their plans for U.S. energy independence. Developers would mine vast tracts of rock in the American West, crush it, and then heat it until the chemical compounds it contained turned into oil. "There's a time for technologies to happen," says Jonas. That wasn't one of them. By the early 1980s, oil prices crashed, government subsidies vanished, and the industry was in ruins. The rest of the U.S. oil business wasn't in great shape either: for the next quarter century, output would fall steadily, with few exceptions. Americans became more pessimistic about the country's oil-production prospects with every passing year.

In 2008, Jonas moved back from Israel and came out of retirement. The outlook for American oil was still gloomy, but he decided to pursue his teenage dream. "If I was going to take the medicine [of going back to work]," he recalls, "I was going to take some of the dessert too."

In January of that year, IDT, still controlled by Jonas, took a majority stake in EGL Oil Shale, a small firm that had recently won a research and development lease for a tract of Colorado land owned by the federal government. It was the same stretch of the country, and the same resource, that had defeated the U.S. oil industry nearly thirty years before. In May, the company became American Shale Oil, or AMSO, and a year later it entered into a joint venture with the French oil giant TOTAL.

Howard Jonas was optimistic about AMSO, but, like most others, he was still pessimistic about the broader landscape of American oil. In June 2010, he posted a stark letter on the firm's website.[1] "Dear Fellow American," it began. "The world is facing a serious fuel crisis." The one-page brief detailed the calamities to come: skyrocketing prices for oil, food, and other necessities, alongside geopolitical competition so intense that "even the U.S. military and NATO may lack sufficient fuel to meet its needs." The rhetoric was hyperbolic, but its basic story of inevitable decline was entirely mainstream.

Yet within less than a year after he posted the letter the conventional wisdom changed entirely. Oil watchers were heralding a stunning boom in U.S. production. In North Dakota and Texas, producers were drilling down and then sideways to extract oil, using the same techniques that have been applied to natural gas. Offshore production was booming despite the Deepwater Horizon disaster, the first major U.S. oil spill since the *Exxon Valdez*. North of the U.S.-Canada border, in the Alberta oil sands, developers were extracting tarlike bitumen in massive mines and by heating deposits buried deep beneath the earth, producing millions of barrels a day of oil in the process and fueling excitement about potential gains further south.

This time around, it seemed, the technologies that were needed to fuel resurgence in American oil were finally ready for prime time. Adam Sieminski, a sober analyst who would soon leave Deutsche Bank to join the White House staff, captured the mood in an interview with *Bloomberg*: "For 40 years, only politicians and the occasional author in *Popular Mechanics* magazine talked about achieving energy independence. Now it doesn't seem such an outlandish idea."[2] Jonas, newer to the oil game but already deep in it, seems sold too. Technology has come to the rescue, he explains: "There will be abundant fossil fuel."

This sort of optimism is characteristic of oilmen and those like Howard Jonas who aspire to join their ranks. The wild and unpredictable nature of their business would crush most anyone who wasn't. Promising prospects can turn out to be worthless, often taking their boosters down with them. As recently as 2002, drillers exploring for new petroleum in the United States found themselves striking out more often than they hit pay dirt.[3] And that state of affairs was considered enormous progress: a decade before, the rule had been roughly three failures for every success. Worse, even if prospectors found oil, there was no guarantee they'd be able to make money producing it. Prices could tumble precipitously just as easily as they could skyrocket, mercilessly wiping out producers and their dreams of fortune.

It's usually a safe bet, then, to meet enthusiastic boasts about prospective oil riches with a skeptical eye. Until a few years ago, the United States had been through two periods of oil optimism since the 1973 oil crisis, only to see its hopes eventually dashed each time. Since the United States reached its peak output in 1970 and started to see oil production decline, it has twice appeared to turn things around.[4] The first run began in 1977 and lasted through 1985. It was propelled by one big development: production from Alaska's North Slope, which began in 1977 and peaked at nearly two million barrels a day in 1988.[5] Production within the United States was bolstered by high oil prices, which kept some aging fields in the lower forty-eight states in business for a few years more than many had expected. By 1985, though, the North Slope was starting to lose steam. A staggering drop in oil prices that year, brought on by a Saudi decision to flood the market with cheap crude, crushed production in the lower forty-eight, permanently ending the eight-year run of increasing output.

The second turnaround was far more short-lived: oil production edged upward between 1990 and 1991 before continuing with its previous decline. Falling crude prices collided with a new ban on most offshore oil and gas development, issued by George H. W. Bush in 1990, to seal the trend.

Yet the third time may turn out to be different. Oil production rose every year between 2008 and 2012—and production was up in fifteen states. Oil prices still swing up and down, but with the average price of a barrel of crude topping sixty dollars in every year since 2005, the betting money now seems to say that oil will fetch big bucks for many more years to come.[6] This would seem to place American oil production on far firmer financial ground than it has enjoyed at any time since the 1970s.

The bulls have another important thing going for them: the sheer diversity of new prospects is unprecedented in recent memory, partly inoculating predictions of plentiful oil to the risk of individual failures. In the 1970s, almost all the action was in Alaska; in the early 1990s, it was mostly offshore. Today boosters talk about prospects ranging from tight oil (often referred to as shale oil) to deepwater drilling to new Alaskan crude to oil shale to enhanced recovery of oil from old fields using carbon dioxide; they also highlight massive production from the Canadian oil sands—not quite America, but close enough to often add to the total. In short, something unseen in almost half a century seems to be under way in American oil. Nowhere is this more apparent than when you look at what's been happening in North Dakota.

"Shale Shock! Could There Be Billions in the Bakken?"[7] It's safe to guess that few reports from the staid U.S. Energy Information Administration have matched the enthusiasm of this November 2006 entry. ("The Availability and Price of Petroleum and Petroleum Products Produced in Countries Other Than Iran" was a more typical example.[8]) It's also reasonable to assume that few people noticed it at the time. But Steven Grape, a petroleum engineer at the U.S. Department of Energy, was on to something big.

If you had to pick one development that's been most responsible for fueling talk of energy abundance, it would have to be the tight oil boom in North Dakota—and the source of the boom is the Bakken. In his report, Grape flagged a sudden surge in oil coming out of neighboring Montana, whose output had more than doubled over the previous five years. The upswing came from a single source: the Elm Coulee Field, which was discovered in 2000 and then proceeded to more than double its output every year. Drillers married horizontal drilling with hydraulic fracturing, just as they had with natural gas, to unlock petroleum that others previously assumed was economically impossible to extract. But few beyond the state paid much attention to the phenomenon. Montana, after all, was still delivering less than a hundred thousand barrels of oil a day—a fraction of a percentage point of U.S. consumption, which totaled nearly twenty million barrels a day.

Within a couple of years, the action moved east to North Dakota, where it would eventually explode. Before 2007, that state's oil production had never exceeded 150,000 barrels a day, and for most of its history daily output remained below 100,000 barrels, about half of 1 percent of U.S. demand for oil.[9] By 2011, though, the techniques used in Montana were becoming widespread. North Dakota was producing well over 400,000 barrels of oil daily. As of early 2012, it was conventional wisdom among industry analysts that the state could produce as much as a million barrels a day by the decade's close.

And the Bakken oil field, though the biggest, was far from the only tight oil story. A similar upsurge was under way in Texas. In 2007, the Eagle Ford shale, which covers ten to twenty thousand square miles between the Mexican border and East Texas, produced a measly 2.99 barrels of oil a day.[10] (That isn't 2.99 million; it's 2.99.) By 2011, it was yielding one hundred thousand barrels every twenty-four hours, up eightfold just from the previous year. In early 2012, analysts projected that the Eagle Ford could quickly catch up to the Bakken and also reach a million barrels a day of production before the decade is out.[11] By September of that year, the Eagle Ford had combined with another oil-producing part of Texas, known as the Permian Basin, to deliver a gain of half a million barrels a day in the span of just a year.[12]

Indeed North American geology means that tight oil is found all over the United States. To date, the most common source has been shale, which explains why tight oil is often confusingly referred to as shale oil. About four hundred million years ago, mud and organic matter settled across bottoms of large water basins covering much of what is today the United States. The thin layers of material from plants and animals, together with silt and mud, added up. Over millions of years, the resulting pressure formed the sedimentary rock known as shale.[13] Trapped in the rock, the organic materials turned into chains of carbon and hydrogen atoms—oil and gas—and began to turn the shale black.[14] Not every shale deposit is ripe for production. Some, buried too deep, found their oil and gas cooked off by intense pressure, while others, too shallow, never found their contents converted to petroleum at all. In much of the country, though, the shale was just right.

This, along with an abundance of other geologies in which oil was trapped, means that discovery of new technologies to unlock tight oil hold the potential to transform the landscape of U.S. oil. As recently as 2008, total crude oil production from the entire lower forty-eight states was 4.3 million barrels a day.[15] By early 2012, a team of Citigroup analysts would tally nearly four million barrels a day of tight oil production that could be realized by the end of this decade. The possible sources they identified spanned the country, from Texas and North Dakota to newer prospects such as Delaware, Wyoming, Colorado, and California. In 2012 alone, U.S. production rose by eight hundred thousand barrels a day, primarily on the back of tight oil development, bringing the country's total daily production up to 6.4 million barrels.

These gains are being supplemented by so-called natural gas liquids (we first encountered these, also known as NGLs, in the previous chapter) that are produced alongside shale gas and have the potential to partly displace oil: ethane can replace naphtha, a refined oil product, in chemicals plants, while propane and butane can replace some oil in petroleum refineries. Analysts debate how interchangeable NGLs really are with oil, but regardless, their volumes are difficult to ignore: between 2005 and 2010, NGL production rose by more than half a million barrels a day, a figure that some expect to grow by as much as another million barrels a day within the next decade.[16]

But tight oil and fracking are far from the whole story. Only a few years ago, had you asked an oil analyst the future of American oil was, odds are that tight oil would have been far from the top of the list. There's a good chance that the analyst would have told you to look at the rigs working in the deep water of the U.S. Gulf of Mexico instead.

"This is not a decision that I've made lightly." Barack Obama wasn't overstating his point. Standing in front of a new F-18 fighter jet christened the "Green Hornet" (it could run on a mix of petroleum-based jet fuel and biofuels), he had some decidedly ungreen news to share. "Today we're announcing the expansion of offshore oil and gas exploration," he explained, ticking off frontiers from the Gulf of Mexico to Alaska that would be opened for business. After decades of pitched battles between the right and the left over the future of offshore drilling, the president had decided to break free. His allies were not impressed. Jacqueline Savitz, a senior campaign director at the environmental group Oceana, captured the sentiment: "We're appalled that the president is unleashing a wholesale assault on the oceans," she fumed.[17] The White House insisted offshore drilling was now safe. Environmental groups weren't so sure.

Less than a month later, the president's plans were in tatters. On April 20, 2010, fifty miles off the coast of Louisiana, an explosion at

BP's Deepwater Horizon oil platform unleashed a devastating chain of events. The shock immediately killed eleven men and injured seventeen more. Five thousand feet below, oil poured into the sea at a rate of as much as sixty thousand barrels a day. Within two days, a sheen was detected on the ocean's surface; for nearly three months, the nation would be transfixed as everything from golf balls to a giant cone was used to try to plug the wild well. When the flow was finally stemmed in early July, Gulf Coast residents—not to mention BP leadership, the White House, and most of America—breathed a sigh of relief.

For the oil industry, though, the fight was only beginning. More than two decades of largely blemish-free operation had finally culminated in a Democratic president deciding to open big new offshore tracts to development. Now a single disaster was throwing the process into reverse. By December, the administration withdrew its offshore plans. Interior Secretary Ken Salazar defended the decision bluntly: "We believe the most appropriate course of action is to focus on development with existing leases and not expand to new areas at this time."[18]

Tight oil might get technology enthusiasts buzzing, and Alaska might raise the most environmental ire, but it's the outer continental shelf (OCS) of the United States that many petro-optimists look to for the biggest gains. Mainstream projections of offshore production typically foresee a steady decline for decades to come. But bullish analysts have argued that offshore production could surge from less than two million barrels a day today to nearly four million a day within a decade or so, and then hold steady near that level.[19]

The secret? Often it's access to new lands: the Atlantic and Pacific parts of the OCS have long been off-limits, as have large parts of the Gulf of Mexico. If this changed, production could ramp up. No one can confidently say precisely how much: given the dearth of exploration in recent decades, knowledge of what lies beneath the surface of the sea is limited. Prices would need to stay above fifty dollars a barrel or so to make new drilling worthwhile, and leaps in technology could change the picture yet again. It's not unreasonable, though, to imagine that another couple million barrels a day of American oil could be within relatively easy reach.

For many on the other side of the fight over the future of American energy, that's precisely what's so worrying. Little time has passed since the Deepwater Horizon disaster gripped the nation. Years of promises that offshore drilling presented virtually no risk of major accidents were gutted in an instant, and trust will be difficult to rebuild. Yet less than a year after the spill, on January 11, 2011, the National Commission on the BP Deepwater Horizon Oil Spill and Offshore Drilling, chartered by the Obama administration and counting at least one die-hard environmental campaigner among its members, came to a blunt conclusion: "Drilling in deepwater does not need to be abandoned. It can be done safely."[20] But theirs was far from a laissez-faire verdict. "The central lesson to be drawn from the catastrophe," they concluded, "is that no less than an overhauling of both current industry practices and government oversight is now required." Despite a broad range of steps taken by government and industry in response to the spill and to the commission's report, many still fear that even though deepwater drilling has returned apace, offshore drilling remains unsafe.[21]

Tight oil and offshore drilling have dominated oil-related headlines in recent years. But before the tight oil boom began to transform North Dakota, and before the Deepwater Horizon oil spill vaulted offshore drilling into every living room, the most important battlefield in the fight between oil developers and environmentalists was a sliver of the Alaska National Wildlife Refuge (ANWR).

There is one big reason the 6,100 square kilometers that make up Area 1002 of the refuge, known in energy circles simply as ANWR, have been the target of industry interest for so long: the oil there is cheap to produce. Long before rising crude prices made it profitable to extract oil locked in shale rock or buried thousands of feet beneath the sea, the economics of ANWR already worked. Back in 2000, when people still expected oil to sell for around twenty dollars a barrel forever, government analysts estimated that the refuge might be able to deliver as much as two million barrels a day of oil within twenty years, and they were confident that peak output of at least a million barrels a day was likely—numbers that most people still believe, give or take a few hundred thousand barrels a year.[22] Contrast that with deepwater drilling, oil sands, tight oil, and other sources that mostly don't make sense at prices below fifty dollars, and the decades-long focus on ANWR is a lot easier to understand.

For as long as industry has wanted to drill in ANWR, environmentalists have wanted to stop it. The refuge is home to polar bears, caribou, and the shaggy muskox, a prehistoric beast that some groups claim is endangered.[23] Three decades of battle have turned ANWR into a critical litmus test: to support its opening is to declare that you are on Team Oil, and to oppose it is to show you are serious about the environment. There has long been no in between: when the U.S. Senate took votes in 2005 on cranking up fuel efficiency in cars and trucks and on opening ANWR to exploration, only three senators out of a hundred said yes to both.[24] Geology and economics may have moved on—ANWR is no longer as important to U.S. oil as it once was, and technology has shrunk the environmental footprint that would accompany development—but the political world has not.

Indeed Alaska could become even more controversial: ANWR might not need high oil prices to work, but high oil prices and melting sea ice have turned the forbidding waters of the offshore Arctic into a tempting target for drillers. In many ways, this is the final frontier of extreme oil: the Beaufort and Chukchi seas can feature waves topping twenty feet, and (at least for now) they are packed with ice from November to May.[25] Dealing with spills would be doubly difficult: beyond the usual challenges, even scattered sea ice can render typical cleanup strategies impotent. No serious analyst expects that the offshore Arctic could deliver much within the next decade. But the National Petroleum Council, a group that advises the U.S. secretary of energy and includes many such analysts, reports that Arctic drilling could potentially deliver upward of a million barrels a day within about fifteen years. This means that when it comes to assessing whether the United States could produce far more oil not just for a few years but also over several decades, the Arctic looms large.

When oil watchers tally up the big prospects for U.S. oil production over the next decade, they typically have tight oil, offshore drilling, and Alaska at the top of their lists. Each source seems to present a simple choice. If regulators allow drilling, production could surge, with each prospect adding well over a million barrels a day to total U.S. oil output (and potentially much more). If big parts of these oil-rich prospects are kept or placed off-limits instead, no oil will be produced.

There is, however, another wild card that some argue could boost U.S. oil production by as much as two million barrels a day over the next two decades without needing to open new lands for oil production: using carbon dioxide to get more oil out of old fields. For decades, U.S. producers have injected carbon dioxide into depleted oil wells in order to boost their pressure and spur continued production; today, roughly a quarter million barrels a day of U.S. oil production comes from this so-called CO_2-EOR, short for carbon dioxide enhanced oil recovery.[26] Advanced Resources International, a consultancy, has estimated that sixty-seven billion barrels of oil (equal to roughly ten years of U.S. demand) could profitably be extracted this way at an oil price of eighty-five dollars per barrel.[27] The Department of Energy has looked at how quickly this oil could be produced, concluding that U.S. production could rise to nearly a million barrels a day by 2035.[28] The Natural Resources Defense Council (NRDC)—hardly a hotbed of oil boosters—has pegged the potential, circa 2030, at closer to two million barrels a day.[29] The 2011 analysis from Advanced Resources International, prepared for the U.S. Department of Energy, tops all of these, pointing to as much as four million barrels a day of potential output.[30]

The catch is that there's no ready source of carbon dioxide to match the scale of the opportunity. The CO_2-EOR projects currently existing in the United States rely largely on natural formations that contain carbon dioxide, like the Bravo Dome in eastern New Mexico, which supplies fields in west Texas, and Mississippi's Jackson Dome, whose CO_2 is used in state and in neighboring Louisiana. A few use artificial sources: the largest group, in Wyoming and Colorado, harnesses CO_2 produced at the LaBarge gas plant in western Wyoming.

The biggest concentrated source of carbon dioxide, though, is in smokestack emissions from power plants. Alas, it's expensive to scour those emissions, condense them, and send them down pipelines to oil-producing sites. The reason the NRDC has talked up enhanced oil recovery (EOR) is that if policymakers want to turbocharge the

CO_2-EOR business, they'll need to make sure that more power plants capture their carbon rather than dump it into the atmosphere. Climate change is largely the subject for the next chapter, but for now what matters is that stopping power plants from emitting carbon dioxide is right at the top of the climate agenda.

There are, of course, doubters about CO_2-EOR. Some argue that all but the most narrowly crafted rules that might encourage power plants to capture their carbon dioxide would spur investment in wind, solar, or nuclear energy instead, leaving the oil industry without a new carbon dioxide source. Others oppose any legislation that actually boosts oil production or prolongs the future of coal, believing such an outcome is unacceptable. And of course, there's the strong possibility that no such legislation or regulation will exist, at least not for a long time.

Still, the prospect of a big boost in enhanced oil recovery remains a genuine possibility. Combined with crude oil from shale, Alaska, and the deep offshore, the further gains to U.S. output could be truly massive, easily exceeding five million barrels a day.

Set against the long span of history, though, all of these resources still fall short. Technically recoverable U.S. oil resources (most of which aren't yet economic to produce) total somewhere around two hundred billion barrels—a massive number, but still less than thirty years of U.S. consumption. Even if the United States could crank up production and, for a time, eliminate imports, it would see its oil output plummet soon thereafter.

Two hundred miles west of Denver, though, a small club of oil developers, Howard Jonas among them, are betting that there's one more trump card to be played: oil shale. If you drive through northwest Colorado, you can literally see this holy grail of American oil without stepping out of your car; massive expanses of shale whiten the stunning cliffs near towns like Rifle. Many Americans can recall oil shale from the 1970s, when it was touted as the answer to dependence on foreign oil, a bigger potential source of oil than Saudi Arabia itself and enough to last the world a hundred years. Then, as oil prices crashed, oil shale seemed to vanish.

Roger Day remembers the moment well. A tall, lanky man with a kind smile, Day earned a degree in mechanical engineering from Michigan Tech before trekking out to California to mine rare earths. In early 1982, he moved to Rifle to join the oil shale rush; soon after, the industry collapsed. Six months after he bought his new home, its value had been slashed by more than half.

Day spent the next twenty-five years in the area developing solution mining of nahcolite. In layperson's terms, he became a pioneer in the extraction of high-quality baking soda from the ground. Then, in the late 2000s, as oil prices began to rise, a company called EGL came calling. They had bid for and won a federal research and development lease (one of only three; the others went to Chevron and Shell) to go after oil shale and they wanted Day to come onboard. The team quickly took shape. Day would be the chief operating officer. Alan Burnham, a careerlong employee of the Lawrence Livermore National Laboratory, where he had pioneered techniques for simulating the cores of nuclear weapons, would join as the chief technology officer. In January 2008, Howard Jonas's company bought a 75 percent interest in EGL. By early 2012, TOTAL had put its own man in the small Rifle office alongside Burnham and Day: John Foulkes, a mustachioed Briton who boasted of having drilled the first well at the famed Kashagan oil field in Kazakhstan.

The trio had few illusions about what they were up against. When I described their efforts as the second attempt to commercialize oil shale after the failed experience of three decades before, they quickly corrected me: it was the fifth. Developers had found their hopes dashed first in the middle of the nineteenth century, then in the years after each of the two world wars, and finally in the early 1980s.

Oil shale is forebidding. Having broken so many hearts so many times over, it still scares most suitors away. "I know that when something has a bad name," Jonas says, "people are very hesitant to go back there, even if things have totally changed."

That change is what a few investors are betting on. Modern oil prices and new technology could eventually make oil shale economically viable. In 2005, Jim Bartis at the RAND Corporation led a team to study the issue. They estimated oil shale could become profitable at an oil price between $80 and $110 a barrel, with costs eventually falling over time as the industry gained experience.[31] (Three years later, Bartis brought together another group of researchers to look at the prospect of turning coal into liquid fuel; they concluded it could work with prices around sixty to seventy dollars per barrel.)[32] But oil shale would take a lot of time to develop at a commercial scale; the RAND teams estimated it would be at least twenty years before production might be brought up to a million barrels a day. Jonas says he thinks he can deliver in twelve, but it's a long way to go from a handful of commercial projects to a full-blown industry.

In any case, when I visited his lease in July 2012, it was supposed to be producing its first oil. The idea is to drill deep within the shale and heat the rock until it essentially melts, yielding flowing oil. Instead, when the engineers had put their massive heater down a two-thousand-foot drill hole, the high-tech equipment had broken. It will take time, and a lot of trial and error, before oil shale had any chance of yielding big results.

Were it to do that, the consequences would be far from universally embraced. If oil shale is the biggest American oil resource, it's probably also the most controversial. Oil shale production, at least historically, is not a pretty business. The traditional approach has involved mining massive amounts of kerogen-bearing rock and then heating it up to temperatures as high as nine hundred degrees Fahrenheit in order to create synthetic oil. The process requires three barrels of water for every barrel of oil produced.[33] It also leaves massive amounts of "spent shale" behind, which can bleed salts and other toxic materials into local water supplies if handled improperly.[34] Most new producers, AMSO among them, are exploring novel methods that convert the kerogen into oil by heating it before drawing it out of the ground, avoiding most of the toxic mess and reducing water demand. (One company, American Soda, wants to produce oil shale and baking soda at the same time.) Yet there are challenges here too: safeguards need to be put in place to make sure that now-mobile oil doesn't seep into aquifers on its way to the surface. Shell is trying to freeze the area around the well to create an impermeable barrier;

AMSO is drilling deep to try to entirely avoid the layers that hold groundwater. Whether any of these will work, and gain public trust, remains to be seen.

❀　❀　❀

Adding up the prospects from all the different U.S. oil resources quickly leads to a conclusion that, in principle, U.S. oil production has the potential for very large gains. But a fundamental question remains: Is this good news just for the oil industry, or could it have much bigger consequences for the United States? After all, oil is special. It evokes intense worries about vulnerability to high prices, hostile foreign producers, and nefarious oil companies closer to home. There is good reason to think that oil is different: if the price of oil spikes, or an oil shortage hits, you have no large-scale alternative to oil-based fuels for your car. Oil has been the subject of frequent fretting since it burst on the scene over a century ago, but contemporary worries can be traced back to the 1970s—those who were alive during the 1973 energy crisis can remember how the U.S. economy was knocked on its back by hostile Middle Eastern suppliers and how U.S. national security was fundamentally undermined as a result. Those who weren't there to experience it have heard the tales of gas lines and economic turmoil, and drivers all continue to confront the reality of high prices at the pump.

For many people, this is why the promise of a renaissance in U.S. oil looks so exciting. Before 1973, the United States didn't depend on imports from abroad, let alone from a shaky Middle East. (It imported some oil, but by choice, not necessity; its goal was to conserve U.S. resources for the future.) After 1973, everything changed. "This is the energy equivalent of the Berlin Wall coming down," says Robin West, an authority on oil markets who served in the Ford and Reagan administrations. "Just as the trauma of the Cold War ended in Berlin, so the trauma of the 1973 oil embargo is ending now."[35]

It's a common sentiment. Critics, though, take umbrage with claims that domestic oil production will slash prices, insulate the economy, or transform U.S. national security. In early 2012, Media Matters, a liberal research organization, collected quotes in a report called "20 Experts

Who Say Drilling Won't Lower Gas Prices."[36] (I made their list, though as you'll see in a moment, I don't quite agree.) They emphasize the fact that, as the Congressional Budget Office has noted, "greater production of oil in the United States would probably not protect U.S. consumers from sudden worldwide increases in oil prices," suggesting the economy as a whole could not be insulated either. And they sharply question the security benefits of greater domestic production: according to the Energy Security Leadership Council, a bipartisan group of prominent business executives and retired military and government leaders from across the political spectrum, "as long as the United States remains a large consumer of oil, no level of domestic fuel production can meaningfully improve energy security."[37]

Open any Economics 101 textbook and you'll learn what determines oil prices: it's the collision of supply and demand. High prices make production more attractive and encourage people to cut back how much they use. If prices get too high, supply outstrips demand, and an oil glut develops; eventually, prices crash. Too low a price will do the opposite, dissuading production while encouraging people to use more oil, which leads to a shortage of crude. Markets eventually settle on prices that avoid both unsustainable outcomes.

This helps in quickly settling one of the battles between oil enthusiasts and skeptics: since oil is traded globally, prices depend on how much is produced in the entire world, not how much is pumped from the ground in the United States. A world where the United States produces ten million barrels of oil every day won't necessarily have lower oil prices than one where it produces five million. After all, U.S. oil production was higher in 2010 than in 2009, but oil prices were higher too.

Score one for the skeptics. But there's less to this victory than meets the eye. If the United States increases its oil production, and output from the rest of the world remains unchanged, total world supply will rise. This means that, everything else being equal, prices will fall below what they otherwise would have been. (If they don't, people will use the same amount of oil they did before, and all the new oil will have nowhere to go.) The big question is how much.

You might think this would be easy to nail down: figure out the historical relationship between oil supply and oil prices and use it to predict the future impact of producing more oil. The first big problem, though, is that there are a lot of things that influence the price of oil. This means teasing out the influence of new supplies isn't straightforward. Worse, if the relationships have changed over time, the results are even less reliable. Still, economists have come up with some reasonable guesses—and the implications are striking. A team at the International Monetary Fund recently estimated that a 5 percent increase in world oil supplies would eventually cut oil prices roughly in half.[38] (Even this was a best guess: they gave nearly one-in-four odds of a drop either twice or only half as large.) This sort of change might be produced by an increase of about five million barrels a day in U.S. oil supplies. The possibility of slashing oil prices in half by increasing U.S. oil supplies by five million barrels sounds huge. The problem, though, is we've seen only half of the story.

When U.S. oil production rises, other countries' oil output usually falls. The economic logic is simple: more U.S. oil output means lower prices; lower prices render some oil projects economically unattractive; those will either shut down or won't reach production in the first place. If the United States increases its oil output by, say, five million barrels a day, this means total world production rises by less. The resulting price drop is also smaller as a result.

This is compounded by an even more important dynamic: most of the world of oil production doesn't work like a real free market. Many countries try to maximize their revenues from oil sales by restraining production and propping up prices. Saudi Arabia, for example, can often profit more by producing less oil. It's not unreasonable, for example, to imagine that a 50 percent increase in Saudi output would cut world oil price in half. But the net impact would be to slash Saudi revenues by a quarter. It's no wonder, then, that Riyadh isn't racing to produce more oil. And things get worse: if several of these "strategic producers" wanting to restrain their oil production can successfully coordinate, the payoff from holding back output rises. This is the goal of OPEC, which still produces 40 percent of the world's oil, a figure that has swung up and down but hasn't changed radically for decades.

All of this has a big upshot for the potential consequences of higher U.S. oil production. As U.S. oil output rises, prices are inclined to fall. That's bad news for oil-exporting countries. In response, some of those countries will tend to try and cut back their own supplies, aiming to neutralize the U.S. boom and prop up prices. This dynamic has the potential to deeply undermine the impact of increased U.S. production on prices. If, for example, a five-million-barrel-a-day increase in U.S. crude output was met with a four-million-barrel-a-day cut in supplies from other countries, the net impact on prices would be slashed by a factor of five.

There is, however, one other tantalizing possibility—and it could mean deeper price cuts rather than smaller ones. Big-enough gains in global oil production could spark a battle among OPEC members and other big producers for market share, leading to a crash in world prices.

To see how this could happen, imagine you're a strategist for a major member of OPEC, perhaps Saudi Arabia, the United Arab Emirates, or Iraq. Oil production outside the cartel is surging; not only is U.S. production on the rise but so is output from Brazil, Canada, and beyond. You're worried about falling prices but don't want to sell less oil. What you'd like most is for others to curb their production; that would keep prices high and spare you the need to throttle back your own output. Everyone else, of course, feels the same way, making this particular outcome unlikely. Your next-best bet is to share the burden of restraint with your fellow cartel members (and perhaps a few others). As new production rises, though, the burden increases too—and although it might be easy to divvy up some minor cutbacks, it's a lot harder to share a smaller pie. At some point, discipline breaks down. You lose faith that others will curb their output; in fact, you fear that if you dial back your own production, other members will just raise theirs and steal your customers. Even worse, with falling prices you have trouble meeting your country's budget. So you turn to a final option: you crank up production in an attempt to sell more oil. The only problem is that several other countries have made similar decisions. Collectively, you flood the market. Prices plummet.

To be certain, there are limits to how far this dynamic can take things. Most new U.S. oil is expensive to produce. If prices drop too far, U.S. oil production will stagnate or even fall, reversing the stimulus that had prompted lower prices in the first place. This makes it tough to see how rising U.S. crude production could drive world oil prices below fifty dollars or so for more than a brief period of time. But that's still a staggeringly different number from the ones people have begun to get used to. So here's the big question for anyone trying to divine the impact of rising U.S. oil production on world prices: What sort of response will other oil producing countries mount, alone or collectively? Will some of them restrain production and put a floor on prices? Or will discipline break down and result in a flood of oil?

Two episodes from history can help us sort through the difference. The first is the late 1960s and early 1970s. Oil production outside OPEC is rising, but consumption is increasing even faster. West Germany and Japan continue to grow as industrial powerhouses after the devastating experience of World War II; the United States and the rest of Europe are increasingly thirsty for oil too. The net result is that OPEC has an ever larger pie to divide: its members can restrain production and raise prices while still ensuring solid revenues for each. And that's exactly what happens: OPEC output doesn't grow a lot, but prices and incomes soar.

Fast-forward to the early 1980s. The Iranian revolution of 1979 has spiked crude prices and crushed global oil demand. For the first time in decades, in fact, consumption is falling year upon year. Supply from outside OPEC, meanwhile, continues to rise. The pie left for OPEC members to divide is now shrinking. Tough collective decisions are essential if prices are to stay high, but producers aren't up to the task. Instead, OPEC members battle each other for the remaining scraps of an ever-smaller market. Prices drop to previously unthinkable lows.

If you want to know whether OPEC countries will muffle or amplify the impact of rising U.S. supplies, then you need to ask whether the growth will be overwhelmed by even bigger increases in demand. That's where China, India, and the rest of the developing world come in—and in a way it doesn't look good for the United States. The International Energy Agency has projected that demand for oil from the developing world will rise from about thirty-two million barrels a day in 2008 to forty-one million barrels a day in 2020; developed world demand, meanwhile, is projected to fall by only a quarter as much. Other projections yield similar results. The net result is a massive new market to divvy up, particularly if no big steps are taken to curtail the world's thirst for oil.

This was all at the front of my mind when I arrived at OPEC headquarters in Vienna on a cool spring day in 2012. OPEC's influence has waxed and waned, but with nearly half of world oil production within its member countries' borders, and a far higher fraction of the world's cheap crude, it still matters. Abdallah Salem el-Badri, a former Libyan oil minister and at the time the secretary general of OPEC, welcomed me warmly. Trained at Florida Southern University, the onetime Esso Standard manager was by then seventy-one and reaching the end of his five-year term. I asked him how he felt about the boom in U.S. oil and gas production and was a bit taken aback by his reply. "This is really good," he told me. Since Richard Nixon, the United States has obsessed over its dependence on Middle Eastern oil; rising U.S. oil output could get OPEC off the hook. "They will blame us less," he predicted. "Look at the [U.S. presidential] campaign," which was just warming up at the time. "Fifty percent of it is about energy!" I pressed el-Badri on whether OPEC could weather growth in U.S. supplies. He was sanguine. "Yes, for us, it is important," he acknowledged. "But there is room for everybody."

He's probably right. In the short run, it's entirely possible the world will overinvest in oil production, leading to a temporary price crash if producers aren't able to hold back. But there seem to be few limits so far to the world's thirst for oil over the long haul. And even though crude output in United States, Canada, and Brazil is on the rise, it is declining in countries such as Norway, China, and the United Kingdom. Rapid turnarounds in producers from Iraq to Venezuela could quickly alter the picture, as could a persistently weak Chinese economy, letting U.S. oil output tip the final balance, but it would be unwise to bet on it. Letting U.S. production rise would help keep a lid on prices, which might otherwise rise more. Anything much beyond that, though, seems unlikely, at least in the long run.

Still it's tough to be too confident. Oil markets are often as much about politics as economics, and predicting future political twists and turns should be done with care.

This doesn't mean, of course, that people will (or should) stop trying. Economic analysts, worried about the health of the economy, constantly try to predict whether the price of oil will go up or down. Between January 2007 and July 2008, oil prices rose from about $50 a barrel to nearly $140. With the United States consuming about ten million barrels more oil than it produced every day, this meant consumers were spending nearly a billion dollars a day more than before on imported oil. Economists would later discover that the economy had entered a recession in December 2007. Jim Hamilton, long a leading analyst of oil and the U.S. economy, would conclude in a much-cited paper that the oil spike helped do it in. For those with memories of the recessions that followed rising oil prices in 1973, 1979, and 1990, this was bad news once again.

It also reinforced a popular perception. The United States depends on imported oil, so when prices rise, it's forced to ship money overseas, sucking life out of its economy. If it produced its own oil, though, this would no longer be the case. Instead of sending money abroad, consumers would now be handing it over to American producers; the two sides of the ledger would cancel out. Whatever rising supplies meant for oil prices themselves, moving toward self-sufficiency in crude production would insulate the United States from the worst effects of expensive oil. If the United States could go so far as to produce all the oil it consumed, it would become energy-independent.

It's a seductively simple picture of how oil affects the U.S. economy, with a similarly straightforward resolution; but unfortunately, it doesn't hold up. The first clue as to why comes from digging deeper into the historical record. It turns out that all but one of the twelve U.S. recessions since World War II were preceded by spikes in the price of oil.[39] This includes recessions that began in 1948, 1953, 1957, and 1969—all years in which the United States did not depend substantially on imported oil. If the United States was vulnerable to price spikes before it became a major oil importer, it might remain vulnerable even if it slashes its imports today.

Basic economic theory does a good job of explaining why. Rapid rises in consumer costs act like a sudden tax. People have less money to spend, so they curtail all sorts of purchases. The beneficiaries of their bigger gasoline bills—oil exporters in places such as Saudi Arabia or Kuwait—don't spend much of their windfall in the United States. The net result is that U.S. firms can no longer sell as much of what they produce as before, forcing them to shrink production or fail; collectively, the economy pulls back, at best slowing down, at worst reversing.[40] There are other ways that price spikes affect the economy—in particular, as we'll see later, they can slam the auto industry—but when it comes to looking at the value of increased domestic oil production, it's the impact on consumers' wallets that matters most.

So what changes if the money those consumers lose goes to an oil producer in Texas instead of to a sheik in Iraq? Less than you might hope. The average American oil user isn't particularly rich, and she does not save a lot of money. Instead, she spends what she has: if you put a dollar in her pocket, she'll spend a dollar more. Rising oil prices, though, create a windfall that flows disproportionately to corporate treasuries. They normally either spend it slowly (it takes time to develop plans for large capital outlays) or distribute it to typically wealthier shareholders (through stock buybacks and dividends) and to executives (through bonuses), who are less likely to quickly spend the extra dollars in their pockets; they already have substantially more money and are more inclined to save the extra cash.

Pinning down exact numbers for this dynamic is thornier than you might imagine; the question of how individual and corporate spending differ in their economic impacts is far from being settled. (Its relevance is not just to this book; it's at the heart of fights over things like tax policy and government stimulus spending.) Reasonable estimates, though, claim that the short-term consequence of taking a dollar from the average individual and giving it to the typical company—basically what happens when oil prices spike over days or months—can be similar to taking seventy-five cents from that person and throwing it in the trash. (If oil prices rise strongly but more slowly, perhaps over the course of several years, greater reliance on domestic oil production can provide more insulation, since companies have more time to reinject their profits into the broader economy.) I hasten to add that this doesn't mean corporate profit or spending is bad; it just means profits often translate slowly into spending—too slowly to immediately compensate for a sudden loss of broad-based individual wealth. The net impact on the U.S. economy isn't as bad as if the money went to the Middle East—some of the windfall is now being quickly spent at home—but it's still nowhere close to removing most of the ugly near-term consequences that may exist.

There is, however, one more important piece of this puzzle: lower average oil prices could also mean smaller price spikes. A sudden loss of a million barrels a day from world oil supplies could raise oil prices by more than 50 percent.[41] If the starting point is one-hundred-dollar-a-barrel oil, that means a fifty dollar rise, which translates into a tax of a billion dollars a day on American consumers. If abundant oil supplies drop average prices to fifty dollars a barrel, though, the starting point is different. The shock to the system still raises prices by 50 percent, but this now works out to just twenty-five dollars. The new tax on Americans is only half what it was before, and the danger to the U.S. economy is reduced. It's this dynamic that may hold the most promise for translating U.S. oil abundance into greater security in a world of volatile oil.

I should pause briefly and point out something important: I haven't actually said anything about how dangerous high and volatile oil prices are, or even claimed they're all that bad. All I've shown is that if they're as bad as many people think they are, more domestic oil production won't change the conclusion much. I'll revisit the more basic question of the real dangers of high oil prices in Chapter 5.

So far, new oil production looks good, though not nearly as good as some of its boosters have claimed. New U.S. oil output would lower world crude prices, but the consequences probably would be marginal rather than dramatic. More U.S. output would also help shield the country from the impacts of price spikes, but unless oil prices collapsed, this protection would be far less than enthusiasts hope.

All of this high theory is unlikely to impress Jennifer Kaiser. Had I met her in June 2011, she probably would not have known the first thing about oil, but by the time we found ourselves chatting outside her Carrollton restaurant a year later, petroleum was a central part of her life. The town got swept up in tight oil fever the previous October, as landmen and drillers moved in to extract crude from the Utica shale thousands of feet beneath the ground. So many oil workers were in town that they started begging her to open the restaurant at four o'clock in the morning, before they headed off to the rigs. The town was short of places to stay, so Kaiser also took in two oil workers as boarders above her restaurant. Her brother did even better: the previous autumn, he had leased his land to an oil and gas company for more than a million dollars. For people from Carrollton, Ohio, to Williston, North Dakota, booming oil production is about something quite simple: jobs.

There's little question the oil industry employs a lot of people. But the actual numbers matter, particularly if you want to extrapolate them to predict how many jobs a growing oil industry could create. The American Petroleum Institute claims that oil and gas together employ nearly ten million Americans.[42] That's too generous. It includes the people who staff nearly two hundred thousand gas stations across America, but it's fair to assume that increased U.S. oil production won't raise their numbers too. It also includes all sorts of people who benefit from the money spent by oil and gas workers. Many of them might get richer, but, like Kaiser, many would still have had jobs without oil.

You'd do better to look at the number of people who are actually engaged in producing oil. Government statistics don't distinguish between jobs in oil and in gas, but together, they report 160,000 people employed as of 2010.[43] It's also reasonable to assume that a similar number have jobs that government statistics classify as "support activities," raising the total to around 300,000. If you want to be particularly generous, you can even go a step further, guessing that for every job that's technically in the oil industry there's another upstream, from producing steel to line the wells, cooking food to cater the drill sites, or some other associated activity. This takes us to somewhere in the neighborhood of half a million jobs. Now let's imagine the figure is doubled by booming U.S. oil production, a stretch but still a useful limit. The result will be somewhere around another half million new jobs; this is not a trivial number, but in an economy with more than a hundred million people who want to work, it's not world-changing either.

Alas, even this can overstate the case. The latest boom in U.S. oil production emerged within a depressed economy. It's plausible that many of the people newly employed in the oil sector would otherwise have been unemployed. But a healthier economy doesn't work that way. Jobs gained from strength in one sector are usually offset by jobs lost in others.[44] Economists have long agreed that the unemployment rate is determined by more fundamental factors such as how easy it is to hire and fire people, how well the education system works, and whether workers can easily move to jobs in new places. Booming oil production won't change any of that.

It can, however, make Americans richer. Think about a barrel of oil as if it's a hundred dollars that's buried deep underground. Now imagine you suddenly discover a massive deposit of a billion barrels that can be dug up at a cost of sixty dollars each. (Equivalently, you develop a new technology that can be used to extract previously unreachable oil at this price.) If you spend sixty billion dollars to extract them, you end up with a hundred billion dollars. The extra forty billion dollars in your pocket is essentially free: it is a pure windfall. Those proceeds are divvied up: the company doing the drilling takes some, its workers grab a slice, and the government has its own take too. Unless you do a massive amount of damage in the process of digging up the oil, the country as a whole is better off.

How much better off? Daniel Ahn, an economist at Citigroup whom I've collaborated with on occasion, developed a model to try to find out. The model looks at historical data for the U.S. economy and extracts relationships among things like oil, technology, employment, and economic growth. It can consequently make tentative forecasts about U.S. economic growth. Then Ahn layers on an optimistic forecast for future U.S. oil production as the result of recent changes in what technology allows us to extract from the ground. The model tells him it could boost U.S. economic output by as much as a couple of percentage points within a decade. This might not sound like much, and the results come with many caveats, but regardless, the numbers are big: the payoff that Ahn predicts works out to more than $300 billion every year.

And there's still one more economic benefit to tally up. For many years, Americans have worried that they import far more than they export; in economic jargon, the United States has a big current account deficit. (Technically, the difference between imports and exports is known as the trade deficit, but for the United States the difference between that and the current account deficit is small and often neglected.) Economists have long debated whether this is a significant problem. Some see it as a sign that the United States is an attractive place in which to invest. Others fear that big current account deficits could collapse through a plunge in the U.S. dollar, or that big current account deficits sustain the sort of cheap credit that fueled the financial crisis only a few years back.

Oil imports superficially look like a big culprit behind the U.S. current account deficit. In recent years, the tab for imported oil has often accounted for more than half of the current account imbalance.[45] Producing far more oil at home, then, would seem to go a long way toward fixing the problem.

This is one of the few advantages from domestic oil that oil-production skeptics tend to concede. In fact, they'd be on firmer ground questioning this claim than many of the others they attack. Economists have long believed that, in the long run, current account deficits have a straightforward explanation: Americans consume more than they produce, so they need to rely on imports to make up the difference. The result is a current account deficit. The thing about oil production is that it has two consequences. The first, of course, is an increase in U.S. output. But because that makes Americans richer, it drives their spending up as well. The two effects should cancel out over the long haul; there's no reason to believe more oil production will make any sustained long-term difference to the U.S. current account. (Still not sure? Then consider this: there are plenty of countries with massive oil import bills that have big current account surpluses. Germany is a great example. So is China.)

The long run, though, can take a long time to come around. In the meantime, rapid run-ups in oil prices tend to blow open the U.S. trade deficit. Spending on oil imports rises, but increased revenues from other exports don't offset it. Even worse, the strategic role of the U.S. dollar means dollars flowing out to pay for oil get recycled back into the U.S. economy more problematically. Instead of coming back in exchange for goods and services, U.S. dollars are often lent back to Americans. This helps sustain U.S. consumption, which can be a good thing for a while, letting Americans ride out bumps in the oil market rather than being buffeted by them. But sustained over time, it can turn ugly. Cheap credit can fuel bubbles that collapse in disaster, much like what happened in real estate before the financial crisis of 2008. History suggests that episodes leading to the accumulation of big external deficits rarely end well.[46] Buying more oil from within the United States rather than from abroad can blunt this danger. Score one more for the promise of domestic oil.

❧ ❧ ❧

All of these concerns about the economic consequences of changes in oil markets are amplified by a basic fact: worries about the impact of oil on the U.S. economy shape national security decisions. The relationship goes back nearly a century, but the most immediate fears date back forty years.

On October 6, 1973, a group of Arab states launched a surprise attack on Israel. As the Jewish state gained the upper hand, though, a coalition of Arab countries hit back at Israel's allies, beginning a painful embargo of their oil supplies. Several months later, Henry Kissinger, then the secretary of state and national security advisor, would sit down with his aides for yet another discussion of how oil had changed the dynamics of world power. He quickly became exasperated: "Don't talk to me about barrels of oil. They might as well be bottles of Coca Cola. I don't understand!"[47]

Similar conversations have undoubtedly taken place many times since: in 1979, when the Iranian revolution ended up sending the U.S. economy into recession; in 1990, when Saddam Hussein invaded Kuwait and threatened the oil fields of Saudi Arabia; in 2011, when revolution in Libya sent oil markets into convulsions. They happen every time U.S. leaders consider intervening in a part of the world where oil is also at stake. U.S. decision making seems to be hopelessly entangled with oil.

It is liberation from this crushing constraint on U.S. freedom of action abroad that the biggest enthusiasts for higher domestic oil production hold out most tantalizingly. "To not be concerned with where our oil is going to come from," Pioneer Natural Resources CEO Scott Sheffield told the *New York Times* in early 2012, "is probably the biggest home run for the country in a hundred years."[48]

Yet for all its promise, larger U.S. oil supplies probably wouldn't do that. We've already seen that the U.S. economy would remain vulnerable to price spikes even if it produced all the oil it consumed. Nor would those price spikes be muted for domestic oil: for example, the price of U.S.-produced oil jumped just as much during the Libyan crisis of 2011 as the price of oil from the Middle East did. Even a technically independent America would still be vulnerable to oil market vagaries (if somewhat less so than it has been for the last few decades) and hence still restrained in what it could do abroad.

There is one potential exception to this logic, but it would come into play only under extreme circumstances. A United States that produced as much oil as it consumed could wall itself off from global oil markets in a crisis by temporarily banning exports of crude. (Otherwise, if the price of oil shot up overseas but not in the United States, people would ship oil from the United States to other higher priced markets where they could make more money, until prices in the United States rose similarly.) This would give it more room to maneuver abroad. But it would be an immensely difficult step to take. Blocking oil outflows during a crisis would in practice mean denying oil and inflicting severe economic damage on others, some of whom might be allies. Those on the receiving end might well retaliate by barring U.S. imports of other critical items, undermining the intention of U.S. policy in the first place. In a war for U.S. survival, these caveats might be set aside, but such a fight is highly unlikely, at least in the coming years. The sorts of contingencies that American policymakers have typically grappled with in recent decades are ones where closing the U.S. borders to crude oil is almost unimaginable. In any case, so long as U.S. production is even slightly smaller than U.S. demand, even this option would be impossible to pursue without substantially raising U.S. oil prices or causing shortages of crude.

That said, if more U.S. oil production might not do much to strengthen the United States against its adversaries, it could do more to weaken those opponents themselves. Iran is fueled by oil sales; so is Russia. Hugo Chavez has dominated Venezuela for a decade by strategically employing oil revenues, something Saddam Hussein managed to do for even longer in Iraq. And although we saw earlier that greater U.S. oil production might not slash oil prices, the reason was important: other producers might curb their own production in response. Either way, oil exporters would suffer, either selling less crude or getting less money per barrel. Not all of them would be hostile—in fact some, like Kuwait and Iraq, are actually U.S. partners in many respects—but many could well be.

Economic logic aside, rising U.S. oil output is also likely to affect geopolitics simply because of how leaders react to it. My colleague Blake Clayton and I have studied how patterns of oil trade affect relationships between countries.[49] One of the most striking findings is that if leaders believe that changes in the oil market will have big political consequences—and leaders often do believe that—they take steps that themselves can change the world. For example, Saudi Arabia underpriced oil that it sold to the United States for decades, in an attempt to remain the largest oil supplier to the United States. Saudi leaders reasoned that many U.S. diplomats and strategists believed the largest supplier of oil to their country must be important and would thus treat Saudi Arabia deferentially. They were probably right. Today, if Middle Eastern oil producers conclude that rising U.S. oil production will weaken U.S. interest in the region, they'll take steps to build new alliances with other world powers. If leaders in Beijing believe that the United States will no longer be as interested in protecting critical sea lanes that link Middle Eastern oil markets to the wider world (including China), they'll build up their navy more quickly, with broader results. All of this can happen even if economic analysts insist that the United States will remain vulnerable to events in the Middle

East, since beliefs about the relationship between oil and international security have a way of creating consequences of their own.

Similarly, with rising prospects within the United States (and Canada), large U.S. oil companies may feel less pressure than they have in the past to invest in politically fraught, war-torn, or corrupt countries abroad. The U.S. government has often been called on to protect and advocate those companies' overseas interests, a task frequently in conflict with other U.S. foreign policy goals, including human rights promotion.[50] One can debate whether the U.S. government should get enmeshed in such fights between private companies and foreign governments; U.S. involvement is often driven by misguided beliefs about what's needed to promote security of U.S. energy supplies. Yet so long as some U.S. policymakers are strongly compelled to intervene on behalf of U.S. oil companies abroad, any trend that turns those companies increasingly toward North America could have benefits for the United States.

The future of American oil looks drastically different from only a few years ago. Back then the big question was how to deal with scarcity. Today it is the possibility of plenty that is at the forefront. What will actually happen depends substantially on two factors: demand for oil and what Americans decide to do with the bounty that's underground. Most of the land that fueled the first stage of the American oil renaissance was private. Going much farther will require making far more inroads into public lands—and whether this happens in a big way will be up to the American people.

High oil prices and technological breakthroughs mean there are often large gains to be had from producing more U.S. oil. Expanding access to oil-rich territory for increasing production will create new economic opportunities; it will also reduce, though far from eliminate, U.S. economic and security vulnerabilities stemming from the critical role of oil in the American economy and in geopolitics. (Greater U.S. oil production might also affect efforts to cut oil use, a possibility we'll explore in Chapter 5.) But there is no magic line beyond which the United States will become energy-independent—no threshold in whose pursuit it would obviously be worth opening up massive tracts of wilderness to drilling or putting another thousand miles of coastline at risk of spills. Whether risks to the local environment are tolerable will depend on whether oil is developed safely, and on where development is pursued. And even though the benefits of U.S. oil development may appear inevitable, the reality is that, as with natural gas, development without proper safeguards could lead to a backlash, undermining the potential of abundant crude. How these environmental unknowns are resolved depends in part on whether governments make wise decisions regarding protection against local risks.

Yet there is still one big question surrounding an American oil renaissance that all the economic benefits in the world cannot straightforwardly answer. Scientists and advocates increasingly warn that aggressively exploiting America's oil will be catastrophic for climate change. Some voice similar skepticism about natural gas. As far as they are concerned, Howard Jonas's dreams for Colorado oil shale, and everyone else's big plans for U.S. oil and gas, are incompatible with a safe future for the planet.

4

"GAME OVER"

On a typically warm late August Sunday in Washington, D.C., which marked the first day of protests against the Keystone XL pipeline, 70 men and women were arrested outside the White House.[1] The next day, another 50 joined them, and by the third day of the action 162 had gone to jail.[2] The following Monday, Bill McKibben, the writer turned activist who masterminded the protests, was released; he had been detained on day one. "I'm a little tired and a lot hungry but I'm happy as can be," he told an interviewer as he exited Central Cell Block, the main D.C. jail.[3] The protests were attracting attention. "This is what starts to happen," he said, "when people show what the stakes are."

For McKibben and the other 1,251 people who would ultimately be arrested over the next two weeks, those stakes were impossible to overstate. First proposed in 2008, the Keystone XL pipeline was supposed to stretch 1,179 miles, from Hardisty, Alberta, to Steel City, Nebraska, before linking up with other lines that would connect to the refineries of the Texas Gulf Coast. At the northern end of the pipe lay the massive Canadian oil sands. Geologists have known for decades that the Athabasca region, which extends over more than a hundred thousand square miles north of the Albertan capital of Edmonton, held within it staggering amounts of potential oil. The problem had always been how to get at it. Unlike conventional crude, which flows easily when tapped, Albertan oil is found in bitumen, a gooey mix of clay, sand, and oil. For decades these deposits were considered too costly to extract. In the early 2000s, though, rising prices and advancing technology combined to begin to change that. By 2010, oil sands production had hit 1.5 million barrels a day.[4] The U.S. Department of Energy has projected that if oil prices rise steeply, oil sands production could reach six million barrels a day by 2030.

Indeed, typical estimates peg the total volume underground at 1.7 trillion barrels, about fifty years' worth of world oil consumption at the current pace. The sheer magnitude of the oil sands has led people on both sides of the fight over the future of U.S. energy to develop a habit of including this source in their vision for U.S. oil. Enthusiasts talk about how Canadian production could deliver U.S. jobs and about the potential for North American energy independence, extrapolating the purported benefits of U.S. oil production to output from north of the border. Environmental advocates have focused their energies on the local environmental impacts of oil sands development, which can be ugly, for several years. But in early 2011, Jim Hansen, a prominent scientist at NASA, published some simple analysis that broadened their focus. His calculations had led him to conclude that if the Albertan deposits were all burned, it would be "game over" for the planet when it came to climate change.[5] Later that year, McKibben put the pieces together and came to a stark conclusion: the Keystone XL pipeline had to be stopped.

He was not the only one who felt that way. A who's who of environmental groups backed the protests. They were joined by conservative Nebraska landowners, afraid of risks posed by a pipeline that would run through their backyards. The disparate group had tapped into something much deeper than concern about a single pipeline. "We've got to get off oil," McKibben emphasized the day after his release. "We don't need one more huge source of oil pouring in."[6]

The sentiment made instinctive sense, and not only when it came to the tar sands. Americans were rapidly tapping into ever bigger pools of petroleum. The outer continental shelf, Alaska, tight oil, oil shale; each source of oil raised alarms when juxtaposed with increasing concerns about climate change, which scientists were confident was being accelerated by the carbon dioxide produced from burning fossil fuels. Massive deposits of shale gas, recently unlocked, had struck many similarly: there was nearly ten times more much carbon in the world's gas fields than in the Alberta oil sands.[7] The Sierra Club, which had campaigned to move "Beyond Coal" since 2002, added "Beyond Oil" after the BP spill in 2010 and then launched "Beyond Natural Gas" in 2012. In a world threatened by climate change, fossil fuels no longer appeared to make any sense.

A brief walk with Jeff Mitton and Scott Ferrenberg through the pine forests of Niwot Ridge nearly a mile above the nearby town of Boulder, Colorado, makes it easy to understand why people are worried. The world has been getting hotter, and so has Niwot Ridge. Mitton, the model of a naturalist with his white beard and big smile, studied evolutionary biology after getting his PhD in 1973. When I visit, he is toting a tripod-mounted camera to record the results of the pair's experiments. Ferrenberg, who's carrying a small axe to slice into trees, is tall and lanky with a salt-and-pepper goatee; he spent time in California, Pennsylvania, and Arizona, working jobs from entomological (insect) research to technical support for forest fire control, before moving to Boulder and becoming a graduate student in Mitton's lab in 2008. They were then part of a team studying the impact of higher temperatures on alpine trees and plants by planting massive heating lamps in the hills above Boulder and watching to see what happened.[8]

The two men were walking in the forest one late spring day when they spotted something odd: mountain pine beetles were moving about. Pine beetles had recently been in the news. In British Columbia, the critters invaded around 2001; ten years later, more than half the loggable pine in the province had been killed, devastating a core part of the local economy.[9] The Rocky Mountains came within the beetles' sights in 1996, but it took a decade before the epidemic there really intensified. By 2010, four million acres in northern Colorado and southern Wyoming had been hit, and beetle watchers were warning of more damage to come.[10] It wasn't unusual to see mountain pine beetles in the Colorado hills: they had been there for as long as anyone could remember. But everyone knew they couldn't live at the high altitudes of Niwot Ridge and that the beetles usually didn't come out until July.

Ferrenberg and Mitton quickly started to guess what was happening. Mountain pine beetles are one of the simplest organisms you can use to study the impact of climate change on living creatures. The life cycles of the cold-blooded beetles are controlled by heat; add more high-temperature days, and the beetles' lives speed up. With rising temperatures, altitudes that were always too cold to support pine beetle populations were suddenly warm enough to host the creatures. More troubling, though, was how quickly the beetles were developing. It used to be that pine beetles would breed one generation before dying off in the cold. Now, propelled by rising temperatures, they were breeding two generations every year, the first in the late spring, the second in the summer. If one generation of beetles used to count sixty members, two generations meant thirty-six hundred. A small change in climate meant big and devastating consequences on the ground.

And it was not just the lowly mountain pine beetles or the trees they feasted on that were feeling the heat. Scientists were now gingerly attributing extreme weather events such as heat waves and droughts to a changing climate, and they confidently predicted worse consequences to come. Raging wildfires, widespread droughts, and devastating storms like Hurricane Sandy, whatever their individual causes, made the sorts of dangers that lurked in a warming world vivid. And many fixated on other ways in which small changes might have big impacts. I visited the Arctic with the Coast Guard in 2008; they wanted to establish a presence in a region that many were heralding as the next frontier of geopolitics, as rising temperatures melted Arctic ice and opened vast new territories to commerce. The boat I was on landed in Kivalina, Alaska, a village under assault by waves that had previously been kept away by massive sheets of now-melted ice. No corner of the earth, it seemed, was being spared. Yet seven billion people around the world continued to use energy largely as if nothing was amiss.

❊ ❊ ❊

Along Niwot Ridge past where Mitton and Ferrenberg study their beetles, scientists have been collecting air samples since 1968.[11] Each one is sealed in a cylinder and later scrutinized with special equipment to determine its concentration of carbon dioxide, known scientifically as CO_2. The pattern that has emerged from this experiment, the second oldest of its kind in the world, is unmistakable: the concentration of CO_2 wiggles from month to month, but year after year it has been rising, at a steadily accelerating pace. When the gathering station opened in 1968, the concentration had just crossed 320 parts per million (ppm)—if you divided a cube of atmosphere into a million little cells, 320 of those would have been full of CO_2—a figure substantially higher than 280, roughly where it had been until industrialization began in the eighteenth century.[12] Every year, as people burn coal, oil, and natural gas and cut down the world's forests, the number rises. When I visited the ridge in 2012, it was quickly closing in on 400. It will continue to rise, by two or three parts per million every year, unless there are fundamental changes in how energy is produced throughout the world.

It has been known for more than a century that carbon dioxide and other so-called greenhouse gases such as methane, water vapor, and nitrous oxide concentrate in the atmosphere and trap heat. Without them, the average temperature on earth would be well below zero; the fact that there has long been a blanket of greenhouse gases surrounding the planet is a big reason we are here. But human activities—most prominently the combustion of coal, oil, and natural gas to generate usable energy—produce massive amounts of carbon dioxide. Some is absorbed in the oceans and in trees, but much of it collects in the atmosphere, further insulating the earth and raising global temperatures. With that come changes in weather patterns and sea level and, as a consequence, impacts on societies and people. Despite attempts by some people to confuse the public, this much is basically uncontested. Even Richard Lindzen, an atmospheric physicist and MIT professor best known for arguing that climate change isn't a significant problem, says that there is nothing controversial among "serious climate scientists" about claims that the world has been warming and that increases in carbon dioxide, which have been extensively documented, ought to cause temperatures to rise.[13]

The fact that burning oil and gas intensifies climate change, though, doesn't tell you much about whether booming U.S. oil and gas production is more to be celebrated or feared. The questions that need to be answered in order to make that sort of judgment are different. Two come down to a mix of climate science and moral judgment: How sensitive is the earth's climate to rising greenhouse gas concentrations? How bad will the consequences that result from global warming be? (This second question has a big moral component: How much should we care about bad consequences that will occur outside the United States or to future generations?) Another two lie more in the realm of economics and politics. How much will developing U.S. oil and gas contribute directly to global greenhouse gas emissions? Moreover, human-caused climate change is a product of emissions from around the world, not just the United States. Given that, what does higher U.S. oil and gas production really mean for emissions and climate change writ large?

Much of the debate over how touchy the earth's thermostat is revolves around a number known as climate sensitivity. This is typically expressed as the amount of warming we should expect to see if atmospheric concentrations of greenhouse gases were to double from their preindustrial levels. It is widely agreed that the direct impact is relatively small, but big questions arise when you start looking at more complex dynamics, particularly those that unfold over longer periods of time. A big part of the debate focuses on what happens to clouds: as temperatures rise because of higher greenhouse gas concentrations, clouds start to behave differently; depending on whom you ask, this could suppress warming slightly (these days a minority position) or enhance it moderately (the dominant view). Another area of contention revolves around what will happen to Arctic ice. As the planet warms, ice melts, and white slabs make way for dark blue seas. Dark colors absorb much more energy from the sun than white ones do (something that anyone who has gone outside on a hot day wearing black knows). The Arctic seas, now much darker than before, trap more heat, leading to more warming. Feedbacks such as this one, which can play out over many years, can boost climate sensitivity well beyond what short-term dynamics would do.

With so many moving pieces, it should be no surprise that estimates of climate sensitivity are all over the map. The most authoritative survey of scientific calculations, published in 2007, looked at eighteen stud-ies.[14] Most of them used a mix of models and historical observations to conclude that global temperatures might rise as little as one degree Celsius if atmospheric greenhouse gas concentrations doubled, an increment that few scientists consider particularly dangerous. But most also found that a temperature rise of between two and four degrees was more likely, and that an increase of six degrees or more—more than ten degrees Fahrenheit—was, though relatively improbable, within the realm of possibility. Scientists and policymakers have often focused on two degrees as a threshold for particularly dangerous climate impacts, and most find a four-degree increase immensely ugly to imagine. Few studies of a world that is six degrees Celsius warmer even exist, because it is so far beyond the realm of experience, and because few scientists even want to consider its troubling implications.

In 2009, a team of MIT researchers built a special roulette wheel to dramatize the risks that result when these dynamics collide with green-house gas concentrations that are currently on track to do far more than double.[15] Each slice represented a different rise in temperatures. Without changes to how people made and used energy, they estimated conservatively, the lowest odds on the wheel were for temperatures to rise by less than four degrees Celsius (about seven degrees Fahrenheit). The best odds lay between four and six (seven and eleven Fahrenheit), and a bet that temperatures would rise by six degrees Celsius or more, marked in bright red on the wheel, showed nearly a one in four chance of paying off. One could debate the numbers the MIT scientists used, but the basic message was tough to shake: extreme and dangerous out-comes are difficult to rule out, and the more carbon dioxide people pump into the atmosphere, the more likely they become.

Predicting temperatures is only the start of the challenge in antici-pating the consequences of climate change. Pick an amount by which you think the earth will warm. Now you still need to connect that to human impacts. Scientists try to estimate the consequences of cli-mate change for everything from food production and storm damage to civil war and international conflict. A lot of this science is at once fascinating, impressive, and inevitably shaky. Mitton and Ferrenberg have spent years carefully marking and excavating trees above Boulder in search of clues about what is happening with the pine beetle. Yet by their own admission, their knowledge about how climate change affects this one simple and much studied organism—and how those consequences play out for trees, forests, and the people and livelihoods that depend on them—is still maddeningly incomplete. Expand this to the thousands of other dynamics that govern life on earth, and you start to appreciate how difficult it is to anticipate precisely what climate change might or might not do to the planet. It is impossible, however, to avoid the conclusion that it could all turn out very badly.

❦ ❦ ❦

All of this haze surrounding the consequences of climate change makes evaluating the impacts of various energy paths immensely difficult. Some people look at the situation and conclude that all new fossil-fuel developments should be stopped. They are implicitly judging the resulting climate damages to be infinitely bad. The logic is simple: burning fossil fuels is raising the risk of deeply dangerous climate change, which naturally makes new development intolerable.

In practice, though, few actually believe that. Consider what might seem like a completely different matter. More often than not, when an American turns on her lights, there's a coal- or gas-fired power plant somewhere that's producing the electricity and, in the process, adding to climate change. But no one is calling for Washington to issue a ban on turning on lights; the benefits of having light outweigh the damages. The same sort of trade-off exists when it comes to developing new fossil-fuel sources. Sometimes the good consequences of developing new fossil fuels will be enough to outweigh the bad ones; other times they won't be.

On the other end of the spectrum are people who insist on more research into climate risks before we judge the consequences of certain developments for climate change, and do anything to confront the climate problem. Once we know what the real dangers are, they say, we can assess costs and benefits and take whatever action is needed. By suggesting that we shouldn't account for emissions in our current decisions, they are implicitly treating the damages from greenhouse gas emissions as zero.

This is unwise, because it's far easier to get into a climate mess than to get out of one. Think of the atmosphere as being like a bathtub with a clogged drain. If you crank open the tap and later realize that the tub's about to overflow, the only way to stop it is to immediately turn off the water. When it comes to climate change, the bathtub is the atmosphere, and burning fossil fuels is the same as keeping the tap running. (Loosely speaking, when you add a carbon dioxide molecule to the atmosphere, it typically takes about a hundred years before its impact on atmospheric carbon dioxide concentration goes away.[16]) We might wake up one day and, because of new research or data, realize that we need to stop generating greenhouse gases immediately in order to avoid particularly nasty consequences. But quickly closing the tap would be tantamount to shutting down the economy, which won't happen. Emissions today will lead to damages in the future.

That makes it essential to confront climate risks today if one wants to avoid damages in the future. There are two reasonable ways to think carefully about how to gauge the gravity of a number of immediate courses for greenhouse gas emissions. The first uses something called the social cost of carbon, which puts a dollar figure on the damages that a ton of carbon dioxide emissions is likely to cause. If, for example, a ton of greenhouse gas emissions causes twenty dollars of damage because of climate change, and each barrel of oil we burn generates half a ton of greenhouse gas emissions, then every barrel of oil we use causes ten dollars of harm. The barrel of oil is worth burning if the amount of good that that does exceeds the downside. In practice, the methods scientists and economists use to come up with figures for social costs of carbon are complicated and controversial; they require assumptions about climate sensitivity, economic damages from various changes in temperature, and even moral judgments about how to value harm that won't occur until the distant future or will affect people beyond the United States. When the U.S. government did its own review of the numbers in 2009, it concluded that every ton of emissions caused just over twenty dollars of harm globally, though it acknowledged that the real figure might be three times larger (or several times smaller).[17] Others have argued that the actual damages are considerably higher.[18]

Still, these figures can yield some useful insight about how the costs of rising U.S. oil production might compare with the benefits. Think about what happens when U.S. oil production increases by one barrel. Remember that some OPEC members, in an attempt to stabilize prices, are likely to cut their own output by nearly as much as the United States boosts its own; imagine, for simplicity, that every barrel the United States adds to the market is offset by four-fifths of a barrel others remove from it, for a net increase of only one-fifth of a barrel. Then the net climate damage from every barrel of added U.S. oil production works out to about two dollars. Even if the U.S. government analysts are way off, and the social cost of carbon is a hundred dollars a ton, the net climate damage from every extra barrel of U.S. oil is likely less than ten dollars. Unless oil production depends on subsidies that are much larger than the ones currently in place, the economic benefit gained from a barrel of U.S. oil production will almost always exceed these costs by more than that.[19]

There is, however, a fundamental problem with focusing too much on the climate cost of each individual barrel of oil or ton of carbon dioxide: it only works well for small shifts in emissions. Many of the biggest climate risks, though, show up only when you look at big changes. Small increments in emissions may each have small consequences, but when added together they might prove catastrophic.

This is why it's often best to measure big fossil-fuel developments against big concrete goals. In recent years many governments have fixated on a goal of preventing global temperatures from rising by more than two degrees Celsius. This sounds sharp and scientific until you notice that it's also 3.6 degrees Fahrenheit, which sounds pretty arbitrary. But so is any other goal. The bigger problem with the two-degree target is that, because we don't really know how sensitive the climate is to greenhouse gas emissions, it's only tenuously connected to concrete changes that might happen to the energy system. The world could slash emissions and end up with temperatures rising far more than two degrees. It could also do a lot less and still get lucky.

It often makes more sense to talk instead about concentrations of greenhouse gases, particularly of carbon dioxide, in the atmosphere. This is basically tantamount to thinking about how high the water in the bathtub can get before the attendant risks become unacceptable. (Looking at things in terms of temperatures is more like worrying about how messy your bathroom might get if the tub overflowed; it's a nice motivation but not all that useful in practice as a way of deciding when to turn off the tap.) There are three popular candidates for this sort of goal among those who spend their lives worrying about climate change: 550, 450, and 350 ppm of carbon dioxide in the atmosphere.

For the first couple of decades during which people started to get worried about climate change, 550 was perhaps the biggest game in town. Part of that was pretty arbitrary. It was popular for scientists' models to look at what would happen if greenhouse gas concentrations doubled from their levels prior to the industrial revolution—which would leave the world at around 550 ppm. Interested policymakers naturally gravitated to a similar target, and scientists also pointed to dangerous developments that might unfold beyond that point.

Over the last decade, though, it's become more popular for many of those who worry about climate change to talk about gunning for a concentration of 450 ppm or less. For all practical purposes, this is what policy discussions typically aim for, even though diplomats still talk about trying to keep global temperatures from rising more than two degrees. (Official assessments estimate that keeping concentrations below 450 would yield roughly even odds of staying below two degrees.) Scientific and economic papers are more and more often using 450 ppm as a benchmark against which to measure developments and assess potential consequences. Studies using models and, more important, examining the history of climate change throughout millions of years have started to worry researchers that substantially higher greenhouse gas concentrations would set off series of events that are difficult to control. Melting Arctic sea ice, for example, could trigger higher temperatures that melt even more ice, with the cycle repeating itself in a runaway chain that scientists call a feedback loop. Similar feedback loops in the Amazon rainforest and in melting Siberian permafrost concern researchers too. As trees in the Amazon grow, they absorb carbon dioxide, keeping it out of the atmosphere. But if rising temperatures kill off trees there, the rainforest will absorb less carbon, leading to higher temperatures, more damage to the rainforest, and even higher temperatures as a result. The Siberian permafrost contains massive quantities of methane, a potent greenhouse gas. Rising temperatures could trigger melting, releasing some of it, which would raise world temperatures further and also accelerate the melt.

Moreover, even if warming itself doesn't get out of control, there are worries that heading much above 450 ppm might lead to big and irreversible changes in the earth's climate. High temperatures could lubricate the West Antarctic Ice Sheet, helping it slowly slip into the ocean; this could raise world sea levels massively over time. Could we stop the process once it was clear it was starting? Researchers don't know, and it will probably take at least a decade to get a better handle on the question. The fact that problems of this kind may be lurking in the climate system makes 450 a reasonable goal—though, as we'll see later, it is perhaps not one that can be met.

But the race to come up with ever more ambitious climate targets doesn't stop at 450. Over the last few years, another number has become popular, particularly among many young people and the most intense activists: 350, the same number that showed up on signs at the anti-fracking rally in Columbus. Largely based on a single paper by James Hansen, 350 has become a worldwide phenomenon.[20] Hansen claimed in his 2008 paper that, looking back at data from the last four hundred thousand years, atmospheric concentrations of carbon dioxide barely above 350 ppm ultimately led to massive changes in climate. Bill McKibben has turned the number into a movement. His 350.org website organizes campaigns and protests around the world. The movement's signature action was originally arranging large gatherings of people in the shape of the numerals "350" and posting the group photos on the Internet. But those in the movement are also deadly serious.

Alas, there are two problems with 350. The first is its relatively weak scientific footing. Hansen can't say whether it took a hundred, a thousand, or ten thousand years or more for greenhouse gas concentrations of 350 ppm to lead to widespread climate impacts, and few other researchers have reinforced his work. This makes the number tough to use as the jumping-off point for massive and immediate global economic change. The second is that it's impractical unless cost-effective technologies for sucking carbon dioxide out of the atmosphere materialize: otherwise, hitting 350 would require promptly mothballing a large slice of the world's infrastructure and replacing it with even more expensive equipment. The steps that one might envision for reaching 350 ppm aren't simply more ambitious versions of those required for other frequently discussed goals; they are radically different measures that are nowhere close to becoming politically possible. This doesn't mean that people should stop thinking about what the consequences would be if 350 ppm turned out to be a truly critical threshold. But it would be dangerous to direct too much attention away from other goals.

Where does that leave us? A good starting point in assessing whether or not big fossil-fuel developments are exceedingly dangerous is to look at what they do to the prospect of holding greenhouse gas concentrations below 450 ppm. That line, though, should not be the end of the story. Holding concentrations below 550 (or some point in between) is also a laudable goal—and it's important to know how developing new sources of carbon dioxide affect the world's ability to meet it. It's also useful to occasionally check developments against 350, but for all practical purposes this target is beyond reach, unless huge changes in technology appear.

By the way, in case you're curious, here are two other numbers for context. The current atmospheric concentration of carbon dioxide is nearly 400 ppm. Because of ever-rising fossil fuel consumption around the globe, most projections expect the world to eventually blow through 1,000 ppm, with or without U.S. oil and gas.[21]

Burning all the oil in North America, or even in the United States alone, would be catastrophic for climate change. The Canadian oil sands contain enough carbon to raise atmospheric concentrations of CO_2 by about 60 parts per million beyond where they are today, blasting right through 450 and making 550 nearly unavoidable.[22] Colorado oil shale contains even more. Even tight oil and offshore oil and Alaskan oil, each providing a smaller increment when considered alone, add up.

Nonetheless, the logic that equates tapping these resources with destroying the climate is awfully weak. What matters isn't how much oil is in the ground; it is how much will be burned in the coming years. It would take three thousand years to extract all the fuel from the Canadian oil sands at the current pace, and it would take even longer to tap out Colorado oil shale if it were developed at the same rate. The future course of climate change will be determined long before that. This means the sheer volumes of each resource matter far less than how much of them is promptly developed.

We can put some numbers on this. As of 2011, the United States produced 5.7 million barrels of oil a day.[23] Imagine, in a massive leap, that this was doubled. What would the extra emissions contribution be? Burning a barrel of oil generates about four hundred kilograms of carbon dioxide emissions; adding in the emissions required to get the oil out of the ground and turn it into fuel at a refinery brings that up to about half a ton.[24] An added 5.7 million barrels of oil every day thus translates into about a billion tons of carbon dioxide annually. This compares to about six billion tons a year of total U.S. emissions and nearly forty billion tons a year of global emissions (and the figure is rising). It's a decent slice, particularly of the U.S. contribution, but measured against the global benchmark it's still relatively small. Figured another way, a billion tons of carbon dioxide emissions adds about 0.07 ppm to the atmospheric carbon dioxide concentrations; sustained over sixty years, the added burden would be about four parts per million. Again, this is far from trivial, but in a world that's on course to see carbon dioxide concentrations rise by many hundreds of parts per million, it's not earth-changing either.

Such arguments, though, can be dangerously slippery. No single action alone, even a big one, will make the difference one way or the other when it comes to dangerous climate change. This means you can't dismiss any particular step as inconsequential unless you look at it in the broader context. Here's the real question we should ask: How might adding this much new oil production in the United States (and perhaps in Canada) affect what others around the world do with their own oil and emissions? And what are the consequences for climate change? It turns out that once you factor in how others are likely to respond, the net impact is better for climate change, not worse.

More American oil production would lower oil prices and thus boost consumption. But it would also probably prompt less oil production elsewhere. We learned earlier that OPEC countries typically cut back on their output in an attempt to prop up oil prices when other countries produce more oil. Moreover, to the extent that prices still fall, other market-based oil producers will find themselves with less incentive to pump crude. Both of these dynamics are at the heart of arguments that boosting U.S. oil production probably won't do a lot to bring down prices at the pump. But they also imply that the climate damage from increased U.S. oil output will probably be smaller than simple calculations suggest.

How much? Imagine that every five barrels of increased U.S. oil production spurs cuts of four barrels elsewhere in the world; the net increase in oil use that results is one barrel. (This is conservative: it may actually overstate the net impact of U.S. oil production on global oil demand.[25]) Then doubling U.S. oil production would raise world emissions by half a percentage point and contribute a bit less than one part in a million to atmospheric carbon dioxide concentrations over the span of sixty years.

There is another way, in principle, that allowing U.S. oil production to rise could undermine efforts to rein in emissions: it might prompt others to follow course by expanding their own production, or deter other major producers from holding back their crude as part of a collective effort to deal with climate change. In practice, though, neither of those outcomes is remotely likely. The world's biggest oil producers by and large depend on oil production for their survival. Six of the ten biggest producers—Russia, Saudi Arabia, Iran, the United Arab Emirates, Kuwait, and Iraq—are intensely dependent on oil.[26] Another seven of the next ten fit in that category. Unlike the United States, which could deeply restrain oil production for an indefinite period of time without vital domestic economic danger (though still not without considerable harm), they cannot slash their oil production, let alone over a long period, without the risk of severely hurting their economies. At a minimum, if they do cut or restrain their oil production, it will be because of a strategic attempt to raise prices and hence revenues, not because the United States—a far more diversified economy—has set the pattern.

There may be one exception to the logic that says U.S. restraint in oil production probably won't be reciprocated by anyone else. China has massive reserves of coal and has flirted with converting large quantities to liquid fuels (though without following through so far). Any decision on such a move would neither make nor break the Chinese economy; as such, it comes down to Beijing's discretion. There is a chance that a U.S. embrace of massively expanded oil production could undermine efforts to persuade China to forgo converting coal to liquid fuels, multiplying the climate impact of the U.S. move. On the other hand, though, because greater U.S. production would push down world oil prices, it would make the already forbidding economics of Chinese coal-to-liquids efforts even less promising.[27]

But we're not quite done yet. If, at some point in the future, countries have deeply cut their greenhouse gas emissions, the relative impact of U.S. oil production would be higher. If the world were able to cut its emissions in half by midcentury, a target often discussed at diplomatic gatherings, the relative contribution of U.S. oil emissions would double. If, by the end of the present century, the world brought its emissions down even more deeply, the relative U.S. contribution could become huge. In either of those worlds, though, oil demand would be deeply reduced as part of the effort to curb emissions. Oil prices would fall along with it, undermining the economics of U.S. oil production. Lower oil output would be the result, not the cause, of efforts to combat climate change.

The last dynamic to keep in mind is one that we encountered when investigating oil prices: a massive increase in American production could prompt conflict among OPEC countries and temporarily flood the market with oil. This would magnify, rather than reduce, the impact of greater U.S. oil production. But the resultant price crash would be short-lived or would wipe out the financial viability of massive American oil production. Either way the climate impact would be limited.

All of this, many scientists and advocates argue, misses something important: carbon emissions from new sources of oil are unusually high. The Canadian oil sands have come in for acute criticism on this front, and many fear U.S. oil shale could have similar problems too. Former Vice President Al Gore claimed for several years that "gasoline made from the tar sands gives a Toyota Prius the same impact on climate as a Hummer using gasoline made from oil."[28] His assertion rested on the fact that some oil sands operations produce three times the emissions of extracting conventional oil. But most emissions from oil come when it's burned in your tank, not when it's removed from the ground. On a "well-to-wheels" basis, oil sands crude entails somewhere between 5 and 15 percent greater emissions than most other oil.[29] That's small beer in the grand scheme of things. Ultimately a Prius using gasoline made from oil sands would generate less than a quarter of the emissions of a Hummer using conventional oil.

The entire matter of climate change looks radically different when it comes to natural gas. Almost every alternative to oil (save synthetic fuels made from coal) is better than crude when it comes to climate change. The same can't be said for alternatives to natural gas. Some, like nuclear power and solar energy, are indeed superior in emissions terms, but others, most notably coal, are decidedly not.

The shale gas boom arrived at an odd moment in American politics. In 2008, both presidential candidates at the time, John McCain and Barack Obama, promised to implement aggressive policies to combat climate change. Both pledged to pursue cap-and-trade systems that would drive down U.S. greenhouse gas emissions by penalizing the use of dirty fuels. Then the drive collapsed. An economic crisis combined with intense political polarization turned cap-and-trade into a dirty word and a political nonstarter. Those people who feared global warming most began to worry that coal, the worst climate polluter of all fuels, would become ascendant again.

And then something strange happened: another fossil fuel appeared to come to the rescue. Just as cap-and-trade was collapsing, the shale boom was rising. Natural gas has long been regarded as the cleanest-burning fossil fuel; estimates typically peg it as only half as bad for climate change as coal when both are used to produce the same amount of electricity. Cheap natural gas would be as powerful a disincentive to coal-plant construction as a strict climate bill could be.

Environmentalists are wary of the local risks posed by fracking, but a powerful weapon against coal looks awfully attractive to many of them too.

A heated debate has thus ensued among experts, activists, and policymakers who worry about climate change. For some, since natural gas is only half as bad as coal, it is a godsend. Switch your electricity source from a typical coal plant to a regular gas one, and emissions are cut in half. For others, gas is infinitely worse than zero carbon energy sources such as wind, nuclear, or even clean coal. Change your power source from a traditional coal plant to a conventional gas one, which dumps its carbon dioxide emissions into the atmosphere, they contend, and you're missing an opportunity to wipe out your emissions entirely.

Which of these is the right way of thinking about natural gas? It all depends on your emissions goal and on the time scale you're thinking about. If you're a 350-or-bust sort of person, only zero carbon fuels will do; the difference between coal and gas is a distinction between shades of disaster. For everyone else, though, natural gas has the potential to play a strong and positive role.

There is little question that the first few years of the shale boom have slammed coal. As of May 2012, U.S. power producers had generated 561 terawatt-hours of electricity from coal for the year, a 25 percent drop from two years before.[30] (A terawatt-hour is a billion kilowatt-hours; a kilowatt-hour is enough to power a normal light bulb for a minute.) Rising natural-gas-fired generation filled in most of the other side of the story.[31] In April 2012, natural gas actually came within a whisker of edging out coal, an event never before seen in the history of American electric power. Replacing half the coal-fired power plants in the United States with gas-fired ones could ultimately cut U.S. carbon dioxide emissions by nearly 20 percent.[32]

The rapid gains seen so far at the expense of coal could not have happened (or at least not so quickly) with renewable energy. Between 2010 and 2012, renewable energy increased its contribution by roughly 50 terawatt-hours, an impressive achievement. But that paled when compared to the decline in coal. The rise in renewables would have had to be more than five times as large to deal coal the same blow that natural gas had. Put another way, instead of rising by about 30 percent, renewable energy production would have had to nearly triple in a very short period of time.

This logic, though, only gets you so far when it comes to designating natural gas the climate savior absent policy intervention. Many coal plants will keep running even with relatively cheap natural gas; low-priced natural gas will also encourage the expansion of gas-consuming industries, generally a good thing for the economy but bad for emissions. (Cheap natural gas could also make it difficult to get zero-carbon nuclear power plants relicensed when they reach the end of their intended lives.[33]) Worse for climate change, if a backlash against shale gas sent natural gas prices heading back toward ten dollars for a thousand cubic feet, construction of new coal plants could start once again. (To those who worry that boosting natural gas use could "lock in" the fuel for decades, this should be a persuasive counterpoint; the alternative is further entrenchment of even more carbon- and capital-intensive coal.) More fundamentally, keeping global carbon dioxide concentrations below 450 ppm could require reductions in U.S. emissions on the order of 80 percent by 2050. Even a goal of 550 would require steep curbs, and eventually emissions that decline to close to zero. Neither of these goals is consistent with a simple shift from traditional burning of coal to conventional use of natural gas. Imagine that you replaced all the coal that's used in the United States with natural gas. Emissions from the U.S. use of natural gas would then total slightly more than two gigatons a year of carbon dioxide. This alone would still be 40 percent of current U.S. emissions, and we haven't even added in the pollution from burning oil-based fuels in cars and trucks. There is simply no way, absent big technological shifts, to square indefinite use of massive amounts of natural gas with the kinds of climate goals that many have sensibly proposed.

The basic truth about natural gas as part of a serious climate strategy is simple: conventional use of gas needs to be an element a genuine bridge between coal and zero carbon fuels, and that bridge must eventually end. It is well-established science that, in order to stabilize greenhouse gas concentrations, carbon dioxide emissions ultimately need to fall close to zero.[34] (You can't stop the bathtub from overflowing unless you turn off the tap.) The only question is when this must happen. In late 2011, intrigued by the question, I decided to investigate. I conjured up a big set of paths that energy production could take and then simulated their climate consequences by using a simple climate model. It turned out that to stick to something like 450 ppm, the world will need to start phasing out conventional combustion of natural gas by around 2030.[35] (We'll look at alternative approaches to using natural gas that might prevent most of their carbon dioxide emissions from accumulating in the atmosphere in Chapter 6.) Indeed, models of what would happen if the United States imposed stringent climate policies consistently predict that traditional natural gas use would first rise for a couple decades and then fall. If the world is going to stabilize at around 550 ppm instead, natural gas could stick around for a two decades or so longer.

The upshot is straightforward. For the next couple of decades, gas is a great way to push out coal, particularly if low-cost renewable energy doesn't emerge as an effective alternative way to do that. Gas plants also happen to be a lot cheaper than coal plants, which makes it easier to ultimately replace them with other plants that don't emit greenhouse gases.[36] This makes natural gas good news for climate change. (Regardless of its impact on climate change, as natural gas drives out coal it also slashes local air pollution, providing immediate health benefits to those who would otherwise be exposed.) Beyond that, if there isn't a transition to zero-carbon fuels, odds are a goal of 450 will be in the rearview mirror. Natural gas would still matter: it could be the difference between stopping at moderate greenhouse gas concentrations like 500 or 550 or blowing way past them if zero-carbon sources don't become viable. Ultimately, though, it can't deliver on the most ambitious goals alone.

There is one big caveat to all this: it is possible to square natural gas with low long-term greenhouse gas emissions if the carbon dioxide that it produces is captured and sequestered underground. Most people who know about this idea, known as carbon capture and sequestration (CCS), have heard it pitched as an expensive way to clean up coal. If natural gas turns out to be as abundant as many believe, though, cleaning up its emissions might turn out to be a better fit for CCS. In this case, the United States could continue to expand natural gas indefinitely while still slashing its emissions. Whether CCS or renewables or something else (or for that matter, nothing) is the future of zero-carbon energy will depend on a complex mix of economics, technology, and public policy.

The last factor is critical: if you want to maximize the odds of hitting ambitious climate targets while also taking advantage of cheap natural gas, you need to use public policy effectively. Carbon taxes, cap-and-trade, or a clean energy standard (CES) could each have the potential to strike the right balance. Carbon taxes are charges that would make coal, oil, and natural gas users pay penalties proportional to their total greenhouse gas emissions. Cap-and-trade would make them buy permits for every ton of carbon dioxide they emit, with a similar effect. A CES would require that electricity producers derive an increasing fraction of their power from cleaner sources, with partial credit for natural gas. All three admit a wide range of options for cutting emissions: whichever technology is most cost-effective—natural gas, zero-carbon coal, nuclear power, renewable energy, or greater efficiency—is the one that will be pursued. So long as each becomes stricter over time (higher carbon taxes, fewer emissions permits, or more clean energy under a CES), this will encourage the conventional use of natural gas to replace coal at first but will eventually tilt the incentives toward zero-carbon power, including natural gas with CCS.

In early 2011, Robert Howarth, Anthony Ingraffea, and Renee Santoro, three researchers at Cornell University, published a bombshell study with a simple implication: everything I've just told you about natural gas is wrong. Natural gas, they argued, was worse for climate change than coal. The announcement reverberated through the energy world and through Washington. The New York Times put the stakes clearly: "Natural gas," it wrote, "with its reputation as a linchpin in the effort to wean the nation off dirtier fossil fuels and reduce global warming, may not be as clean overall as its proponents say."[37] Environmental groups previously torn between supporting gas because of its climate benefits and opposing it because of its local risks suddenly had a way out. There was no trade-off to be made: natural gas was simply bad.

The scholars' argument was straightforward. Chemically, natural gas is methane, a combination of one carbon and four hydrogen atoms. When it's burned in a power plant, one of the products is carbon dioxide. This is why using natural gas contributes to climate change. But methane itself is an immensely potent greenhouse gas. A molecule of methane in the atmosphere traps far more heat than a molecule of carbon dioxide does. This means that if small amounts of methane leak from natural gas operations such as wells and transport pipelines, the climate consequences can in principle be severe. The one big thing weighing against this is that methane doesn't stay in the atmosphere for nearly as long as carbon dioxide does. To go back to our bathtub analogy, the methane drain isn't nearly as clogged as the carbon dioxide one. If you look at a span of twenty years, a molecule of methane traps about seventy times as much heat as a molecule of carbon dioxide does, but if you look over a hundred years, the factor falls to about twenty-five.[38]

Howarth and his colleagues used this fact to their advantage. Exploiting crude data from the field, they estimated that between 3.6 and 7.9 percent of produced natural gas was leaking into the atmosphere.[39] And, pointing out that climate change was an urgent problem, they argued that people should be looking at impacts over a span of twenty years, greatly boosting the relative impact of methane. The consequence was that gas was indeed worse for the climate than coal. Early in 2012, their case seemed to get some real-world reinforcement: a team of thirty scholars led by researchers at the National Oceanic and Atmospheric Administration (NOAA) had taken careful measurements of leakage around gas fields in Colorado and had come to similar conclusions.[40]

However, there were three big problems with the analysis. The estimates that Howarth and his colleagues used were wrong. As several other Cornell professors later explained, they misread the data.[41] They looked at how much gas was coming out of wells and at how much was being delivered to customers, and inferred that the difference between the two was what had leaked. In reality, though, most of the missing gas was being used to power generators and the compressors that make gas pipelines work. The researchers also used real-world data to estimate leaks from pipelines, but those data were for massive pipelines in the former Soviet Union, not for facilities in the United States. This list of misunderstandings went on, but when they were all accounted for, it was hard to say much about the rate of gas leaks based on the apparently bombshell work.

That wasn't the only problem. As several observers pointed out, the scholars were comparing apples and oranges. They had estimated the amount of methane that leaks for each "megajoule" of gas or coal. A megajoule is a measure of how much energy the fuel contains. It typically takes fewer megajoules of natural gas than coal to keep your lights on, because most power plants that use gas are more efficient than ones that use coal. As a result, substituting gas for coal would cause less methane to leak than the authors claimed. The Cornell scientists retorted that not all gas is used to make electricity—indeed, as of 2012, a little more than a quarter of U.S. gas was used this way—but if you're talking about replacing coal with gas in power plants, that's beside the point.[42]

The last problem was with using the twenty-year timeline. The scholars were right that hitting ambitious climate goals requires rapid action. But this is mostly because the consequences of what we do today will still be felt in a hundred years, not because the near-term impact of emissions matters more than their long-term consequences. Because the world already has so much infrastructure pumping out carbon, and so much heat built up in the oceans that will eventually bubble out, it's stuck with rising temperatures for the rest of the century. This would be true even if it stabilized greenhouse gas concentrations at low levels. If you want to know what something will do to the ultimate scale of global warming, then you must ask how it will change the ultimate temperature peak. Because the high point is closer to a hundred years away than to twenty, a hundred years is the time scale you need in studying methane. If you combine this with the fact that methane emissions from natural gas are still far smaller than carbon dioxide emissions, and then crunch the numbers, you find that methane isn't nearly as big a problem as people have claimed.[43]

And what about that NOAA study of the rampant leaks in Colorado? Soon after it came out, I started digging into the data. The measurements were impressive. The team had driven a carefully designed mobile labo-ratory around the region in order to collect copious measurements of the concentrations of all sorts of molecules in the air. Back at their desks, they combined these data with other information about oil and gas operations in the region to infer the volume of methane that was leaking. The results were even more troubling than the ones reported by Howarth and his colleagues.

The data were great. But as I started trying to reproduce the bigger conclusions myself, I became concerned. The authors' interpretation of what the data meant didn't make sense. They had made some big assump-tions about the mix of methane and other chemicals in the leaking wells. They treated those as routine, but my math told me they were very conse-quential, and once you got rid of the assumptions then their calculations didn't actually tell you much at all about how much methane was leaking from local wells. The results, published in the same journal as the original NOAA analysis, further reinforced my basic conviction: it is valuable to reduce methane emissions in the natural gas industry, and important to get a better idea of their precise nature, but the available evidence points strongly to the conclusion that methane leaks aren't coming close to mak-ing gas as bad for climate change as coal is.[44]

❧ ❧ ❧

As I curled up in my rented apartment in Copenhagen's Nørreport neighborhood in the early hours of December 19, 2009, the possibility that U.S. greenhouse gas emissions could tip the planetary balance one way or the other was not the first thing on my mind. Like everyone else who spends time worrying about climate change, I knew U.S. emissions weren't ultimately what mattered most. When it came to determining how bad climate change would get, global greenhouse gas emissions were paramount.

For the previous two weeks, delegates from 193 countries had gath-ered at the Bella Center just outside town to hammer out a global cli-mate change agreement. Their assigned task was at once simple and monumental: to negotiate a legally binding treaty that would spare the world the worst of global warming. When I arrived a week into the conference, the meeting was already in disarray. Progress was stalled. It wasn't just that countries couldn't agree on what to do; they couldn't even agree on whether they should be talking to each other at all. Outside, UN and Danish security corralled thousands of angry attendees trapped in the freezing cold by logistical planning that was no better than the diplomatic preparations. Seven hours of this left me with no voice. That's why, as the Copenhagen climate summit came to a close, I was holed up in my Danish Modern apartment with only email and Twitter as my lifelines to the outside world.

It turned out that most people thought I wasn't missing much. The headlines that greeted the end of the conference were punishing. The *Financial Times*, hardly a world headquarters for hardcore environmentalists but recently an advocate for a binding global treaty, called it a "dismal outcome" and a "fiasco."[45] The assembled leaders failed to conclude a legally binding agreement. They did not even set a target to cut their emissions. And the aspirational, nonbinding text that they finally cobbled together was rejected by the assembled countries as a whole. Instead, its existence was simply "noted."

To many people who worried about climate change, this was a sign that any emissions cuts by the United States would be for naught. Climate change is a global problem. The United States currently accounts for a little less than 20 percent of global carbon dioxide emissions from energy use, and it is an even smaller fraction once you add in things like deforestation and emissions of other gases.[46] The figure is expected to decline steadily over time: the International Energy Agency projects that the U.S. part will fall to as little as 12 percent over the next twenty or so years. If Americans and Europeans cut their emissions but the Chinese and Indians crank theirs up, the U.S. effort will be almost pointless. This seemed to be the lesson from Copenhagen: climate change is hopeless, and it isn't worth your effort to try.

But that's a mistaken reading of how international politics works. The apparent Copenhagen failure had signaled that a legally binding treaty wasn't in the cards. But there are other ways to make progress on climate change, and they all benefit from action by the United States. Even the deal made at Copenhagen, many would convincingly argue, was an important step forward, even if not revolutionary, for climate change.[47]

There is little reason to equate rejection of a binding global treaty detailing strict emissions cuts with rejection of action to deal with climate change. Binding treaties are tough to conclude. As countries pursue increasingly ambitious policies, uncertainty about those policies' outcomes will rise, because the farther away a country moves from its past experience, the more difficult it is to predict how things will evolve. Uncertainty can be a deal killer when it comes to promising specific outcomes. Scholars of international relations generally agree that countries are less likely to commit to outcomes over which they have relatively low confidence and control.[48]

Moreover, certainty and legal strength aren't as neatly connected as some might imagine. Even if countries had made strong commitments at Copenhagen, that would not have ensured that emissions would be satisfactorily reduced. People have taken too many lessons from the history of negotiations over areas such as nuclear weapons, where governments have enormous control over outcomes. If leaders promise to remove a thousand missiles from active deployment, they can usually deliver, even if they must sometimes deal with political and bureaucratic barriers. But when it comes to complex energy systems that are largely not run by governments, the link between policies and outcomes becomes far more tenuous. Execution matters at least as much as intent. The Chinese government, for example, has said it wishes to reduce its carbon intensity by 40 to 45 percent from 2005 to 2020, but given the hodgepodge of policies being put in place to accomplish that, no one knows for certain whether it will be achieved. The failure at Copenhagen to conclude a treaty did not change the future as much as many people believe.

There is no reason to believe that successful international agreements need to focus on emission-cutting targets in the way that many negotiators and advocates sought at Copenhagen. Instead, they could direct their attention toward specific policies, such as tax credits for low-carbon power, and narrower goals, such as boosting energy efficiency by a particular amount. Commitments like these are easier for governments to deliver because they're more tightly within their control. They're also easier to verify: it's more straightforward to check whether tax policy has changed than to determine whether emissions have fallen by some promised quantity. Many argue that such an approach would provide less certainty than one based on emissions targets, but this is largely because they give too much credit to the supposed certainty that targets deliver.

And one needn't conclude an international treaty to have effective international cooperation. Less formal mechanisms—for example, national action combined with international transparency—have often done just as well.[49] The intuition is straightforward even if the examples can be complex: the basic purpose of a climate treaty (as opposed to changes in energy systems that might curb climate change) is to help involved parties gain more confidence in each other's actions and intentions, and arrangements other than treaties that promote these same ends can thus serve the same goals. By removing the fear of a binding treaty from the minds of policymakers, more informal approaches can occasionally liberate leaders to pursue bigger goals.[50] To be certain, everything else being equal, a hard international agreement usually works best. But the potential to leverage U.S. action exists even if a treaty remains remote.

The ability of the United States to deliver strong emissions cuts is being enhanced by abundant shale gas. Gas is cutting greenhouse gas emissions right now, deterring construction of high-emissions coal-fired power plants that might remain in service for decades, and making emissions-cutting policies cheaper than they otherwise would be. But abundant natural gas, however valuable, isn't going to come close to solving the climate problem alone—indeed, in the long run, burning natural gas as we do today is incompatible with seriously confronting climate change. In contrast with natural gas, there is no way to claim that gains in U.S. oil output are good news for climate change. U.S. oil production, though, will have at most a small impact on global emissions, even if production grows strongly, so long as it isn't heavily subsidized. Conversely, restricting U.S. oil production deliberately (rather than seeing it curbed as a consequence of lower oil prices), even if done in conjunction with a group of like-minded oil producers, would do little to address climate change. Slashing U.S. emissions requires a second revolution in American energy: one that cuts emissions from power generation by using zero-carbon technologies and reduces oil consumption with new cars, trucks, and fuels. Precisely such a revolution has recently begun to emerge—and people are promising far more than just climate benefits if it realizes its full potential.

THE CAR OF THE FUTURE

There are many cars that scream conspicuous consumption, but none quite like the Hummer. A beast weighing in at as much as six thousand pounds and delivering as little as nine miles to a gallon of gasoline, by the mid-2000s, it had come to symbolize the American addiction to oil.[1] When U.S. Hummer sales broke thirty thousand in 2003, people noticed; when they climbed over seventy thousand in 2006 despite rising oil prices, many were appalled.[2]

Those days are looking increasingly ancient. Fewer than ten thousand Hummers were sold in 2009, and after an aborted attempt to sell the brand to China's Sichuan Tengzhong Heavy Industrial Machinery Company that year, General Motors announced it would be shutting the brand down.[3] For a time it seemed as if the American automobile industry would go the same way. In 2009, GM and Chrysler both filed for bankruptcy; later, they turned to Washington for bailouts. Meanwhile, revenues from U.S. automobile sales plunged, crashing from a pace of $110 billion a year in mid-2008 to a mere $40 billion only six months later.[4]

Yet the death of the American automobile industry never materialized. Instead a second revolution is under way in American energy that has nothing to do with increased production of oil and natural gas: new technologies that cut consumption and pollution are on the rise, the American automobile is being reborn, and motorists are changing too. By late 2011, auto sales had rebounded close to their precrisis pace, but the cars and trucks being sold were different. After barely budging for a quarter century, the average fuel economy of a new U.S. vehicle has risen nearly 15 percent in the last five years.[5] Hybrids made up a mere one in two hundred vehicles sold in 2004; by 2011, they accounted for one in twenty-five sales.[6]

Moreover, when Americans fuel up, they're increasingly putting something other than gasoline or diesel in their tanks. Annual U.S. consumption of ethanol, mostly made from grain, crossed the ten billion gallon mark in 2009, and by 2010 ethanol made up a tenth of all gasoline sold in the United States. Americans are driving less too, racking up fewer miles in 2011 than in 2010, the first drop outside a recession in at least twenty-five years.

With cars and trucks responsible for more than two-thirds of U.S. oil consumption, the combined impact of all these shifts has been powerful. Oil consumption within the United States once looked as if it would rise forever, but between 2007 and 2011 it fell by nearly 10 percent.[7] In the five years ending in 2011, U.S. oil consumption fell by three times as much as U.S. production rose.[8] These shifts could be chalked up in part to the economic recession that began in 2007, but alone the recession couldn't come close to explaining the strong and steady declines.

Indeed, independent analysts project that fuel consumption could continue to dive over the coming decade.[9] Combined with rising U.S. oil production, this is making the prospect that the United States will stop importing oil from outside North America more realistic than it has been in forty years. It promises to put a big dent in greenhouse gas emissions at the same time.

But not everyone is so optimistic about the numbers, and many aren't particularly thrilled about what they mean. People are fighting over whether curbing consumption or boosting production is the right route to economic strength and increased security. Those who want to use government to make people burn less fuel face attacks for meddling in the economy and increasing costs for consumers. Skeptics warn that the technologies promised by boosters aren't ready for prime time. Biofuels are tarred as taking food out of people's mouths and doing more harm than good for climate change. And some security hawks worry that adopting electric cars could leave the United States free of oil but dangerously dependent on exotic minerals that are under foreign control.

The steep decline in U.S. gasoline consumption is due mostly to one overwhelming factor: the rising price of fuel. If you're paying two dollars for a gallon of gasoline, it might not be worth shelling out an extra ten thousand dollars to buy a car that gets thirty miles a gallon instead of fifteen. If you're paying four dollars a gallon, though, it certainly is. At the turn of the present century, anticipating stable oil costs, the U.S. government projected that a gallon of gasoline would cost about $1.65 for the next two decades.[10] Things turned out differently.

This is the biggest reason fuel consumption has been falling. It takes time, though, for the full impact of higher prices to be felt throughout the system. People don't junk their cars just because gas is more expensive; they wait until it's time to replace them and buy leaner models. Even then, their used cars usually remain on the road (and one person's "new" car is often someone else's old one). Because the typical car is driven for between ten and twenty years the full fleet turns over slowly.[11] But high gas prices are making their mark, and the trend has yet to fully run its course. Analysts who otherwise differ on important energy issues have looked at things like car buying and driving habits and generally conclude that U.S. gasoline consumption will fall gradually over the next decade or so.[12] If prices crash, though, the pattern may well reverse, though even then big increases in U.S. fuel consumption aren't in the offing.

Yet if history is any guide, high prices alone probably won't bring about dramatic drops in oil consumption. To be certain, economists have an incredibly poor understanding of what prompts people to change their car buying and driving habits. It's entirely possible that the psychological impact of gasoline at a sustained four or five dollars a gallon could encourage surprisingly radical change. But it's also quite possible that it won't.

History provides more than one cautionary tale. This is not the first time that U.S. oil consumption has declined. It first occurred between 1973 and 1975, then between 1978 and 1982, and finally between 1989 and 1991. Each episode featured high oil prices and subsequent recession. The first two coincided with the two Middle Eastern oil crises that shook the 1970s; the third came in the wake of the first Gulf War. In every case, U.S. oil consumption eventually resumed its rise.

This time around, though, the odds are higher that the trend will stick. The first factor that drove lower consumption in the 1970s was high oil prices, and ultimately they came down to earth. There's a strong case to be made, though, that oil prices will stay high this time. Nonetheless, there are also wild cards, including greater U.S. crude production, that could change things. The second big factor shaping the 1970s was policy. In the wake of the oil embargoes, the United States adopted its first fuel economy standards for cars and light trucks. They grew progressively tighter, until fuel prices fell in the mid-1980s and the U.S. government promptly relaxed them.[13] The current trend in U.S. fuel economy is also driven in part by regulations that have been sustained for several years. Yet a policy reversal on that front is possible—and could help swing the overall trend toward lower oil consumption. The possibility that oil use could start heading back up is compounded by the prospect that future policymakers might decide to abandon mandates that encourage people to use biofuels instead of oil.

How far could oil use fall? Analysts at the U.S. Energy Information Administration estimate that high oil prices and existing fuel economy rules that were in place as of early 2012 will drive U.S. oil consumption from just shy of fifteen million barrels a day today down to thirteen or fourteen million barrels by 2020.[14] The same team has also modeled the consequences of new fuel economy regulations that were put in place later in 2012. Those standards don't take effect until after 2017, which means they won't do much to oil consumption during the current decade, but by 2030 they could shave another million barrels a day off demand, for a total reduction of three million barrels a day. (The same analysts estimate that achieving the similar reductions without the new fuel economy rules would require oil to cost nearly two hundred dollars a barrel, equivalent to five dollars for a gallon of gasoline.)[15] Some people are also counting on federal mandates for biofuels use—a law currently in place requires refiners to add the biofuels equivalent of nearly another million barrels a day of oil to their sales by 2022—to push U.S. oil demand down even further.[16]

If you add up these potential shifts in demand for oil, you'll find them comparable to what many production enthusiasts tout for supply, particularly looking a couple of decades out. Like the claims about crude production, though, they entail large uncertainties as well.

❈ ❈ ❈

Those unknowns are embodied in the changes under way in two places: Detroit and California. When Americans think about the future of the automobile, they don't usually have regulators or oil traders in mind. They think about performance, safety, design, and technology. Bob Lutz, a famed auto executive, titled his best-selling book *Car Guys vs Bean Counters: The Battle for the Soul of American Business*, and it is clear which side most of his readers wanted to win.[17]

The instinct to focus on the car itself, and on technology in particular, is wise. High oil prices can spur drivers to buy smaller and often less capable cars, but there's a limit to how far that can go. Unless new technology delivers the kind of comfort and performance they insist on while reducing fuel demand at the same time, they'll simply pay more for their rides, continuing to guzzle gas while cutting back on spending elsewhere.

Regulators are beholden to the progress of technology too. They develop new fuel efficiency standards through intensive negotiations with automakers; along the way those rules are painstakingly tested for balance between costs and benefits. Unless there are technologies in place (or at least on the horizon) that make big efficiency advances plausible to the car makers, and that make the costs of fuel-sipping vehicles tolerable to consumers (many of whom vote), those regulations won't ever be put in place. Fortunately for the future of the American car, recent years have been good for automotive technology. From the heart of the American auto industry in Detroit to the coast of California, engineers are pushing the technological edge. Many of them are chasing a new holy grail: the electric car.

"All four wheels have to stay on the ground at any one time." It is the only instruction Kevin Layden has for me as I get ready to take his new electric car for a spin just outside of Detroit. Layden, a twenty-six-year veteran of Ford, is most definitely a car guy. Stocky with neat blond hair and wire-rimmed glasses, he's the kind of person who regularly injects himself into conversation with new ideas, but in a way that no one else seems to mind. Layden joined the company after getting his degree in mechanical engineering at Ohio State; he started off working on engines and eventually spent time in twenty countries overseas. He became the company's top engineer in charge of electrification, an increasingly important position, and two weeks before my visit the company released its first all-electric car. Visitors embraced the peppy Ford Focus Electric enthusiastically, so much so that one of them managed to tip it on its side on the closed track.

"It's a nondisruptive technology," he explains. As best I can tell, this is news to everyone who watches the industry. But Layden's case makes sense: "We've got the infrastructure required to support plug-in hybrids and battery electric vehicles. Fuel cells—we're going to have to figure out how to get hydrogen to people.... Natural gas, again, it's disruptive." Electricity, as he sees it, is fundamentally different. The infrastructure—basically the electric grid—is already there. And there is an evolutionary pathway in sight. Hybrid electric cars like the Toyota Prius are already mainstream and are letting engineers and developers learn about and improve engines and batteries. Next will come plug-in hybrids, which combine twin gasoline and electric engines to propel cars further on electricity while keeping gasoline around for longer trips. The final stage, already being rolled out in small numbers, is the pure electric car.

It is the basic hybrid, though, that has really cracked the old skepticism. The Prius has barely been around for a decade, but the idea of a hybrid car that uses twin gasoline and electric engines is a lot older. The first patent for a hybrid engine appeared in 1905, and at least one commercial model was sold in that decade.[18] The basic concept of pairing an internal combustion engine with a battery-operated electric motor hasn't changed since.[19]

For most of the next century, though, conventional wisdom held that hybrid electric vehicles faced dim prospects for success. They were too expensive, and given the design challenge that wasn't a surprise.[20] Engines were complex and costly, and hybrids needed two.[21] This added not only cost but also weight, which in turn required bigger engines. And when spiking oil prices started to enter the cost equation in the 1970s, hybrids ran into another problem: enthusiasm for battery-only cars made them seem tame. As late as 1990, one group of analysts suggested that "the very attractiveness of the hybrid concept might discourage development of, and compete in the marketplace with, advanced battery-only vehicles with longer range than today's best vehicles and emissions benefits superior to those of the hybrid."[22] Hybrid cars were caught in a no-man's-land: too alternative for hardcore oil boosters, too traditional for die-hard advocates of alternatives.

But there was some progress. In 1972, Victor Wouk, a Caltech-trained researcher, modified a 1972 Buick Skylark into a successful hybrid.[23] His prototype could reach 85 mph while slashing fuel consumption.[24] A Ford experiment in 1976 demonstrated that hybrid engines could deliver fuel economy gains of 70 percent.[25] But Wouk's Environmental Protection Agency-funded project was cut short for lack of long-term government interest in the technology.[26]

More typical were hybrids that showed the technology's limitations. The Hybrid Test Vehicle (HTV-1), the Department of Energy's only prototype during the decade following the first Arab oil crisis, was close to two tons in total weight.[27] Compared to other cars on the road at the time, it was almost a thousand pounds heavier.[28] Private companies' designs didn't do much better. The Briggs and Stratton Corporation's 1979 prototype hybrid was considered promising, but it needed six wheels so that the extra battery weight wouldn't collapse the car. The electric motor on the vehicle accelerated from 0 to 30 mph in an appallingly slow 10.5 seconds, and the car's top speed was 55 mph.[29] A report from the Congressional Office of Technology Assessment lamented in 1982 that "substantial penetration by electric and/or hybrid vehicles (EHVs) before the end of the century is unlikely, and doubtful even thereafter."[30]

Nonetheless, some persisted. In 1993, President Bill Clinton announced the New Generation of Vehicles (PNGV) program, a research consortium among the U.S. government and Ford, GM, and Chrysler.[31] For perhaps the first time, government-funded research in hybrid technology was substantial: the program included an investment of $1.25 billion in order to create an 80-mile-per-gallon car by 2004.[32] (PNGV was canceled before the milestone could be met.) While the project was under way, Toyota unveiled its Prius hybrid sedan at the 1995 Tokyo Motor Show.[33] The car made its U.S. debut in 2000. By 2012, it occupied the number three spot in global car sales, third only to the Ford F150 truck and the Toyota Corolla.[34]

The surprising success of hybridization was making many people bullish on a much bigger step, the move to fully electric cars. But something important was missing: there needed to be batteries that could store enough juice to power cars over hundreds of miles, deliver acceleration in powerful bursts, and be small, light, and inexpensive enough to actually fit in most cars.

Mark Schulz, recently retired from one of the top positions at Ford, has been looking at batteries for a long time. "California mandated zero emissions vehicles, so we had to do electrics," he explains over iced teas at a country club outside Detroit, as he reflects on the experience from the early 1990s. "Back then you used heavy lead acid-type batteries.... You could dial in whatever performance you wanted. A lot of the young engineers thought this was great. You could dial in zero to sixty in five seconds. But your cruise range would go from thirty-five miles to four." Batteries have come a long way since, but they still aren't ready for prime time, at least not at a tolerable price. The Focus Electric has a range of only seventy-six miles, and that's after using up what looks like half its trunk space to fit in more electric cells.

Atul Kapadia, the Silicon Valley battery executive who in Chapter 2 bragged to me about his natural gas car, is determined to change that. Kapadia worked most of his life in the information technology business. In the seven years he spent as a venture capitalist at Bay Partners, the firm made dozens of investments, backing everything from shopping software and semiconductor manufacturing to online poker. Only twice, though, did it venture into energy.[35] In 2007, as oil prices skyrocketed,

Silicon Valley was swept by energy fever; for a time, it seemed as if every investor and entrepreneur who had made it big in information technology was getting into the game. Kapadia caught the bug too, and he joined the board of Envia a couple months after its founding, kicking in $250,000, the company's first investment. The next October, Bay Partners bought into the company, and early the following year it invested in Enphase Energy, a company that made microinverters for solar power.[36] In August 2010, Kapadia left to run Envia full-time.

"Two things were the core drivers of the founding," Kapadia explains. "We were convinced that oil prices are not going to go back down to twenty dollars a barrel, as it was fifteen years ago, and we were convinced that A123"—then the hottest battery company on the planet—"was not going to succeed." A123, in his view, had misunderstood the challenge, focusing its efforts on driving down the costs of manufacturing. To Kapadia, though, the challenge remained technology: "We needed to increase the amount of energy we encapsulate in a battery because each ounce of energy determines how many miles you can drive that car." Envia and a handful of other companies focused squarely on the goal. "We have done exactly that," Kapadia claims, "which is to focus on the innovation required to double or triple the amount of energy per unit weight." He is certainly right about A123. Within a week of going public in September 2009, the company stock topped twenty-five dollars a share, but by July 2012 a share could be bought for less than fifty cents.

"The only risk now is the demand," says Kapadia, a sentiment that is widely shared but understates the challenge. "Can we bring the cost down fast enough?" Any progress will be evolutionary: "You start out with the smallest battery possible. And then gradually, as the cost comes down, you increase the size of the battery. As you increase the size of the battery, the amount of miles goes up." Whether this will happen rapidly, delivering the 250-mile range at a modest cost, which Kapadia seeks by 2020, or far more slowly, as many more skeptical analysts believe, will be revealed only in time.

Layden is also optimistic that technological progress will be faster than many naysayers project. He reflects on an engine that he worked on back in 1986: "We were happy to get ten miles a gallon." Layden ticks off the then-exotic systems they were trying to incorporate and says, "There was a huge technology terror. Oh my god, we'll never make the cost work, we'll never be able to get technology like fuel injection"—something that now seems simple and ancient to carmakers—"on these vehicles. It's just going to be too expensive. It's never going to work." A quarter century later, talk about electric cars sounds awfully similar to him: "I see the same kind of fears now with the battery. You tell an engineer, 'Hey, your job is to do this,' [they'll tell you] it can't be done and they give you a hundred reasons they can't do it." Then Layden reveals his engineering roots: "Then we go away and put a team together and do it in about half the time you thought it was going to happen and a third of the cost."

All the excitement, though, makes Schulz, the old-school executive, a bit nervous. "You can get some academic to come up with some vehicle made out of toothpicks and it's lightweight and it's the same size as an SUV," he tells me. "But in the car industry you gotta make millions of them." Companies also need to deal with mundane things like warranties and liability. "I look at these Teslas," says Schulz. "They're from Silicon Valley and they're smarter than Midwesterners and all that good stuff." But he has a warning: "You get one safety recall, where they've got to take their whole fleet and replace stuff and disassemble the whole vehicle to do that, they're done, they're toast, and they haven't tasted that yet." The message is clear: electric cars are far from a mature technology, and there are many things that can still throw them off course.

When I headed to the test track to try out the Focus Electric, another car caught my eye. It was the new Ford Mustang, a powerful-looking sportscar, and it would surely be really fun to drive. I asked Layden whether I could take the 444-horsepower beast for a spin, but that wasn't going to be possible.

A few weeks later, I fly into Grand Junction, Colorado, to begin a week on the road. The man at the airport rental counter politely informs me that the fuel-sipping compact I have booked is unavailable. Would I like a Mustang instead? My first instinct is joy. My second is terror: I'm planning to drive nearly a thousand miles over the next three days, and there's no way I'm willing to foot the bill for the gas-guzzling monster. After some back and forth, I settle on a Chevy Impala, a far more sensible option.

Before I drive away, though, I take a quick peek online. The clerk told me that the Impala would get thirty miles to the gallon on the highway, which sounded good. But as I look up the Mustang, I am taken aback: its miles-per-gallon rating is thirty-one. I go back to the desk and trade in my keys. The rest of the trip is a blast.

Electric cars and plug-in hybrids might be the next big thing, but for now the biggest fuel savings are coming from changes in conventional cars. "We're spending a lot of time in the near term on...our advanced gasoline engine technology," explained John Viera, head of sustainability and environment for Ford. "And a lot of people would say, 'That's not sexy, why aren't you working on electric vehicles?' We are working on electric vehicles. But from a volume standpoint, the most cost-effective technology solution in the near term...is still to work on improvements of advanced ICE [internal combustion] engines and diesel engines."

Indeed, when you take a look at how the Environmental Protection Agency and Department of Transportation believe that automakers will hit their fuel economy targets over the next decade, the overwhelming changes come in traditional cars and trucks. The volumes sold don't change much (though they do drop a little), but the vehicles' characteristics shift dramatically.[37] The average fuel economy of a new gasoline-powered car, for example, rises from about thirty-two miles-per-gallon today to about fifty-one by 2025; every other class of conventional vehicle sees a similar shift too.[38] Automakers are counting on advances in high-tech materials and automobile design to allow them to build lighter cars—particularly lighter big cars and small trucks—without sacrificing safety.[39] Because lighter cars take less energy to move, this leads to much-improved fuel economy. The companies are also pinning hopes on technologies that make engines more efficient. One of them, called stoichiometric gasoline direct injection, uses advanced computing to control fuel injection far more precisely than before; it could improve the efficiency of big cars by more than 15 percent. Another, called cooled exhaust gas recirculation, takes advantage of the fact that lots of energy is lost when hot exhaust gas is pumped into the engine;

by partly cooling it first, efficiency improves. It could knock another 30 percent off fuel consumption, and the U.S. Department of Transport projects it could move from the fringe of the U.S. fleet to as much as a third of new U.S. cars by 2025.[40]

The other big reason for the decline in U.S. oil use in recent years has been the rising consumption of ethanol, which now comes close to a million barrels each day, up from barely a hundred thousand ten years ago.[41] Most of that ethanol, which can be added to gasoline or used instead of it, is made from corn. People have tried for over a century to turn crops into fuel, often using technologies that aren't so different from those used to brew beer. The task has been challenging primarily because of its expense, which has left biofuels in general, and ethanol in particular, largely uncompetitive with fossil fuels. Recent gains in ethanol production have been driven by strong support from governments, which have mandated minimum levels of ethanol use and provided direct subsidies to producers, helping production succeed despite its relatively high costs. For this reason alone, if for no other, ethanol has come under particularly heated attack.

The big question now is whether biofuels will make big gains in the future. A few years ago, many people were betting on it, but more recently, enthusiasm has faltered. Technologies haven't matured quickly enough to make biofuels competitive without government support—and the political appetite for biofuels mandates has faltered, a trend that problems with corn ethanol make worse.

Perhaps the most controversial and politically difficult issue with ethanol is its possible effect on the price of food. The outrage comes from every part of the political spectrum. One left-wing website put the tension starkly: "Drive 1,000 Miles or Feed a Person for a Year?"[42] At the other end of the spectrum, Rick Perry, the governor of Texas, attacked ethanol in 2008 for hurting cattle ranchers in his state.[43] Perry and others like him were also allergic to federal mandates. Most oil producers, prominent in his state, disliked biofuels too.

The scientific debate over the links between biofuels production and high food costs is murky. Between January 2002 and January 2008, world food prices more than doubled; the final year alone saw a 56 percent increase.[44] Grains and soybeans, which are in demand for biofuels, saw particularly spectacular rises, both tripling over the same period and more than doubling in the period's final year.[45] But separating out cause from effect is devilishly difficult, because many forces affect the price of food. At the same time that biofuels production was rising, new land was being cultivated for food. Energy costs, which are important to farming costs, also rose, while the U.S. dollar, in which rising food prices are typically measured, fell. Speculative interest in food commodities grew simultaneously, and several countries, responding to rising food prices, cut off exports, further fueling price rises beyond their borders.

In 2008, a team at the International Monetary Fund dug through the data. It estimated that a massive part of the price rise between 2002 and 2008 was due to biofuels production—as much as 70 percent in the case of corn and 40 percent for soy.[46] Others, using different models, came to similar conclusions. Some analysts, emphasizing that most food isn't corn, countered that the price impacts had to be far smaller.[47] But rising corn prices can lift the cost of other crops, like rice, along with them, as people abandon ever more expensive corn for cheaper food and start planting corn instead of other crops on their available land.

Whatever the truth behind biofuels production and fuel prices, though, the political consequences were clear. When Congress extended the biofuels mandate in 2007, it drew a hard line: almost all of the gains would have to come from fuels that did not compete for feedstock with food. The new mandate focused on these so-called advanced biofuels: a total of twenty-one billion gallons of them were to be produced by 2022, equivalent to nearly a million barrels of oil every day.[48]

The target has been greeted with immense skepticism. The law aimed to yield 250 million gallons of cellulosic ethanol by 2011. (Cellulosic ethanol is a type of advanced biofuel that is critical to meeting the goals set out in the law; it aims to make fuel from things like switch grass and the cores of corn cobs that can't be used as food.) But only six million gallons were ultimately produced, and few other near-term gains appeared in sight.[49] In October 2011, after extensive study, a blue-ribbon panel of the National Academy of Sciences came to a stark conclusion: "Absent major technological innovation or policy changes, the [mandated] consumption of 16 billion gallons of ethanol-equivalent cel-lulosic biofuels is unlikely to be met in 2022."[50] The reason was simple: advanced biofuels remained considerably more expensive than fuels pro-duced from oil, and there was little hope for a major change in sight. Meanwhile regulators in Washington kept relaxing the biofuels standard, providing little incentive for anyone to comply.

❀ ❀ ❀

Wherever you looked, the questions invariably came back to govern-ment. In 2007, George W. Bush signed a new law to raise U.S. fuel economy by 40 percent, to a target of thirty-five miles per gallon, by 2020. In 2009, Barack Obama tore up those rules, announcing that auto companies would need to hit the same target by 2016 instead. Two years later he announced an even more ambitious goal: U.S. cars and light trucks would be required to deliver 54.5 mpg by 2025.[51]

This is a staggering number. When the rules were first announced in July 2011, only seven cars for sale in the United States were getting more than thirty-nine miles per gallon.[52] Only four models—all of them small electric cars—were capable of hitting the 54.5 mpg target.[53] Even the Prius, at fifty miles per gallon, fell short.[54] To come anywhere close to meeting the new targets, there would need to be massive changes in the cars that Americans drove.

"When we talk about the future fuel economy targets," Ford's Viera told me, "between now and 2022—I think we have a good feel in terms of the technology.... Where frankly it becomes challenging is from 2022 to 2025, which is a pretty big jump at that point. I can't tell you that we have a roadmap that gets us to the 2025 number." Many people predict-ing the future of energy assume that the details of the fuel economy standards are set in stone. They are anything but.

To the contrary the standards explicitly create opportunities for future revisions. "We as an auto company, which in the past we would never do, agreed to a standard that we don't have an idea of how we're going to meet it," Viera explained. So they made a deal: in exchange for the companies agreeing to the target, the government agreed to review it in 2018. "We don't know," he confided. "I mean gas prices are going to have an impact. You don't know how fast technology is going to move. I mean we have an idea, but we're going to know a lot more six years from now." One need only look at the decision in 1985, to stop raising fuel efficiency standards, to appreciate how tenuous such standards really are.

And there is a second problem. Government standards don't really mandate better fuel efficiency; they merely encourage it. Companies have always had a choice of meeting fuel economy targets or paying penalties for falling short. In practice, U.S. automakers are loath to pay the fines: in fact, none of them have ever needed to, because they didn't violate the standards. That's not because the standards were easy to meet. European automakers have regularly failed to meet them, and routinely paid a price. Many observers have guessed that U.S. auto companies are simply scared of being branded as rule breakers. Whether this could change in the future, if compliance costs rise, is anyone's guess.

Not that these are the problems that concern most skeptics and opponents of strict fuel economy standards. Beyond a general distaste for government meddling in the economy, and in many cases a belief that rising oil supplies will fix whatever problems fuel economy standards are supposed to solve, they tend to focus their worries on three areas: alternatives, safety, and cost.

Some people are open to government steps that would promote purchases of more efficient cars; they just think that fuel economy standards are the wrong way to do it. This camp, typically concentrated in university economics departments, would much prefer to see higher taxes on fuel. Motorists might respond by buying more efficient cars or by driving less. Alternatively, they might choose to not respond at all. Either way, studies consistently show, the same goal of cutting fuel consumption could be achieved at lower cost.[55] The only problem with this is that substantial fuel taxes have long been a political nonstarter. For the time being, at least, they are an alternative to standards only on paper.

Safety is another matter entirely. For decades, improved fuel economy has been synonymous with small cars, and there are broad worries that smaller cars are more dangerous to drive. Technological progress has helped blunt this trade-off; it's now possible to make pretty big cars that don't gulp fuel. Recent rounds of fuel economy rules have also been designed so that companies trying to cut their cars' fuel consumption simply by making them smaller won't get any credit. This means that the new regulations won't create any incentive to make smaller cars.

But one of the big ways auto companies still foresee cutting their cars' fuel demand is by making those cars lighter. This still concerns people who worry about what would happen to drivers in a car crash. In 2010, the U.S. Department of Transportation weighed in on the controversy.[56] New fuel economy rules passed three years earlier would make small cars lighter, increasing the number of occupants killed in accidents, but it would also make big cars lighter, decreasing the number of people killed when those cars struck others. The net impact, they determined, would be zero. Later, they revisited the analysis, applying it to the new rules being put in place for 2025. This time they concluded that although more people would be killed in small, light cars as the result of the new regulations, it would be more than offset by the saved lives of people struck by now-lighter trucks.[57] This sort of cost-benefit analysis is done all the time. Still, when you break it down, it's a bit morbid. It's easy to see why some people blanch at government mandates that yield consequences of this kind.

The final challenge comes down to cost. No one seriously disputes the fact that fuel economy standards raise the costs of cars and trucks and that tougher standards will raise them more. The debate is over how big those costs are and whether they outweigh any benefits. Analysts at the Department of Transportation have looked at this question with a computer model that attempts to predict the changes car manufacturers will make in order to comply with its new rules for cars and truck sold between 2017 and 2025. They have concluded that, by 2025, a new car will cost somewhere around two thousand dollars more to produce, and sticker prices will rise by a bit more as a result.[58] Whether the right number is half this, or double, is tough to pin down—governments usually overestimate the costs of complying with new rules—but the basic trend is certainly right.[59]

The big question is whether this cost is outweighed by the benefits from driving more efficient vehicles. The Department of Transportation analysts estimate it would take drivers an average of four years to make up for the extra money they spend by saving money on fuel, and in the long run they'd save twice what they spend.[60] The conclusion is sensitive, though, to assumptions about future fuel prices and to exactly how much the new vehicles turn out to cost.

When terrorists struck on September 11, 2001, when Hurricane Katrina hit New Orleans in 2005, and when the U.S. economy cratered in 2008, many people's thoughts turned to oil. But they weren't debating the finer details of fuel economy regulations; they were focused on the broader vulnerabilities the United States suffers because of its dependence on crude. Their instinct was correct: cutting oil consumption, whether through more efficient cars and trucks or through alternative fuels, has the potential to deliver economic, security, and environmental benefits that extend well beyond the money consumers save at the pump.

Start with the economic and security benefits, which are intimately linked. In Chapter 3, I argued that importing less crude by producing more oil at home could help shield the U.S. economy from the vagaries of expensive and volatile oil prices. This has direct economic value but is also important for national security, because the risks of high and volatile oil prices often prompt the United States to take military action abroad, force it to be restrained when it would otherwise take action, and more generally alter its foreign and defense policies. I also concluded, though, that the benefits are considerably smaller than many instinctively assume. In particular, even if the United States were to produce all the oil it consumed, it would still be vulnerable to volatile prices and would be pinned in when considering action abroad.

Reducing imports by cutting oil consumption is different. Take the issue to its extreme: if the United States consumed no oil, it would suffer no direct economic consequences from rising oil prices; moreover, it would not need to worry much about the oil market consequences of its actions abroad. (It would still be concerned about what happened to oil-dependent allies.) No one is talking about getting the United States off of oil anytime soon, but millions of barrels a day in reduced consumption over the next ten years or so, and substantially more in the decades beyond that, could make a big difference.

The most basic facts are simple. A given change in oil prices has a smaller impact on people's pocketbooks if they consume less oil, which in turn insulates the broader economy. (If they consume ethanol instead of oil, though, they aren't protected, because whenever gasoline prices spike, ethanol prices do too.) Something similar is true for industry: the less oil it uses, the less likely it is to be hurt when oil prices spike. It's difficult to quantify these consequences, but it isn't impossible to try; in fact something of a cottage industry aimed at estimating the impacts has flourished over the past thirty years. In 2007, a team of economists at Oak Ridge National Laboratory, whose scientists study everything from nanotechnology to national security, produced an updated estimate of the benefits.[61] They looked carefully at historical patterns in oil-price volatility and U.S. economic performance, using statistical methods to estimate the relationship between the two, and they concluded that every time the United States reduced its oil consumption by one barrel, the broader economy benefited to the tune of somewhere between three and twelve dollars because it became less vulnerable to jittery crude prices.[62] This works out to between one and four billion dollars of annual benefits for every million-barrel-a-day cut in U.S. oil consumption.

Cutting oil consumption also brings a second benefit: just as raising U.S. oil production does, it can help reduce the world price of oil. The logic and the numbers for consumption are almost a mirror image of those for production. Less demand for oil means less oil must be produced. The way the market tells producers to cut production is by driving down prices. The only limit, just like with new U.S. supplies, is that some producer may respond by preemptively cutting its own production, helping to prop prices back up. The Oak Ridge economists have created a model of how the world oil market would respond to a cut in U.S. oil consumption and what this would mean for oil prices. Then they look at how much money those lower prices would save consumers. In the end, they find that every time the United States cuts its oil consumption by a barrel a day, prices fall a tiny bit; when you add up those savings across the millions of barrels the United States imports, the savings total somewhere between five and twenty-three dollars. That's equivalent to between two and nine billion dollars a year for every million-barrel-a-day cut in U.S. demand for crude.

One might go so far as to wonder whether these benefits from reducing oil consumption are reasons to oppose any effort to boost U.S. oil production; after all, more U.S. oil output lowers oil prices, and U.S. oil use rises as a result. But the impact of higher U.S. oil production on U.S. oil consumption would be small. More U.S. oil production will always lower imports, even if consumption rises as a result.[63] And when it comes to the biggest economic and security vulnerabilities stemming from U.S. oil consumption, all of which arise from the massive amount of money the United States spends on oil of all origins, increased production remains on solid ground. Economists find that every 1 percent drop in the price of oil yields less than a 1 percent increase in U.S. oil use.[64] That means lower oil prices resulting from increased production always lead to lower total spending on oil.

It is also sensible to ask about the reverse. Increased U.S. oil production benefits the U.S. economy and national security. But cutting U.S. oil consumption, by lowering oil prices, would undermine U.S. oil output (if only a little bit). Could that be fatal to the benefits of using less oil? The answer is again no. It is impossible for cuts in U.S. oil use to undermine U.S. oil production so deeply that spending on oil imports (one root of U.S. economic and security vulnerabilities) doesn't drop.[65] Nor would the fact that Americans would make less money selling oil be a problem. Workers who would otherwise be pumping crude could use their time to produce other valuable things; capital that would otherwise be used for oil-drilling equipment could be applied to other productive pursuits; scientists and engineers might stop directing as much energy toward inventing new oil-drilling technologies and instead steer it toward breakthroughs in other fields (not just energy); and the United States would still have the oil it needed to run its economy—at lower cost.

So when exactly do gains from greater fuel economy outweigh the costs? Answering that question can help draw the line between smart pushes for greater automobile efficiency and foolish ones. To see how, drill down on an example. The typical U.S. driver tallies about thirteen thousand miles on the road every year.[66] Imagine that she starts with a car that gets thirty miles from a gallon of gas. That's a bit worse than the average car sold in the United States in 2012.[67] Suppose gasoline costs four dollars a gallon. Our driver spends about $1,700 every year on gas for her car. Now imagine she's offered a similar car that gets forty miles to the gallon instead. This would save her (or a future owner) about five thousand dollars over the lifetime of the car.[68]

The broader economy, though, would benefit more than that from her new purchase. If you use the Oak Ridge numbers, you conclude that the new car would create extra economywide savings of as much as forty dollars for every barrel of lower oil consumption, or about a dollar a gallon, because of reduced oil prices, greater economic resilience, and lower climate damages, none of which the driver would include in her own calculations. The extra benefit to society would be more than a thousand dollars over the life of the car.[69] If the new car gets fifty miles to the gallon instead, our driver will now save more than eight thousand dollars, and society might reap another two thousand dollars in benefits. If performance were boosted to a hundred miles per gallon, the driver would save around fifteen thousand, with gains to society approaching four thousand dollars more.

The most obvious lesson here is that the benefits to the country collectively from cutting oil use are greater than benefits to individual car buyers. Just because people won't buy more efficient cars without government intervention doesn't mean the more efficient cars wouldn't help the overall economy. The case becomes stronger as the costs of efficient vehicles drop and oil prices rise. Today, the United States benefits when consumers shift to slightly more efficient cars and trucks, leveraging inexpensive improvements in conventional engines. But the country loses if it pushes too quickly into expensive vehicles, like electric cars, that provide limited additional fuel savings. In a decade or two, though, if the price of ultra-efficient vehicles drops a lot, the case for pushing people to use them will become stronger.

What happens if the United States reduces its oil consumption not through efficiency or by shifting to electricity as a fuel but by using natural gas to power cars and trucks? It still gets the benefit of lower world oil prices that result from a reduced demand for oil.

When it comes to protection from volatile oil prices, though, the situation gets more complicated. Even if people cut their oil consumption by using liquid fuels that are produced using gas-to-liquids technology, they, and thus the economy, remain exposed to volatile oil prices. That's because the prices of liquid fuels such as gasoline and diesel that are almost entirely produced from oil swing up and down with world oil prices; as a result, so do the prices of similar fuels produced from natural gas. In contrast, when people cut their oil consumption by switching to cars and trucks that use compressed or liquefied natural gas directly, they shield themselves and thus the economy from the pain of gyrating oil prices, just as those who buy more efficient vehicles do.

The increased use of fuel-efficient cars and trucks may also be upending another element of U.S. vulnerability to oil shocks: the automobile industry itself. When I visited Youngstown, Ohio, I regularly heard stories about what had happened a few years back in its sister town of Warren. Warren is next door to the GM Lordstown Assembly Complex, which opened at the heyday of the auto industry in 1966 and produces hundreds of thousands of cars every year. In 2008, when oil prices spiked, car companies laid people off by the thousands. But Lordstown wasn't just spared, it flourished, moving from one shift to three. The secret? The plant manufactured the Chevrolet Cobalt, the second-most-fuel-efficient car in the GM line.[70] High oil prices crushed demand for most vehicles, but appetite for the Cobalt soared.

Paul Edelstein and Lutz Killian, two economists then at the University of Michigan, would probably not have found this a surprise. Their study of decades of data confirmed that when oil prices rise, consumers shift their purchases to more efficient cars and trucks.[71] Historically, U.S. automakers have biased their production toward gas guzzlers; this suggests that oil-price spikes should hurt domestic auto sales much more than they do foreign ones. When Edelstein and Killian did a careful statistical analysis, they found "a strong and highly significant decline in new domestic automobile consumption" following any jump in oil prices. In contrast, they found that "consumption of new foreign automobiles initially increases," though "after four months, [it] slumps as well."[72] In any case, the hit to domestic auto sales is historically much larger and more persistent than the one to foreign cars and trucks.

But this may be changing, thanks to historic shifts in how Detroit does business, with more fuel-efficient cars in its fleets. Now, when high oil prices hit, the pain is likely to be spread more evenly between U.S. and foreign producers of cars and trucks. This is not an entirely new trend: according to Edelstein and Killian, "In the 1970s, U.S. auto manufacturers were simply not producing any small, energy-efficient cars."[73] That changed substantially by the 2000s, despite the prominent presence of SUVs in U.S. automakers' lineups. The fact that the U.S. auto industry isn't just Detroit and its surroundings anymore—it's spread across the country—helps spread any vulnerability too.

It's important to be cautious, though, about just how far the United States has come and what sorts of gains it might see in the future. Economists regularly churned out papers in the first half of the 2000s explaining why the U.S. economy was no longer particularly vulnerable to oil prices. The biggest factor was its falling oil consumption relative to the size of the economy: crude prices could now double without having a massive impact at the national level. But people missed the flip-side of this positive effect. Once upon a time, hundred-dollar-a-barrel oil wasn't really plausible because the economy would be knocked on its back, bringing prices down with it, well before the market could get to that point. Paradoxically, though, energy efficiency helped make the world safer for much-higher-priced crude, as developed economies could now tolerate higher prices without tipping into recession. By the end of the decade, the United States was spending a far higher percentage of its income on oil than it had a decade before, even though it was actually using much less oil for every dollar of GDP it produced.

In principle, something similar might play out with the current trend toward greater efficiency, allowing prices to rise even higher. But there are reasons to be more optimistic this time. In particular, as U.S. oil consumption shrinks, the U.S. economy will be a smaller piece of the oil-price puzzle; constraints on economic growth in places such as China and India in the face of expensive oil (and efforts by oil producers to keep prices at levels that those economies find manageable) may help restrain price increases before they really hurt the United States. There is good reason to believe that, this time, better oil efficiency will really pay off.

Nevertheless, it's possible to overstate the value of using less oil. Oil shocks typically precede recessions, but after forty years of careful studies economists still can't agree on whether oil shocks actually cause big economic downturns. (One economist I know likes to quip that oil price spikes have preceded six of the last three recessions.) Even studies of the biggest oil spike of them all—the result of the 1973 Arab embargo—aren't conclusive when it comes to how much of the ensuing recession should be pinned on oil. Scholars have thrown every model and statistical technique in the book at the problem but haven't yet come to definitive conclusions. Food prices were rising rapidly around the same time the oil shock occurred, hurting the U.S. economy, and it's difficult to disentangle that from the impact oil prices had at the same time. Moreover, the U.S. Federal Reserve hiked interest rates in the face of oil- and food-driven inflation. Many economists contend that, rather than the price rises themselves, the interest-rate hikes are a big part of what did the economy in.

Moreover, in the years since, the U.S. economy has become more resilient to volatile oil prices. The Federal Reserve no longer pays attention to swinging costs of oil when setting its interest rates; because changes in rates can send the whole economy into recession, this removes one big source of danger. (The Fed sets interest rates in part on the basis of inflation; in measuring inflation, it now ignores changes in the price of oil.) Many also argue it has become easier for people to move between jobs, something that rapidly changing conditions can require, which makes the economy more resilient (though mobility appears to have declined in recent years).[74] Cutting U.S. oil consumption surely makes the economy safer, but the benefits may not be as large as in the past, because the problems it tries to solve may now be smaller in the first place.

The best way to think about lower oil consumption in the face of considerable uncertainty about benefits is that it's a way of reducing risk. Lower oil demand reduces the odds that price spikes will harm the United States. Even the mere perception of reduced risk among decision makers would also increase U.S. freedom to act around the world. The national security benefits of greater flexibility would be real and potentially large.

But many worry there will also be big national security costs stemming from a transition away from oil.

O n September 7, 2010, in the choppy waters off a string of uninhabited islands in the South China Sea, a Chinese fishing boat found itself in trouble.[75] If you ask the Japanese, the islands are the Senkaku, under Tokyo's control since 1972.[76] According to Beijing, they are the Diaoyu, a Chinese possession for many centuries before.[77] The dispute meant both countries plied the waters, and on that Tuesday the Chinese boat struck two Japanese coast guard ships. The captain was hauled ashore on Ishigaki Island and arrested.

In the weeks after Zhan Qixiong was detained, Beijing appeared to strike back. Its customs officials began blocking shipments of rare-earth metals destined for Japan.[78] Rare-earth metals span an exotic stretch of the periodic table, from scandium to lutetium, encompassing elements that include cerium, samarium, and neodymium in between. In recent years, these minerals have moved from obscurity to a central place in many modern technologies, including those that make cars more efficient and clean energy cheaper to produce.

The Chinese cutoff, which Beijing denied was connected to the fishing boat incident, sent Japanese officials into a panic. Hybrids such as the Toyota Prius use the metals in their batteries and in the systems that propel the cars.[79] Wind turbines use them in their magnets; efficient lighting often depends on them too. Leaders in Tokyo did not want to take the risk, so days after the Chinese ban went into effect Japan released the boat captain. It would be months, however, before China allowed the rare-earth trade to resume.[80]

To many observers, this heralded the dawn of a new sort of geopolitics. Many fear that clean energy, including electric cars, will simply substitute a new set of security risks for the old ones involving oil. If manufacturing new energy products requires the use of particular natural resources, those who control them may be able to use their position to dominate industries or extract political concessions. They might reserve those resources for their own domestic manufacturers, shutting others out, or choose to sell only to firms based in countries that follow their political lead. (This sort of behavior might ultimately backfire for those countries undertaking it, but that doesn't mean they won't pursue it anyhow, to the detriment of others.)

The United States might also find itself increasingly tempted to intervene in distant parts of the world whose stability is critical to the new energy industries, just as it has in the past in oil-producing regions. The vulnerability has certainly crossed the mind of Atul Kapadia. He's worried about one material in particular: cobalt. "A lot of cobalt is found in Congo," he explains. "Congo is an unstable country." Envia has been trying to cut down on the amount of cobalt it uses: "Our most active research program is trying to make it zero percent."

Worries over dynamics like these have been particularly pronounced in the area of rare-earth elements, whose production China dominates. This is why the incident that pitted Beijing against Tokyo in 2010 alarmed so many strategists. But was it really a harbinger of things to come, or were people just overreacting?

Successfully manipulating natural resource supplies to gain control over energy industries and to use that to influence international politics is possible only if the stars align correctly. Oil has become subject to successful manipulation for three basic reasons. Much of the world's production is concentrated within a small number of countries, and on occasion political circumstances (such as wars against a common enemy) have helped those countries collude. If production were more diverse, manipulation would be far more difficult. Oil also has few substitutes. Once upon a time, when lots of oil was used to produce electricity, countries could respond to manipulation by shifting away, mostly to coal and nuclear power. Today, with oil used predominantly in transportation, there are few options for substitution. Oil's special role is sealed by the fact that most responses to market manipulation, such as buying more efficient cars and exploring new oil fields, take time to bear fruit. Alas, the pain caused by volatile markets can be immediate and acute. This gives those with influence over those markets more power.

How do rare earth metals stack up? The top five holders of proven oil reserves as of the end of 2010—Saudi Arabia, Venezuela, Iran, Iraq, and Kuwait—collectively accounted for a massive 60 percent of the world's total.[81] (The United States made up about 2 percent if you don't count decades-from-commercial oil shale.) Those five countries, along with the next five down the list, also feature strong state intervention in their economies, which makes manipulation easier. When it comes to rare earth metals, China is dominant: figures are sketchy at best, but the U.S. Geological Survey estimates that China boasts fully half of the world's reserves.[82]

The U.S. position when it comes to rare earth metals, though, is stronger than in the case of oil: the United States appears to be home to more than 10 percent of world reserves. Neighboring Canada also sits atop massive amounts of rare earth material, including heavier elements that are particularly critical for electric cars.[83] Moreover, demand for rare earth metals is nowhere near the potential supply. Consumption of such materials clocked in at around 136,000 tons in 2010.[84] Even if the figure were to rise tenfold, world reserves would still be a whopping one hundred times annual demand.

Most rare earth elements that are important to new energy technologies also have greater prospects for economically attractive substitutes than oil does. Battery manufacturers, for example, are already responding to short-term supply concerns by turning to lithium ion materials as a substitute for nickel-metal hydride.[85] Even as the 2010 skirmish between China and Japan reached its peak, Toyota debuted "a new magnet system that eliminated the need for neodymium," a particularly scarce rare earth.[86] Opportunities for rare earth efficiency and recycling will also rise if the materials' prices remain stubbornly high.

Rare earth metals, though, are not the only materials that raise eyebrows. Lithium, a volatile silver-gray metal whose reserves are dominated by Bolivia, comes up just as often in debate over new vulnerabilities.[87] World lithium resources are estimated to total about thirty-three million tons, a whopping thirteen hundred times its 2010 production level.[88] But what would happen if electric vehicle sales skyrocketed, pulling lithium demand up with them? Linda Gaines and Paul Nelson, both scientists at Argonne National Laboratory, have put together some estimates that test the limits of what might happen.[89] They started with an aggressive scenario where pure electric vehicles rose to a fifth of global sales by midcentury, and sales of plug-in hybrids reached nearly twice that share.[90] The impact on lithium demand depends on what you think the new cars would be like; the study assumed they'd be a mix of long-distance vehicles, city cars, and electric bicycles in parts of the developing world. On this basis, it concluded that demand would rise to eight times the current level, and that recycling lithium from used batteries could meet half of the need. The ultimate annual world demand for new lithium would still be three hundred times smaller than current world reserves.

In fact the United States is likely even safer than this suggests. Gaines and Nelson sketch out another scenario where U.S. sales of electric cars and plug-in hybrids take off powerfully around 2020. Plug-in hybrids reach just shy of a third of U.S. sales by 2030, while pure electric vehicles make up around one in twenty sales, and simple hybrids, such as today's Prius, total a quarter of all cars sold. All told, by midcentury nine in ten cars and trucks sold in the United States are at least part electric. As a result, U.S. lithium demand rises steadily, hitting twenty-five thousand tons a year around 2030 and continuing to grow after that. As the stock of electric vehicles rises, though, more material also becomes available for recycling. Demand for new lithium tops out at around twenty-five thousand tons a year in 2030 and falls after that. U.S. lithium resources, by contrast, are estimated to total more than a thousand times this number. Pressed to the wall, the United States could rely on its own resources, which suggests physical availability of lithium supply is unlikely to become a major U.S. problem.

Nor is cost. The price of lithium carbonate, the chemical form in which lithium is typically supplied, has held steady between two and seven dollars a kilogram over the last twenty years.[91] Because the typical electric car uses no more than about fifteen kilograms of the material, the cost of the lithium in it comes out to less than a hundred dollars.[92] Even if lithium prices rise tenfold above their highest historical level, the cost of the lithium in an electric car will still be only a small fraction of the cost of the vehicle. Contrast that with the typical contemporary automobile, which uses around five thousand gallons of gasoline in a ten-year period, at a likely cost of well over ten thousand dollars.[93] That's a hundred times the current cost of the lithium in the typical electric car.

There is one more thing that differs between exotic metals and oil when it comes to economic vulnerability and national security. If the United States were to suddenly find itself without oil, the entire economy would shut down. If, instead, it were to suddenly find itself without one or another special mineral, it might have to cease building new electric cars or wind turbines. The economic impact could be harsh, particularly on a handful of industries, but it still would be far smaller and more contained than if the United States ran short of oil. After all, people could still keep driving their existing cars.

When I visited the Ford R&D laboratories outside of Detroit in early 2012, my first stop wasn't to see their electric cars or to understand their dependence on special minerals. My hosts, having heard that I was interested in efficient technologies, assumed I was there to talk about the environment. They immediately took me to see all the automobile components that they've managed to make out of hemp.

It wasn't an unreasonable instinct: some of the keenest interest in cutting oil consumption is driven by environmental concerns, and the benefits of cutting oil consumption for confronting environmental problems often seem like the clearest benefits of all. Burn a million barrels of oil and you pump about half a million tons of carbon dioxide into the atmosphere. This means that every million barrels a day you can shave off U.S. oil demand results in nearly two hundred million tons less carbon dioxide annually, equivalent to nearly 4 percent of U.S. emissions. That's as big an impact as replacing about fifty big coal-fired power plants with solar.[94]

But the real climate consequences of getting off of oil aren't quite so straightforward. Lower U.S. oil consumption reduces world oil prices, which encourages others to use more crude oil. This partly offsets the climate benefits of U.S. conservation. There are good odds, though, that this effect is pretty limited, for the same reason that the impact that lower U.S. consumption has on prices isn't as big as some might guess: lower U.S. oil use prompts strategic producers to cut back output in an attempt to prop up prices. If, for example, you make the same assumptions about this dynamic as we did in Chapter 3, the upshot is that for every five-barrel reduction in U.S. oil consumption, world demand falls by four barrels in total, thus preserving most of the climate benefits of any cut in U.S. oil use.

As we saw in Chapter 3, though, there is a small but not trivial risk that big cutbacks in U.S. and others' oil consumption, probably combined with gains in U.S. and other oil supplies, could create a fight among strategic producers for share of a shrinking or stagnant global oil market, leading to an oil price crash in the process. Low oil prices would prompt people to use more oil, which would undermine the climate gains from the cutback in U.S. oil consumption, even as low oil prices increase its economic and security benefits. This possibility is worth keeping in mind.

The second potential problem with a move toward more efficient cars and trucks owes its intellectual heritage to William Stanley Jevons, a towering figure in nineteenth-century economics. Born in Liverpool, he had a front-row seat for the first great fossil-fuel revolution: the rise of coal. Yet as the use of coal became ever more efficient, Jevons observed, coal use did not fall; instead, it increased even more rapidly. By 1865, coal production had skyrocketed, which made the book Jevons published that year—*The Coal Question*—all the more persuasive.[95] Warning of the eventual exhaustion of British coal resources, Jevons made an argument that would last well beyond his time.

His case was simple: greater efficiency in the use of natural resources should reduce demand for them. The same factory that once used a hundred tons of coal a day might be able to get away with using only fifty once it becomes more efficient. We all know, though, that falling demand for anything, coal included, results in falling prices—and when something gets cheaper, people will buy more. Perhaps, having become more efficient, each factory will double in size, or perhaps other industries will start using newly cheap coal. In any case, the upshot is straightforward: greater efficiency need not ultimately lead to lower consumption. It can actually result in more.

The claim that efficiency does not actually reduce resource consumption became known as the Jevons Paradox, and more than a century after his death it lives on in fights over the true promise of greater efficiency in American energy use. "Mr. Wizard, meet Mr. Jevons," one prominent skeptic of improved fuel efficiency wrote mockingly on his blog.[96] Yet reality appears to disagree with the strong skeptics.

When it comes to cars, the naïve invocation of the Jevons Paradox leads to a simple conclusion: if all Americans start buying new cars that are twice as fuel efficient as their old ones, they will drive more, because the cost of driving will have been cut in half. In the worst case, they will drive twice as much, entirely negating the value of the efficiency bump.

This logic is deeply flawed. It might sometimes seem as if the most expensive part of driving is the cost of gasoline—after all, every time you fill up, the often staggering cost is right in your face. But the biggest cost of driving is actually the value of your time. Say you drive your car, which gets twenty miles per gallon, a distance of ten miles. That uses half a gallon of gas; if gas costs four dollars a gallon, you're out two bucks. Now imagine you're driving at twenty miles an hour, so your trip takes thirty minutes. For the typical American (who makes about twenty dollars an hour), that much time is worth ten dollars. The biggest cost of your trip isn't the gas: by a factor of five-to-one, it's you. This is why, if you were to replace your car with one that was twice as efficient, you wouldn't drive much more.[97] It's not surprising that when researchers carefully study how greater efficiency affects driving habits in the real world, they find only a small effect: a person might drive 10 percent more as the fuel efficiency of their car doubles, but most of the savings, including in greenhouse gas emissions, can be taken to the bank.[98]

There is a different problem when it comes to cutting oil consumption by using more biofuels: the biofuels themselves can increase emissions. For a long time, the knock on corn ethanol focused on a simple problem: it can take as much energy to make a gallon of ethanol as you get out. The corn, of course, harnesses energy from the sun that isn't going to be used for anything else. But running the farm where it grows means burning diesel in tractors; so does hauling the harvested crop to a refinery. Once it gets there, it still needs to be turned into fuel, a process that requires a lot of natural gas. When you do the math, many ethanol operations actually turn out to be energy losers, particularly if they use corn.[99]

For many ethanol opponents, this is case closed for the fuel. But things aren't so simple; whether this arithmetic really matters depends on the problem you're trying to solve. Most of the energy gobbled up by an ethanol operation comes from natural gas. The United States, though, doesn't have a natural gas problem, at least not in the same way it has an oil problem. From this perspective, biofuels look like just any another technology that converts natural gas into liquid fuels that can displace oil. In a country long on gas and short on oil, this is a good deal.

Unless, that is, you're worried about climate change. Biofuels have long been touted as a way to cut U.S. greenhouse gas emissions. The basic reaction that propels plants' growth pulls carbon dioxide out of the air and produces carbohydrates, oxygen, and water. When biofuels are ultimately burned, the carbon dioxide is released back into the atmosphere, just like carbon dioxide that is released by burning gasoline or diesel. In the case of biofuels, though, the two parts of the cycle balance out. The net result, which scientists refer to as "life-cycle" emissions, should be zero emissions. That's a big environmental boon.

But it doesn't count all the emissions involved in converting crops into fuel. Estimates are all over the map. Some scientists conclude that, when you add everything in, the life-cycle emissions from corn ethanol are nearly as bad as those from gasoline. Others note that if ethanol refineries are powered with natural gas, their environmental performance increases, with the corn ethanol they produce turning out to be about 30 percent better than gasoline.[100] Either way, the emissions reductions aren't radical. And most other crops grown in the United States do barely better than corn. Unless the country can move to cellulosic fuels, which do far better from a carbon standpoint, it's hard to think that greater use of U.S. biofuels will do much for climate change.

This is often contrasted with ethanol made from sugarcane. In the wake of the first energy crisis of the 1970s, Brazil was stung even more than the United States. In response, it launched a massive program to convert sugarcane into fuel, something that turns out to be unusually easy to do. That was good for Brazil because it kept costs down: sugarcane ethanol is widely regarded as the most cost-effective biofuel. But it also meant conversion didn't take much energy, which meant the net greenhouse gas emissions were unusually low.

There is, however, still one more potential problem with biofuels, and skeptics have latched onto it with zeal. If you want to grow crops for biofuels, you need land, and to get it you usually need to do one of two things. You can clear land that's already covered with plants or trees but not being used for agriculture. Since whatever you're clearing was storing carbon before you cut it down, you've just caused massive greenhouse gas emissions. Brazil was long accused of cutting down ancient rainforests to cultivate ethanol. To the extent this was true (in many cases it actually wasn't), the climate benefits of biofuels vanished.[101]

The United States, of course, isn't home to any ancient rainforests: it already cut down the bulk of its old forests a couple hundred years ago.[102] So American biofuels producers take the second path: they plant their crops on land that would otherwise have been used to grow food. In 2008, though, a bombshell paper in the prestigious journal *Science* sounded an alarm: the practice was setting off a chain reaction that was almost as bad as chopping down centuries-old trees.[103]

The story the scientists told was simple. People need to eat. When one person takes land out of food production and uses it to make fuel, someone else needs to clear another swath of land to produce the now-missing food. Odds are that a bunch of the newly cleared territory is coming at the expense of really old trees and other territory that stores lots of carbon. When the researchers ran the numbers, the results were staggering. The title of their paper said it all: "Use of U.S. Croplands for Biofuels Increases Greenhouse Gases Through Emissions from Land-Use Change." The details were just as troubling. Corn-based ethanol, they concluded, "increases greenhouse gases for 167 years."

Those methods and numbers were enormously controversial.[104] This was to be expected: modeling the dynamics of all the food and land use around the world is not a straightforward task. But the basic bottom line was simple: together with the controversy over rising fuel prices, the new analysis meant new government support for corn-based ethanol was a nonstarter. New kinds of biofuels, including cellulosic ones, though still controversial in some quarters, provide hope to those who want to see a future where biofuels play a big role.

Electric vehicles have a different potential climate problem: their emissions depend on the source of their electricity. "Electric cars," as one wag put it, "are really coal cars."[105] He was trying to point out that if you plug your car into an electric grid that is being powered by coal, you are still causing a lot of carbon dioxide emissions.

I decided to dig into the numbers behind the Focus Electric I'd driven. The car takes thirty-two kilowatt-hours of electricity to travel a hundred miles.[106] In Dearborn, Michigan, where I took the car out for a drive, most of the electricity came from coal; producing a kilowatt-hour of electricity yielded about three quarters of a kilogram of carbon dioxide.[107] Put together, this meant I was generating twenty-four kilograms of carbon dioxide for every hundred miles I drove. That was slightly more than the damage I would have done to the climate had I driven a Prius fueled with normal gasoline.[108]

Michigan, though, turned out to be one of the worst places in the country to drive an electric car. In 2012, a team at the Union of Concerned Scientists, an environmental advocacy group, worked through the numbers for every state.[109] Nearly half of the country lived in places where electric cars were better for the climate than even the best hybrid vehicles, and another two out of five made their homes in places where electrics were comparable to the best alternatives.

And the picture is improving as natural gas replaces coal and emissions from the U.S. electricity system drops. Indeed, what matters to the climate for the next decade or so isn't really how much carbon dioxide emissions an electric car causes; there won't be enough of those cars to make a big difference. What matters is the trend: Can electric cars improve enough over ten years or so to really start to take off after that? Only if that happened would it make sense for the debate over electric cars to return to the future of American electricity.

All of this remains in the future. Advances in automotive technology have already made it possible for Americans to drive ever more efficient cars and trucks, and, together with high oil prices, made it more cost-effective for the U.S. government to mandate and otherwise encourage their adoption. The move toward more efficient vehicles is bringing benefits for the U.S. economy, the environment, and national security, even if sometimes overstated. If the trends all continue, the pay-offs will grow too. Fully taking advantage of the opportunity to cut U.S. oil consumption would require some support from government—we have seen that individual car buyers don't fully account for the national benefits of more efficient vehicles when they shop for a new ride—but markets will do a lot of the heavy lifting by themselves. Very little of this would be undermined by a simultaneous trend toward more U.S. oil production, making the two beneficial developments compatible with each other.

Novel cars and trucks and new ways to fuel them, though, aren't the only part of the unfolding revolution in new and cleaner energy sources. The change extends to how the United States produces power.

"WIN, WIN, WIN, WIN"

It's June 8, 2011, a scorching hot day in Midland, Texas.[1] In an average year, the mercury would max out at 93 degrees Fahrenheit, but by noon that reading is in the dust. By three o'clock, the previous record of 102 degrees, set in 1962, has been broken, and by late afternoon the temperature hits 105 degrees.[2] It is the second day of what will turn out to be a record two-week-long streak of hundred-plus-degree heat.[3]

This sort of oppressive heat comes with predictable consequences. Sweltering residents take refuge indoors and crank up their air conditioning to full blast, sending demand for power soaring. On cue, electricity prices skyrocket. Indeed, three weeks later, faced with similar heat, wholesale electricity will be selling in West Texas at almost a hundred times the typical rate.[4]

This June day, though, plays out differently. The hot weather has its usual impact, and electricity consumption begins its typical rise. Starting around noon, prices begin to pick up, and by the time families sit down for dinner, it costs nearly ten times as much to buy electricity as it did at lunchtime. But then the pattern reverses. Prices begin to crash. By the time people have settled in for prime-time TV, prices briefly dip below zero. Despite a surge in demand for electricity, generators are actually paying companies to take their power.

This kind of occurrence is rare but not unheard of, and the explanation typically blends several factors. The most obvious culprit this time, though, is the wind. Over the previous five years, Texas has been installing massive wind turbines at a record pace. By 2011, the state is home to nearly ten gigawatts of wind capacity, more than triple its amount half a decade before. That figure is greater than the total power-producing potential—not just wind, but also coal, natural gas, nuclear, and everything else—of sixteen other states.[5] Texas officials have taken to boasting that if their state were a separate country, it would be the sixth biggest wind energy producer in the world.[6]

The distinction, though, comes and goes from day to day, depending on the wind. On June 8, soon after most Midland residents begin returning home and turning up their air conditioners, the wind picks up. Wind speeds reach close to thirty miles an hour, a highly unusual occurrence for this time of year.[7] To the east and south, the massive blades of thousands of wind turbines churn at a soaring pace. The owners of the wind farms have already paid up front to build the giant towers. Now, with the wind driving, they are producing more renewable power than anyone can use—and they are generating it essentially for free.

Clean energy has become a big business. Investments in renewable energy and energy efficiency in the United States blasted through the fifty-billion-dollar barrier in 2011—nearly as much as the oil and gas industry spent on exploration and production that year.[8] Many advocates and investors long aspired to such heights for alternative fuels, but few of them would have actually predicted this powerful growth in U.S. clean energy a decade ago. Sales of biofuels and efficient cars and trucks have been a big part of that story, but renewable energy has been a massive element too.

In December 2000, the U.S. Department of Energy published its annual projections for the coming decade.[9] Renewable energy capacity, excluding conventional hydroelectric power, stood at a hair below ten gigawatts at the time. (Hydropower—energy derived from water—has little potential for growth in the United States and can obscure statistics for other renewable energy sources. It's excluded from renewable energy totals in this book unless stated otherwise.) Wind and solar, today a central focus of discussions about clean energy, contributed less than three gigawatts combined. Looking out to 2020, the modelers expected wind and solar put together to never top seven gigawatts. That projection was squarely in the mainstream.

Fast-forward to today. In 2010, renewable capacity hit forty-eight gigawatts, triple the projections of a decade earlier, a trend that can mostly be chalked up to wind farms like those that had popped up around West Texas.[10] The pattern of outperformance is expected to continue. When the U.S. government released its annual analysis in late 2012, it projected sixty-five gigawatts from wind and solar energy by 2020, nearly ten times what had been predicted a decade before. This assumed no new policies to promote alternative energy. With new government action, of course, the numbers are likely to clock in even higher.

This is all still relatively small potatoes in the context of the U.S. energy scene. The United States boasts nearly a thousand gigawatts of electric-generating capacity; wind and solar are only about 5 percent of the total. And because the wind doesn't always blow and the sun doesn't always shine, even this overstates their current contribution; a better measure would put it at somewhere around 2.5 percent.[11] But there is another way to look at the situation, and that lens places new energy technologies in a far more central position. The U.S. Department of Energy projected in 2012 that fully three quarters of net additions to U.S. electric generation in the next decade are likely to come from renewable power.[12] This was more than it projected for natural gas, despite the massive growth in shale. And if the U.S. government and the states, seized by a desire to confront climate change or promote new industries, decide to push clean energy more forcefully, the numbers could outperform even these projections. To be certain, not everyone agrees, particularly on the precise figures. One way or another, though, new sources of clean energy seem poised to play a large role when it comes to adding new power-generating capacity in the United States.

These gains appear to come at an opportune time. In the wake of the financial crisis of 2008, the United States was looking for new sources of competitive advantage, and clean energy technology seemed to many to be a perfect choice. Cheap renewable energy also offered hope to those who desperately sought a solution to climate change—particularly those who were skeptical of nuclear power—but could not convince the public to pay much for one. Texas, not the place that jumps to most people's minds when they think about aggressive emission reductions, bested forty other states in cutting its carbon intensity between 2000 and 2009, largely on the back of wind power.[13] (California, often held out as the national leader on environmental protection, didn't come close.) In July 2008, at the height of the presidential campaign, former vice president Al Gore called for the United States to produce all of its electricity from renewable energy and other "truly clean carbon-free sources" within a decade.[14] Most analysts thought this a stretch, but not a ridiculous one to at least raise. Barack Obama, then the Democratic candidate for president, was effusive in his praise. A spokesman for John McCain, the Republican candidate, also greeted the speech warmly, explaining how the senator's plans lined up with Gore's goals.[15] Indeed, when McCain unveiled his energy policy two months earlier, he chose a wind energy-training facility in Portland, Oregon, as the venue.[16] The new consensus seemed clear: after decades of playing second fiddle to oil and gas, it was time for renewable energy to thrive.

But bright prospects for renewable energy were not the first thing on people's minds on August 31, 2011. That day Solyndra, a previously obscure solar company headquartered in Fremont, California, announced that it was filing for bankruptcy and laying off eleven hundred employees.[17] This would not normally have been an unusual event in a year that saw 131 companies file for bankruptcy every day, but Solyndra was not a normal company.[18] The firm, founded in 2005 and backed by a roster of previously successful venture capitalists, had bet that its product would thrive in a booming market for solar power. By 2009, the Obama administration had made clean energy a centerpiece of its strategy for rescuing the U.S. economy, and Solyndra was one of its star cases. In March of that year, the U.S. Department of Energy agreed to backstop a $535 million loan to the company that would help it expand facilities for manufacturing cylindrical solar panels, the first of many similar guarantees offered to other clean energy firms. In May 2010, President Obama himself visited the company, further establishing it as a model not just for American energy but also for the economy at large.[19]

The bankruptcy announcement quickly turned an example of everything good about renewable energy into a symbol of all its flaws. Alternative energy, critics declared, was not ready for prime time; had there been a real market for its products, Solyndra would not have failed. Worse was what the episode apparently revealed about the relationship between renewable energy and government. Solyndra, they said, existed only because government bureaucrats had handed it hundreds of millions of taxpayer dollars. At best, its executives squandered that money, in the process destroying more than a thousand jobs. At worst, some pundits and political operatives darkly suggested, the pile of cash was an invitation to crony capitalism, with money simply steered to the president's political friends.[20]

Here, in one small company, was everything that many people found wrong with alternative energy. The technology was nowhere close to being ready to compete with fossil fuels. This meant it required so much government intervention that corruption and incompetence were inevitable results. It certainly wasn't a recipe for economic revival; one merely needed to ask the laid-off Solyndra employees about that. Nor did an economically unviable suite of technologies hold much promise for dealing with climate change. Meanwhile, as the public began to question the prospects of new energy technologies, the shale gas boom began to unfold.

The apparent convergence around alternatives that seemed at hand in 2008 was shattered. Renewable energy was at once thriving and under intense fire. One side pointed to falling costs, opportunities for innovation, a growing number of clean energy jobs, and lower greenhouse gas emissions. The other emphasized the relatively high price of renewable energy, insisted that government was ill positioned to boost jobs or innovation, and noted there were other ways to cut emissions; it also emphasized that renewable energy had environmental risks of its own. The battle lines between old and new energy, and between governments and markets, were again formed. But the arguments coming from both sides had important flaws.

In April 2012, I found myself in London. Two years earlier, a group of energy ministers had joined to create something called the Clean Energy Ministerial (CEM), a regular summit of governments, companies, advocates, and experts, all of whom aimed to accelerate the progress of clean energy technologies. London would be holding the third CEM summit, and I was to moderate a discussion about solar power.[21]

The group gathered at Lancaster House, an imposing neoclassical mansion built in the early nineteenth century. It was a typically dreary spring London day, and as the drizzle continued more than one participant thought it clever to observe that this was the wrong time to be discussing power from the sun. Once our discussion commenced, though, it was clear that there were bigger challenges at hand. Solar, everyone agreed, had made enormous progress. Additional sessions came to similar conclusions about wind, energy efficiency, and other alternative energy technologies. But agreement among the captains of government and industry mostly ended there. Two big questions remained unresolved: How close were these technologies to competing with traditional fuels? And what role, if any, would governments need to play if alternatives were to fully flourish?

A few weeks before the meeting, three analysts at McKinsey and Company, the strategy consultancy, released a study that caught summit-goers' attention.[22] The analysts had surveyed the landscape and found that the cost of solar power was rapidly declining. The holy grail of solar power has long been a solar module that costs a dollar a watt. (Sixty watts is enough to power a typical incandescent light bulb; look for a "60 W" mark on old bulbs around your home.) According to the National Renewable Energy Laboratory, costs have followed a steady downward trend, declining from ten dollars a watt in the mid-1980s to three dollars by 2009, an average of 7 percent a year.[23] Since then, prices have fallen off a cliff, hitting $1.50 in mid-2011 and continuing to decline from there.[24] Along with falling module prices have come bold predictions for cost competitiveness. Enthusiasts project that electricity from solar panels (which combine many modules) will cost the same as electricity from fossil fuels before the present decade is out.[25]

The McKinsey study revealed this view in full force. The authors added up possible gains in productivity, system design, and technology and concluded that dollar-a-watt solar was fully possible by 2020. Despite solar prices already at $1.50 a watt, this was bolder than it sounded, because there was broad agreement that solar prices had been temporarily driven down by overinvestment in solar module production factories in China; solar would need to make big gains to achieve the dollar-a-watt goal. But reaching the target would spur nothing less than a revolution: the consultants compared the new solar costs with what they expected for other technologies, and they projected that a hundred gigawatts of solar would be installed by 2020, ten times the amount that already existed. This would be only the start of the solar boom; the analysts estimated up to five hundred gigawatts of additional pent-up demand for solar by the decade's end.

Similar claims were already grabbing headlines in the wind energy world. In November 2011, Bloomberg New Energy Finance, a research firm, released a stunning projection: the average wind farm would be "fully competitive" with power from coal and natural gas by 2016.[26] Turbine prices, they pointed out, had been cut by more than half in the past two decades as global installations rose by a factor of nearly a thousand. At the same time, turbines were becoming far more efficient. Combining those two trends and projecting them into the future, they anticipated that both wind and fossil fuels would provide power for around the same price—about seven cents for a kilowatt-hour—within a few years.[27]

But these sorts of claims attracted more than their share of skeptics. Most mainstream forecasters anticipate far more modest gains. The U.S. Energy Information Administration has estimated that, without new policies, U.S. solar energy capacity will barely breach seven gigawatts by 2020, nearly eight times its size ten years earlier but still a small fraction of what the more aggressive forecasters foresee.[28] Wind would continue to be the biggest source of U.S. renewable electricity other than hydroelectric power, but after continuing its climb through 2013 it would flatten off. This was not the behavior of a power source that has become cheaper than fossil fuels. The International Energy Agency is considerably more enthusiastic, anticipating a near tripling in wind capacity and a tenfold increase in solar from its 2012 level to twenty-five gigawatts by the end of the decade.[29] But this assumes that government tax credits for renewable energy and other policies in place in 2011 will be extended through the full decade—hardly a given.[30] Even then, it would still leave those fuels in the minority, with renewables other than hydroelectricity delivering a scant 4 percent of U.S. power.[31]

Indeed, despite the real prospects of strong gains, there is good reason to be skeptical of the most aggressive claims about the likely growth of wind and solar power in the near future. Start with cost projections. Analysts at the Lawrence Berkeley National Laboratory calculated that the average cost of delivering a megawatt-hour of electricity using wind power fell from $150 in 1992 to barely more than $50 in some installations by 2005.[32] Costs then started to edge upward as supply chains got jammed (there were only so many facilities capable of turning out the components required) and the price of essential building blocks such as cement and steel rose on the back of global demand. By 2012, though, prices were again touching record lows, buoyed by technological gains and by a global economic slowdown that dropped the price of steel and cement.[33] Wind power might continue to see prices fall at the same pace as in the past; however, it might not, because onshore wind power is widely agreed to be relatively mature. In particular, wind is fighting an uphill battle in much of the United States, since many of the windiest sites (or at least the ones that don't require expensive new systems of power lines) are already occupied. Improving technology has to fight a constant battle against weaker wind.

Solar has more room to improve. There's more opportunity for innovation, including advances that leverage progress in the broader semiconductor industry. And sunny land isn't nearly as scarce. The problem is that solar is starting from a tougher place than some backers admit. Part of the price crash in 2012 was due to a flood of modules coming from government-subsidized Chinese manufacturers; it's far from clear, though, that those subsidies will continue. Moreover, at least half of the cost of solar power typically comes from components other than the modules and from the costs of installing and maintaining the equipment.[34] Alas, those numbers don't necessarily follow the same ever-declining patterns that module prices do. This doesn't mean solar won't make big gains in the coming decade or two; it just means that making confident predictions, one way or the other, may not be wise.

The second challenge to the more aggressive numbers is what experts call grid integration. The sun doesn't always shine and the wind doesn't always blow. And electricity, unlike oil, usually can't be stored: once you've generated it, you need to use it right away. Operators dealing with renewable energy typically need to carefully integrate intermittent sources into the electric grid. If those variable sources reach substantial scale, an operator has two choices. It can make sure there are a lot of other power plants on standby, ready to fill in when the renewable sources aren't able to deliver. But this costs money, and if wind farms and solar plants are required to pay at least some of it, their own costs will rise and they will become less competitive. The other option is to build up lots of traditional power plants alongside the renewable ones. That, in part, is what Texas has done, which explains why it sometimes needs to pay users to take electricity off its hands. This sort of redundancy undermines whatever edge in costs alternative energy might have. Down the road, the world might develop large-scale storage systems that would buffer these problems. But those storage solutions don't exist yet, and it would be unwise to assume they'll be in place anytime soon.

Perhaps the trickiest part, though, comes from the use of a single simple number to describe and compare the costs of different sources of power. When analysts say that wind will be as cheap as natural gas, they're usually talking about something called the "levelized cost of electricity" (LCOE). The idea is simple: tally up the amount of power produced over the lifetime of a facility and divide it by the cost of producing that power. That's your levelized cost.

But comparing levelized costs of electricity is enormously misleading, because electricity that is available on demand, like that produced by coal or natural gas, is worth more than electricity that is available whenever the sun happens to shine or the wind blows. In this sense, it's like any other product. You'd pay more for a computer you can use whenever you want than for one that's available only for a random hour every day or for one you can only use in the middle of the night.

According to Paul Joskow, then an MIT energy economist, "Levelized cost comparisons overvalue intermittent generating technologies [such as wind] compared to dispatchable base load generating technologies [such as coal or gas]."[35] To show how big a deal this is, he sketches out an example. Imagine two big power plants, each of which will last for thirty years.[36] One costs the equivalent of $4.5 billion to build and maintain over its lifetime, and it would need another two cents for every kilowatt-hour of electricity generated. Being a base load plant—let's say one that uses natural gas—it delivers power 90 percent of the time. The electricity provided costs about 5.8 cents per kilowatt-hour. The second plant costs half as much to build and nothing to operate, because the fuel—the wind or the sun—is free. The output is also intermittent; on average, it's able to produce power only 30 percent of the time. Nonetheless, due to being so much cheaper to run, it delivers electricity costing a smidge less than that from the other plant—only 5.7 cents for each kilowatt-hour.

The second power plant seems better, but there's a problem. Electricity is worth more when in high demand and less when there's reduced need for power. Joskow assumes that about a third of the time, electricity is worth nine cents for each kilowatt-hour, and the rest of the time it's worth only four cents. Then he does the math to see how each power plant will fare. The owner of the expensive but steady power plant makes a predictable but modest profit of about $3.8 million each year. But the fate of the less consistent plant depends strongly on when it delivers. In the worst case, it produces power only when the price is lowest, and the owner loses more than twenty-two million dollars a year. At the other extreme, the second plant produces power precisely when the price is highest; the owner nets a whopping forty-three million dollars every year.

It turns out that wind turbines are a lot like the imaginary power plants that crank out power mostly when people don't want it. Wind power might seem superficially to be within striking distance of other sources, but when you unpack things some of the competitive edge goes away.

Solar power, though, gets a boost. It does best on sunny days, like that West Texas scorcher, because those are when the demand for electricity usually skyrockets. That makes the electricity it supplies unusually valuable. Alas, since solar remains considerably more expensive than traditional fossil fuels, solar remains unable to aggressively and consistently compete on its own.

Some people suspect that the economic viability of wind and solar power would change radically if natural gas prices weren't so low as a result of the shale gas boom: if wind and solar could instead compete with high-cost natural gas, those technologies would be in much better shape. But the logic isn't as powerful as it might intuitively seem. If natural gas prices were a lot higher, the competition for renewable energy often wouldn't be high-priced natural gas; it would be the coal-fired power that cheap gas is currently displacing, still a formidable competitor when it comes to price.[37] (Things are slightly more complicated than this—wind and solar don't compete head to head with coal—but in essence this is correct.) Odds are strong that simply boosting natural gas prices would, at least for the next decade if not longer, lead primarily to more coal power and less electricity use rather than to big growth in wind and solar power.[38] It might, however, blunt growth in renewable power enough to stunt incentives and opportunities for developers to create ever-cheaper alternative energy solutions. This is a real risk to renewables.

That said, cheap natural gas can help renewable energy if it's used properly. The fact that renewable energy is as unpredictable as the wind and sun is a big problem. Power plants that use natural gas can easily be turned on and off to make up for those sudden bursts and shortfalls. (Coal and nuclear plants can't.) This has the potential to help facilitate growth in wind and solar power.

But even though cheap natural gas isn't the main barrier to triumph for wind or solar, abundant gas won't be their savior either. Something else needs to tip the balance for renewables to truly thrive.

This takes us back to the debate around Solyndra. There's no way to avoid it: if you want to be assured of really big growth in renewable energy, you need government to get involved in one way or another. To be certain, costs still matter a lot, because it's easier for government to promote something that's relatively cheap than something that's much more expensive than the alternatives. Moreover, people can still debate whether big renewable energy gains are something society should spend a lot of money going after in the first place. (I'll tackle that later in this chapter.) For now, though, there's a simpler question that needs answering: What sort of government role would be necessary for alternative energy to thrive?

For the past decade, support has mostly come in two forms. Federal government programs provide a mix of tax credits and grants. As of 2012, wind farm developers got a credit worth 2.2 cents for every kilowatt-hour of electricity generated, for the first ten years of operation.[39] (This is in part why the West Texas wind farms kept cranking out power on July 8, 2011, even when prices went negative: they could only collect the subsidies if they stayed online.) Solar installations have benefited too, receiving an investment tax credit worth 30 percent of their upfront capital costs.[40] For one of the mammoth facilities being built in California or Nevada, that can be worth as much as $800 million.[41] At the same time, states have stepped up, mixing their own subsidies with rules called renewable portfolio standards. Those schemes, which existed in twenty-nine states as of mid-2012, require generators to produce a minimum fraction of their power from alternative fuels.[42] In order to meet that standard, generators are willing to pay top dollar for renewable power, which in turn makes producers' economics work.

But without government support of one form or another, the U.S. renewable energy industry would collapse. In 2011, David Victor and Kassia Yanosek, a political science professor and clean energy investor, respectively, described the prospect of a government pullback from clean energy as a "coming crisis."[43] Other analysts and advocates hold out hope that ending government support for traditional fuels, which still receive substantial subsidies, would do the trick; with all fuels competing on a level playing field, clean energy would win.[44] They're wrong: the amount of subsidy that goes to each bit of fossil-fuel electricity is far smaller than the amount that a similar amount of renewable energy receives.

What would it take to make renewable energy reach even greater heights? The policy options tend to fall into two categories: those making traditional energy more expensive and those seeking to make alternative energy cheap. The first category is diverse. It features things like carbon pricing, cap-and-trade, and clean energy standards, all of which we encountered in Chapter 4. Their common hallmark is flexibility: whatever way of reducing emission is most cost-effective is likely to prevail. But the common problem for renewables is that these sorts of policies are unlikely to provide a big boost to those sources for many years.

To see why, we need to do a little math. Imagine that a new policy initially penalizes carbon dioxide emissions at a rate of twenty dollars for every ton. This is at the high end of what anyone has seriously tried to pass in Congress; as we saw in Chapter 4, it's also consistent with U.S. government estimates of the damages caused by every ton of greenhouse gas emissions. A kilowatt-hour of electricity generated using a new gas-fired power plant produces about two-fifths of a kilogram of carbon dioxide; it would incur a penalty of a little less than a penny as a result.[45] This is far smaller than the difference between the cost of gas-fired and renewable electricity in almost all of the United States, so it wouldn't tip the balance. If the policy-imposed penalty rose to a hundred dollars for a ton of carbon dioxide—at the extreme of what policymakers might try in the next couple of decades, and at the high end of recent estimates of the damage carbon dioxide emissions currently do—then natural gas would be hit with a charge of about four cents for each kilowatt-hour. This is still far from enough to consistently close the gap between natural gas and either wind or solar (with some few exceptions). It also implies that, for now, even when one takes the economic benefits of avoiding climate damage into account, renewable energy is rarely as good a deal as the cleaner fossil fuels. Over time, though, declining costs for either wind or solar could change the equation.

A renewable energy standard (RES), in contrast with the other policies, would more narrowly set goals for raising the amount of renewable energy generation. By not allowing gas or nuclear to count toward the target, the standard would ensure that wind and solar grow (assuming that companies complied with the rules), though probably at greater cost. At the far end of the spectrum are tools known as performance standards. They explicitly dictate requirements for individual power plants. In 2012, for example, the U.S. government set a standard requiring that carbon emissions from new plants fall below a certain threshold; the line was low enough that it effectively ruled out new facilities using coal. These are usually the least flexible of all the options. They tend to be relatively unambitious (the 2012 standard would have done nothing for renewable power) in order to make up for their lack of flexibility. If they aren't, they can be dangerous; for example, meeting overly aggressive rules requiring renewable energy could require huge and unpredictable sums of money.

The other set of tools seeks to make clean energy cheaper, often a far more politically palatable enterprise on its face than one that might raise electricity bills. The typical way this has been done is through broad-based subsidies. The big problem with subsidies, though, is that they're cheap only so long as they're relatively ineffective; once they start spurring large-scale growth, their total costs mount, and they come under political fire. Germany is a great example here. It is often ridiculed for subsidizing solar power despite its cloudy weather, but in some ways that's precisely the point: if Germany were sunny, the subsidies would encourage so much deployment of solar power that the government bill would go through the roof. The same thing is true in the United States. Insofar as the country could afford the sorts of subsidies it handed out to wind and solar over the last decade, affordability would be trashed if the technologies took off considerably further and maintenance of high levels of subsidies continued.

This is why people in the "make clean energy cheap" camp have increasingly focused on support for innovation. The idea is to use government support in the near term to permanently reduce the cost of clean energy, ultimately obviating any need for subsidies, mandates, or things like carbon taxes. Some advocates focus on support for research and development (R&D), like the chemistry behind better batteries and the nanoscience that could yield stronger materials for wind turbine blades. This sort of role for government is relatively uncontroversial: Washington has been supporting basic R&D for a long time.

Few believe, though, that this is enough to close the gap, at least not any time in the near future. Basic research takes decades to filter through to products in the marketplace. Really accelerating innovation, many analysts and policymakers have argued, requires backing companies with innovative products that might be able to transform energy systems much sooner. But this means governments need to pick particular firms to support—which takes us right back to companies like Solyndra.

MiaSolé fits the bill too. The firm, headquartered in a drab Santa Clara, California, office park next to a string of data storage and computer network outfits, has staked its bets on thin-film solar photovoltaic technology. Its modules are being made from copper indium gallium selenide, a blend of materials that promises high efficiency and, in a crucial business twist, protection from rising silicon costs. MiaSolé is engaged in innovation but is not doing much traditional R&D. It is the sort of company that many are counting on to upend the energy world.

Bob Baker embodies what MiaSolé is and what it isn't. A thirty-two-year veteran of the semiconductor industry, Baker recently retired from chip-giant Intel when MiaSolé made him its new president in September 2010. When I meet with him at the company's headquarters, a slab of flexible solar panels is spread out on the table, and another heavier block stands against the wall. Rooms in the building have signs with symbols from the periodic table for chemicals found in the firm's solar cells. We are sitting in one labeled "Cu" for copper.

Baker's responsibilities at Intel included all of the company's manufacturing and supply-chain activities. That, he explains, was why MiaSolé brought him on board. "The first factory was coming up," he recalls. His big challenge was straightforward if daunting: "How do you grow cost-effectively and compete with the Chinese juggernaut in crystalline silicon?" Soon after he joined the firm, he quickly concluded that manufacturing wasn't the only challenge: "Commercial was the issue. Great technology, great product, outstanding features, but we didn't have a sales force." This was a far cry from the world of research and development that most people assume the big solar players are immersed in.

In early 2010, MiaSolé received provisional support from the U.S. government to build out its manufacturing facility. The details were different from the Solyndra case—among other things, MiaSolé received the option to draw on a pair of Advanced Energy Manufacturing Tax Credits worth $101.8 million rather than a loan guarantee—but the basic theory behind the subsidy was similar.[46]

There was, in principle, a case to be made for such intervention. Most economists agree that the free market alone does a weak job of promoting as much radical innovation as society could use. Because individual firms and inventors don't capture the full economic benefits of their innovations, they're likely to underinvest in them. Imagine, for example, that after spending years of your life and millions of dollars of financiers' money, you discover a new physical principle that can be used to massively boost the performance of solar panels. The innovation is too fundamental to be eligible for a patent; as a consequence, all of your competitors can use it to beat you at your own game. Looking forward to that possibility, will you invest in the research effort in the first place? Will your bankers put up the money you need to succeed?

Or suppose that your company is deciding whether to build a first-of-a-kind coal plant that captures and buries all of its carbon dioxide emissions. Scientists and engineers have explained for years that such plants are possible, but to date none are in operation. As a result, companies can't fully judge the costs and risks of building such facilities themselves. If you build a new plant, everyone—including your competitors—will learn a lot about what it takes to succeed in the business. Having proven the viability of such an advanced facility, you may actually find the information you generate being used to push your company aside. At a minimum, this will make you think twice about risking the billions of dollars that such a project requires.

Lots of innovation, of course, still happens without government support. Venture capitalists regularly put up money against small odds of a major success. But as those high-risk investors have gradually moved from areas such as information technology and biological sciences to clean energy and related fields, they have discovered that existing models for financing big advances don't always work quite as well. Energy technologies can take decades to mature, but few investors have more than a few years of patience. They can also take hundreds of millions, if not billions, of dollars just to get off the ground. Most venture capitalists prefer to take their risks on more bite-sized chunks.

When the free market looks as though it isn't delivering on needed innovation, economists often suggest governments should intervene. By subsidizing innovative activity, governments can, in principle, help correct the problem. This was the theory behind support for companies like MiaSolé: it, and pretty much any similar company, would require lots of capital and patience to scale up, and it might still fall victim to competitors that could learn from its gains. Policymakers concluded that, as a result, private investors might be unwilling to step up. That, the U.S. government decided, was a good-enough reason to back the firm.

The theory is solid, but the real challenge is what happens when it is put into practice. There are doubtless many occasions in which more innovation would be beneficial. But it is far from clear that governments are much good at identifying them. Government analysts evaluating projects for potential support don't face the same financial incentives to get things right that private sector financiers do. Worse, this all can quickly be compounded by politics. That doesn't require anything nefarious, like the debunked claims of crony capitalism surrounding Solyndra; it simply requires governments and their agencies to seek their own survival, as they are wont to do. Regular failures of government-backed companies make for awful politics, so in the long run big-ticket risk-taking government programs are rare. Instead, those programs often end up supporting less-than-innovative activities; alternatively, they sometimes just die.

And there's a final problem with government efforts to drive innovation so extensively that renewable energy beats fossil fuels: even if they work the way they ought to in theory, it's far from clear that they will actually succeed in their ultimate goals.

The first reason is that innovations that drive down the cost of new energy sources may well lower the costs of traditional ones too. Many of the biggest advances in clean energy, for example, have been due to the availability of cheap computers. This allowed developers to optimize wind turbine design and precisely aim solar panels to maximize their performance, but it's also allowed oil and gas drillers to pinpoint petroleum deposits that were once impossible to exploit economically. Cheap and strong materials, often identified as important to bringing the cost of clean energy down, could also improve the performance of things like natural-gas-fired power plants, whose turbines must operate at staggeringly high temperatures and pressures.

There are, of course, innovations that would benefit new sources of power but not older ones. Technologies that let companies store massive amounts of electricity and then sell when demand is high will help smooth delivery of electricity from new intermittent sources. This will turn equality in levelized cost into something closer to a real equality of performance. But society can also expect big innovations that are far more useful for traditional fuels than for new ones, particularly since the massive size of the existing energy industry creates hugely tilted incentives for companies to spend money on innovation in established areas. The technological advances that led to the commercial extraction of shale gas, for example, will do nothing to directly propel cleaner sources of fuel.[47]

Even if new low-carbon power plants reach a point where they can compete with new fossil-fuel facilities, a final barrier remains. New power plants often aren't competing with new facilities; they're competing with existing power plants to break into the market. Alas, much of the cost of the power those existing plants produce has already been paid for. About 1.3 cents of the cost of a kilowatt-hour of natural gas power is spent when you build the plant in the first place.[48] A new low-carbon power plant therefore needs to beat the all-in cost of gas-fired power by at least that much to muscle its way in. Coal makes for even tougher competition. Once you've built a coal-fired power plant, you've already paid for as much as five cents of the cost of every kilowatt-hour; the actual cost of generating a kilowatt-hour of electricity is in the neighborhood of only three cents.[49] That's an extremely difficult bar to clear.

To be certain, power companies will retire some U.S. coal- and gas-fired capacity, opening up space for new technologies to compete on more even footing. But this will likely require new laws or regulations. The United States currently boasts just over 310 gigawatts of coal-fired generating capacity; less than 10 percent of that is expected to be retired in the next twenty-five years.[50] But this is still not all that large a piece of the power system.[51] Moreover, some of the generation pushed aside by stricter environmental rules wouldn't be replaced by new power sources; instead, it would be offset by lower overall consumption of power.

All of this makes policy aimed narrowly at cutting the cost of clean energy a bad bet if you're looking for massive scale that solves big national problems anytime in the near future. The simplest subsidy schemes become expensive once they start to succeed. Subtler efforts aimed at boosting innovation run into thorny problems with execution—and even if they succeed in battle they might not win the war.

But none of this is reason alone to not pursue these sorts of efforts. If a shift to clean energy produces other economic, security, or environmental benefits for society, it's possible in principle for it to be good for the country even if clean energy comes with a higher sticker price. Moreover, as the cost of clean energy falls, including as a result of government support, the possibility grows that the benefits of shifting toward it will outweigh the associated costs. Making the case that clean energy delivers benefits in excess of its costs, though, requires a careful look at the benefits that clean energy can deliver. Exhibit A, for many enthusiasts, has been jobs.

❦ ❦ ❦

Manufacturing employment has been in a free fall for decades. Brackenridge, Pennsylvania, just outside of Pittsburgh, is no exception. During the first ten years of the twenty-first century, nearly a third of all manufacturing jobs in the area vanished, tracking the trend in the country at large.[52] When FLABEG, a large German maker of automotive mirrors (look for their stamp on your rearview mirror the next time you drive), announced in November 2011 that it would be closing its Brackenridge plant, the news wasn't surprising.[53]

Ten miles down the road in Clinton, though, the same company is writing a different story. Most days dozens of mirrors come off the line at a 230,000-square-foot manufacturing plant, which began operating in late 2009. The unwieldy mirrors range in size, but most are around five feet square. Looking at them directly is like staring into an unfinished carnival mirror: the light is distorted in a precise yet unflattering way. The mirrors start as flat glass; then, using black suction cups, yellow robotic arms grab the seventy-pound slabs one at a time and place them in special ovens. The glass is heated to extreme temperatures, and as it cools, the glass is molded into precise shapes. This part of the operation is off-limits to outsiders; it is what FLABEG believes to be its big edge over the competition. After the glass is molded, a coating of silver adds reflectivity; then a copper layer provides protection. Other coatings are added to ensure that the mirrors can withstand hot, dry, and dusty environments. The mirrors, by now backed with white ceramic, are stacked upright in special particle-board pallets, waiting to be shipped around the country and the world.

These mirrors will never end up installed in cars or trucks. They're being built for solar power. Some of the mirrors will concentrate heat from the sun on specially designed fluids, raising their temperature and ultimately turning electric turbines in a technology known as concentrating solar power. Others will focus the sun's rays on solar panels in order to boost performance; that scheme is known as concentrating photovoltaic power. Both approaches require immense precision. Even the paint on the mirrors is subjected to taxing tolerances: its thickness needs to meet specs within thirty micrometers, about the width of a human hair.[54] Delivering on demands of this kind requires a lot of advanced machinery. The FLABEG plant, which still wasn't fully built as of the middle of 2012, cost thirty million dollars to equip.[55]

This type of work also requires skills that many people desperately seeking jobs appear to have. When I visited the plant, the assembly line was down, and new workers were being trained to operate the controls. A fortyish man with a ponytail and wearing a blue tank top was learning to clean mirrors for concentrating photovoltaic power. Torsten Koehler, president of the company, explained that the on-the-job training was "a very critical part" of what FLABEG does.

Scenes like this are ever more common across the United States. Most mainstream economic studies have long predicted that modest environmental regulation, including steps that boost renewable energy, would slightly slow economic growth and job creation. This is true despite increasing demand for environmental goods and services, including clean energy technologies, because losses elsewhere in the economy would offset that. But proponents of new energy technologies are now attempting to seize the economic mantle for themselves. Tom Friedman, the *New York Times* columnist, made the argument succinctly in his best-selling book *Hot, Flat, and Crowded*, in which he claimed that even if climate change and energy security turn out to be bogus problems, the U.S. economy will benefit enormously from aggressive efforts to address them. Clean energy, he writes, is a "win-win-win-win" opportunity.[56]

The headline numbers are striking. According to a study published by the Brookings Institution, a Washington research organization, 138,000 people were employed in renewable energy industries as of 2010, up 24 percent since 2003.[57] And those numbers are dwarfed by projections for the future. A 2009 study from analysts at the University of Massachusetts at Amherst and the Center for American Progress, a liberal Washington research group, argued that $150 billion in annual government spending could support the creation of 2.5 million clean energy jobs.[58] Another study from the Economic Policy Institute, also based in Washington, concluded that $100 billion a year in spending spread over a decade could create 1.1 million new jobs, even after accounting for jobs lost in coal, oil, and natural gas. Industry advocates have been even more aggressive with their predictions: the American Solar Energy Society, for example, promises a net increase of 4.5 million so-called green jobs if only the United States adopts an aggressive climate change strategy.

Such numbers are met by many with immense skepticism. Perhaps the most celebrated piece of counterevidence, at least among political opponents of green jobs claims, is what has come to be known as the "Spanish study." Published in March 2009 to great fanfare, the fifty-two-page study by Gabriel Calzada, a professor at Juan Carlos University in Madrid, had a stark bottom line: Spanish renewable energy policy had destroyed 113,000 jobs—a full 2.2 jobs for every one created. The *Wall Street Journal* editorial page welcomed the study with the headline "Green Joblessness: Spain Shows the Folly of Eco-employment

Policies." In case the message wasn't clear, it concluded that "Spanish policy shows that green dreams like renewable energy are achievable only through massive transfers of money from productive sectors to those seeking to get rich quick thanks to government mandates." The *National Review*, a conservative political magazine, gleefully calculated that if U.S. government schemes managed to create five million green jobs—a number Barack Obama had bandied about—the Spanish study implied that they would also kill at least eleven million jobs elsewhere in the economy. In an economy that employs somewhere around 150 million people, this is a massive number: by implication, unemployment could jump more than five percentage points as the result of a clean energy drive.

Yet this research was deeply flawed. Calzada's logic was straightforward. He started by estimating that the Spanish government had spent 571,138 euros for every green job created. Then he observed that the total Spanish "capital stock"—the sum of all machines, equipment, knowledge, and so forth workers were using to produce goods and services—amounted to 259,143 euros for each worker. Each euro directed toward renewable energy, he argued, was a "forcible loss of resources" that no longer could be employed toward those other ends. Dividing one number by the other brought Calzada quickly to his conclusion: 2.2 jobs would be lost for every green job that was created.

But there was a massive problem with this argument: the value of a country's capital stock—its sum of machines, skills, and the like—has nothing to do with the number of jobs it supports. China has a much smaller capital stock than the United States, yet it employs several times the number of people that the United States does. Spanish capital stock is several times what it was in 1980, yet the number of people employed has barely changed. Capital accumulation matters—it lets each worker produce more with his or her time and therefore become wealthier—but it doesn't have any long-term impact on the total number of people employed.

Nor is there reason, in any case, to believe that subsidies to renewable energy translate directly into lost money for other sectors. Some of the money directed toward renewables ends up boosting salaries and profits, which in turn may well be invested in boosting the Spanish economy more broadly. Besides, government has a funny habit of spending whatever money it has. Were tax collections not used to support clean energy, they could well have been spent on something else.

So much for the dour Spanish precedent. Yet just because critics have used specious arguments to attack claims in favor of green jobs doesn't mean the original claims themselves are correct. It is easy to count jobs building wind farms and installing solar panels, but there is little in the way of rigorous research or argument to support claims that workers will benefit on net, let alone that clean energy is the future of the U.S. economy. Most of the macroeconomic models that are used to project the long-term consequences of a shift to new energy sources find that the United States suffers, usually just slightly, from the transition. New energy sources are typically more expensive than traditional ones, so increasing reliance on them slows economic activity; this phenomenon is exacerbated if the transition is so rapid that people are forced to replace old energy-using equipment before they otherwise would have.

That said, these models are usually ill designed to capture potential growth in new energy industries.[59] Their conclusions that the economy will be hurt are thus inevitable. Analysts have tried to remedy these shortfalls by performing industry-by-industry estimates. They often find that significant economic benefits in new energy industries can outweigh losses in traditional ones such as coal mining and oil production. But they still usually miss the bigger picture: the rest of the economy consistently suffers from slightly higher energy costs, as well as from the diversion of people and machines to energy production. The penalty elsewhere is usually modest, so long as the transition isn't too fast and the new technologies aren't exorbitantly expensive. But over the whole economy, it can add up. Without new economic models that carefully combine industry-level insight with broader economic constraints, the most it seems one can say overall about the impact of new energy industries is that, so long as there's an orderly transition between technologies over time, it is likely to be pretty small either way.

That is, of course, unless there's another big force capable of transforming the entire picture. Those who claim that clean energy is critical to the future of the U.S. economy believe they've identified two: exports and innovation.

The case for exports is straightforward. Unlike with fossil-fuel energy production, the scope of the U.S. clean energy business isn't constrained by physical fundamentals such as how much oil the United States has underground. Once one includes the potential for exports, then, the possible market for clean energy technology becomes enormous. The International Energy Agency, for example, analyzed one scenario involving an ambitious global pursuit of clean energy and found that the market for clean energy technologies could top a trillion dollars by 2030, equivalent to nearly 5 percent of the U.S. economy.[60] Yet even capturing that entire market (much of which, incidentally, involves things such as construction and installation services that are inherently local and hence can't be imported or exported) wouldn't fundamentally change the United States.

One can push the case even further, though, assuming that clean energy ultimately becomes the dominant way of fueling the global economy. Figures for world spending on energy are tough to come by, but some basic estimates can help. Suppose the world spends a tenth of its income on energy, including everything from fuel to power plants to energy-consuming technologies such as cars, trucks, and air conditioners. (This is probably a conservative number.) Then the total size of the global energy market is equal to 40 percent of the U.S. economy, a figure that would increase as the world economy grew faster than the United States. Capturing a big slice of that could deliver a massive economic windfall to the United States. Yet it is difficult to see how it could grab a wildly oversized chunk of the market. The basic ingredients required for being a big player in energy technology markets— well-trained scientists, engineers, and managers, as well as strong fiscal and regulatory environments—are not areas where the United States has, or will ever have, anything close to a monopoly.

Nor is there any reason to believe that technology initially developed in the United States will consistently be commercialized and manufactured there. Less than a year after I visited MiaSolé, under pressure from a glut of cheap Chinese solar panels the company was sold to a

Chinese firm specializing in hydroelectric power, for a small fraction of what its investors had put in. Hanergy, the buyer, announced that it would keep MiaSolé's Santa Clara–based operations in place but would build a new and larger manufacturing plant in China. MiaSolé had faced down the "Chinese juggernaut" that Bob Baker warned of, but the juggernaut won.

Individual stories, of course, can't prove that the United States won't gain a big overall advantage from clean energy. After all, clean energy enthusiasts have stories of their own. Many are particularly fond of pointing to the information and communications technology (ICT) revolution of the 1990s, which drove massive gains in U.S. economic growth. Yet even though Internet technology is based largely on innovations developed in the United States, the ICT sector is barely more prominent there than in the average developed country.[61] Countries such as Sweden, Ireland, and Israel all have far larger ICT sectors relative to their overall economies, despite having been historical laggards in the area. Moreover, researchers find that the presence of a large ICT sector has little consequence for national economic performance, and there is no reason to expect energy technology will be any different. Economists have, instead, found significant correlations between the *use* of ICT and national economic performance, much as one might expect national economic performance to be influenced by how a country *uses* energy.

So much for the prospect of the United States grabbing a massively outsized share of the global clean energy market. What about the risk that it might end up performing well short of other countries? This has become a worry in recent years, with concerned observers flagging foreign trade protections and subsidies that shut the United States out of overseas clean energy markets, as well as a lack of the kind of local regulations and incentives in the United States that would build up domestic demand for clean energy. When I visited the FLABEG plant outside of Pittsburgh, it was struggling because U.S. demand had not materialized, at least in part because government policy fell short of FLABEG's expectations. One of the few glimmers of hope for its outlook was the prospect of shipping dozens of its seventy-pound mirrors halfway around the world to India, which was mandating greater purchases of concentrating solar power. New Delhi imposed a host of regulations designed to shut foreign competitors out of the market for photovoltaic power, but it left the rest of the solar sector open. Were India to seal off that part of the market too, the FLABEG facilities could well close.

Governments may be particularly tempted to erect barriers that protect clean energy industries: government support for those industries is often sold by promising job creation, and the best way to reassure voters that jobs will materialize is by legally requiring that clean energy products, among them turbine blades and solar panels, be produced domestically.[62] Careful U.S. efforts to open up clean energy markets can thus pay dividends, but regardless, the prospect of being shut out of foreign markets isn't exactly a point in clean energy's favor.

Claims that domestic demand is essential to U.S. export potential are more complicated. Domestic demand is often at most tenuously connected to the potential for capturing a big share of the global market. Shifting the U.S. energy system, for example, from coal-fired power supplied by U.S. coal plants to solar power supplied by U.S. solar plants won't generally help U.S. firms export more. The one possible exception comes in cases where a base of domestic demand for new energy technologies provides a reliable foundation for U.S. companies to achieve substantial scale, which they can then exploit in their efforts to export equipment and expertise. The economic literature is ambiguous when it comes to assessing the contribution of domestic markets to global competitiveness.[63] The potential role, though, may be one place where the pure economic case for boosting domestic demand as part of an effort to increase competitiveness is on solid, though still modest, ground.

There is a final argument in favor of the economically transformative potential of clean energy, or more specifically, clean energy policy. We learned earlier that most economists agree that the market alone does a poor job of promoting as much radical innovation as society could use, and that government can potentially play an important role in correcting this flaw. But it can be immensely difficult to generate political support for the kind of government spending that's promotes innovation; simply pointing to the value of science and technology often doesn't seem to be enough. If policymakers can get people excited about the potential of clean energy and by doing so mobilize new money to support innovation, it might have widespread economic benefits. Indeed, there's an important precedent for this: national defense. Defense has long dominated federal research and development spending.[64] Since 1976, it has never fallen below half of federal R&D outlays, and as of 2009, it accounted for 58 percent of total investment.[65] (Health, another politically potent category, took up a further forty percent of the remaining share.) Careful scholars have persuasively argued that without the motivation provided by a tangible threat—the Soviet Union for much of the period in question—R&D spending would never have been nearly this high.[66] There's little question that the money spent would probably have done more for the broader economy had it been budgeted with broader goals (rather than just defense) in mind. But there's also a strong argument to be made that, without defense concerns, the money wouldn't have been there in the first place.

In principle, the same could ultimately be true for energy: if worries about economics, security, and the environment prompt the government to effectively spend more on innovation than it would otherwise, this could benefit the U.S. economy far more broadly, just as spending on defense technology has in the past. But betting on concern about energy to get the government to invest more in innovation is a long shot. For now, defense technology spending seems to be a far easier path to boosting U.S. innovation. Indeed, energy technology enthusiasts regularly discuss the possibility of steering more defense money toward energy, on the grounds that military demand for fuel is enormous, and Pentagon R&D budgets are huge. Government spending on energy innovation is unlikely to become as central as past spending on defense, at least not anytime soon.

❀ ❀ ❀

But all of this is only one way of looking at prosperity. In the same way that many contend boosting U.S. oil supplies and cutting U.S. oil demand would benefit the United States by keeping it out of foreign wars, many argue that boosting renewable energy would benefit the country—and the world—by thwarting catastrophic climate change.

The real question is not whether it would be good to curb U.S. carbon dioxide emissions, or whether using more renewable energy could in principle do so; the answer to both questions is yes. What ultimately matters is whether renewable energy is the best way to answer the climate challenge. The answer to this question ultimately comes down to whether renewable energy, or instead some other zero-carbon energy source, will prove to be a cost-effective and environmentally sound way to cut U.S. emissions.

Kurt Zenz House and Justin Dawe are sold on the need to cut greenhouse gas emissions, but they are betting on another way to do it. The pair launched their small startup, perched next door to a nail salon and a Goodwill shop a couple of blocks from the campus of the University of California, Berkeley, after meeting at the Harvard Energy Journal Club. House, an athletic man then in his late twenties, was completing a PhD in geosciences; Dawe, a few years older, was finishing his MBA. While House finished up his dissertation (winningly titled "On the Physics and Chemistry of Carbon Dioxide Capture and Storage in Terrestrial and Marine Environments"), Dawe went off to work for Horizon Wind Energy, a Houston-based developer of wind power projects.

"We're oilmen who vote for Democrats," House quips. Dawe laughs. He left Horizon, a true alternative energy firm, to launch C12, which seeks to capture the carbon emissions from fossil-fueled power plants and use them to produce oil. We first encountered this tantalizing prospect in Chapter 2: carbon-dioxide-enhanced oil recovery, known as CO_2-EOR, promises to boost U.S. oil production by as much as two million barrels a day, if only there is a big source of carbon dioxide. "What is the goal of low carbon energy?" Dawe asks rhetorically. "If your goal is to come up with an alternative source of energy, then this is not particularly alternative. If your goal is to have a societal-scale energy system that emits small amounts of CO_2, this is fabulous."

The idea behind carbon capture and sequestration (CCS) is simple. Power plants that burn coal or natural gas emit carbon dioxide; operators can install equipment to separate out the carbon dioxide and bury it deep underground. This costs extra money—the equipment is expensive and requires lots of energy to run—but the end result is fossil-fuel-fired energy without most of the climate penalty. It would let the United States maintain the touted security and economic advantages of coal and gas, minimize disruption to communities that depend on them, and still tackle climate change. As House and Dawe have explained in an open letter, "Modern society is powered with fossil fuel because no alternative energy source rivals its energy density, its cost effectiveness, or its reliability."[67] C12, therefore, will be "dedicated to building the low-carbon fossil fuel industry so that humankind can continue to use fossil fuels while preventing the resulting CO_2 from entering the atmosphere."

But even though renewable energy, at least in principle, might one day survive on its own, there is zero chance that CCS will work at a sufficient scale to take a big chunk out of U.S. emissions without perpetual help from government. Even with the prospect of enhanced oil recovery, most carbon dioxide produced by power plants is worthless, and spending money to produce a valueless product is not something successful businesses do.

House and Dawe learned that lesson quickly. When they launched their company, named C12 after the scientific name for the carbon atom, they had great hopes for federal climate legislation that would have made it profitable for power plants to clean up their carbon pollution. Their plan was to buy up the best underground storage areas for carbon dioxide and then sell them to operators who needed a place to put their waste. Then the federal legislative process collapsed, and with it so did their business model.

Even before the collapse of cap-and-trade, skepticism about CCS abounded. Engineers could sketch out systems on paper that would capture carbon dioxide and bury it for around eighty dollars a ton.[68] But the numbers were shaky, because no full-scale power plant using CCS had ever been built. Moreover, everyone agreed, the first plants to be built would certainly cost far more.[69] This posed a big problem: a typical coal-fired plant with CCS would inevitably cost north of a billion dollars to build. The only interested institution with enough cash and enough appetite for risk to step up was the federal government—and politics were conspiring to prevent it from getting deeply involved.

So the pair regrouped. They quickly noticed two trends: natural gas prices were collapsing and oil prices were on the rise. Cheap natural gas made it relatively inexpensive to capture carbon dioxide from gas-fired power plants. Expensive oil made it increasingly profitable to produce crude. The combination presented an opportunity: C12 could try to capture carbon dioxide from gas-fired power plants and make money by using it to produce oil. This won't come close to solving the carbon problem by itself—there aren't enough oil fields to use up all of the nation's carbon dioxide—but it might be enough to get some experience operating CCS systems and bring their costs down. In the meantime, House and Dawe figure they'll get rich.

No one knows if their initiative will pan out. But it highlights some essential things about the arguments that some make for CCS over renewables. Carbon capture requires government action just as renewable energy does. Carbon capture also remains too expensive for mass deployment, and it will require risky investments, whether from companies or governments, to bring costs down. CCS also comes with other environmental challenges. Fueling it requires extensive production of coal and gas, and storing carbon underground needs a massive network of pipelines and storage sites. These are not exactly environmentalists' favorite things. For some, CCS may still be a holy grail for carbon emissions reductions, but for now it's an aspiration rather than a certainty.

This is a big part of why another group focuses on a different alternative: nuclear power. Unlike renewable energy, nuclear power isn't intermittent, turning on and off with the sun and the wind. Unlike CCS, atomic energy isn't just an idea that engineers have on paper; it has been a critical part of the U.S. energy system for decades, and it currently generates around 20 percent of the country's electric power (not to mention more 75 percent of the electricity in France).[70] And unlike either renewable energy or CCS, its local environmental footprint is relatively small, at least according to some.

March 11, 2011, provided a powerful counterargument. That day, just before three o'clock in the afternoon, a massive earthquake shook Japan. Offshore, a tsunami gathered strength, and an hour after the earthquake hit, a fifty-foot-high wall of water struck the coast. The Fukushima nuclear power plant, comprising six atomic reactors, rapidly descended into emergency. Three hundred thousand people were relocated as responders mounted an unprecedented effort to bring the reactors under control.[71] No acute deaths from radiation were recorded, but the long-term toll remains unknown.

There were more immediate consequences, though, for atomic power. In Germany, Chancellor Angela Merkel announced a phase-out of the country's nuclear plants. Italy turned against nuclear power too. Even China, suspected around the world of taking a more lax attitude toward safety than others, announced a moratorium and review. In the United States, debate again flared about the future of nuclear power.

For the time being, though, the fight was only theoretical. Nuclear power had long struggled with challenging economics. Plants were big and took many years to build, and in the meantime developers racked up big bills with their bankers. Before Fukushima, the U.S. Energy Information Administration had projected that only five or six plants would be built over the next quarter century, a prognosis that found few dissenters. Fukushima couldn't kill American nuclear power. It didn't have the chance.

This could all change, though, if the United States adopted an aggressive plan to cut its carbon emissions. The U.S. government projects that if the United States was to impose a modest penalty on carbon dioxide emissions, that would eventually deliver a bonanza for nuclear energy. Little would change over the next decade—nuclear plants take time to develop—but within twenty years nuclear electricity could easily double.[72] The same thing could happen with a clean energy standard that lets power producers choose how to cut emissions.

This outcome, of course, is far from certain, even if the government takes big steps to try to make it happen. It has been decades since a new nuclear plant went from conception to launch in the United States, which makes the cost of nuclear power enormously uncertain. Moreover, although opposition to nuclear power has been relatively modest in recent years, that could change quickly in the face of a surge in new construction interest. Fights over how to dispose of used nuclear waste could again become critical. Fears of another Fukushima or Chernobyl could rise too. The reality remains that no zero-carbon electricity source—renewable energy, coal or gas with CCS, or nuclear—is ready to replace traditional fossil-fuel-fired electricity across the United States without incurring large costs and confronting big unknowns.

❀   ❀   ❀

For many who care about the environment, though, the fixation on carbon emissions itself appears to be misguided. Laura Israel, a documentary filmmaker, took time to come to this conclusion when wind developers moved into the small New York town where she had spent her weekends for twenty years. "I have a little log cabin in the woods," she told me; "I just go there to look at stars. It's practically off the grid anyway. So when I heard about wind turbines, I thought great! It would be perfect."

But there was controversy brewing in the town. Neighbors were fighting with the wind companies over leases. They were also fighting with each other over whether the massive turbines belonged so close to people's homes. "I work at a place that does a lot of green programming," Israel explained to me over coffee, nearly five years later. She was wearing a black flower print shirt and spoke with a mix of calm and punctuated excitement. "There was a producer in the office and he was doing something on wind energy." She became worried that he was only looking at its upside. "And I said to him, 'You know you might want to look a little bit more into the story. You might want to talk to some people who are going through this.'" It made sense given what she saw. "And he started shouting at me... 'Do you want a coal plant? Do you want a nuclear plant? You should not investigate this. You shouldn't be looking into this. You shouldn't be doing this.'" That was enough to convince Israel, then just shy of fifty, that there was something to see. In 2010, her independent documentary film *Windfall* made its festival premiere.

The scenes in it reminded me of the fracking fight around Athens, Ohio, and of the anti-shale-gas movie *Gasland* that had shaken up the energy world. Every theme was an echo: farmers against urbanites, corporate secrecy, money pitting neighbor against neighbor, and unexpected consequences tearing a town apart. (In another parallel, the story for *Promised Land*, the Matt Damon movie about fracking that was released in early 2013, was originally intended to be about wind farms.)[73] When Israel hit the festival circuit, her suspicions were confirmed. "That's the same thing that happened in my town," people would tell her. "I heard it all over the Midwest, I heard it in Hawaii, I heard it in California, I heard it in North Carolina, I heard it in Florida, I heard it in Maine. So I'm sure it's not just a one-off type of thing."

Climate change is a big environmental problem, but it isn't the only one. It isn't just that gaining climate safety at the expense of new nuclear risks or more natural gas drilling seems like a ridiculous trade to many; the issue appears to extend to renewable energy too. A quick scan of the news is all it takes to confirm the sentiment: from protests against solar power development in California's Mojave desert to fierce opposition to the Cape Wind project off the shore of Nantucket, renewable energy certainly isn't immune to environmental opposition.

And when it comes to impacts on land use, renewable energy skeptics sometimes appear to have the numbers on their side. Extracting coal can leave deep scars on previously pristine landscapes, but producing similar amounts of energy from centralized solar plants can actually affect considerably larger tracts of land.[74] The same is true when you compare normal natural gas extraction with wind power. Perhaps the most shocking contrast is between oil and biofuels, where a tenfold advantage is merely a lower limit; in many cases, the ratio is more like a thousand to one in favor of oil.

But, as with much else regarding energy, these scales may be slowly shifting. Better efficiency from wind turbines and solar farms means less land is needed to produce the same amount of power. New biofuels promise to be far more efficient in their use of land than ethanol production from traditional crops can be. On the other side of the equation, unconventional fossil-fuel production can be far more land-intensive than traditional extraction. Sarah Jordaan and her colleagues at the University of Calgary estimated that producing a hundred barrels a year of synthetic crude oil by mining Canadian oil sands requires disturbing about an acre of land and that producing this much from the oil sands using other techniques uses double the affected land area.[75] This is at least ten times worse than conventional oil production.[76]

The other knock against unconventional oil and gas production is that even if drilling is restricted to small pads, the operations tend to break up landscapes with access roads and pipelines, rendering much wider spaces unusable, just as arrays of wind turbines and solar panels do. The cumulative impact in both cases can be large.

Yet there are limits to how much worse fossil fuels can get when it comes to land use, as well as how much alternative energy sources can improve, leaving alternatives still often facing substantial public resistance. Moreover, the battle over local environmental consequences doesn't just apply to energy itself; it often rises to the most intense level when it's turned to moving energy from place to place, using pipelines and power lines, as with Keystone XL. (Being able to build new power lines that connect windy and sunny locations to places that use a lot of power is ultimately essential to building out renewable energy.) People might not like having drilling pads in their backyard or wind turbines in their fields, but they can usually extract good money from developers in exchange for the rights to their land. Pipelines and power lines present a fundamentally different challenge. They can cross thousands of miles, and hence a huge number of properties, posing a challenge with each one. At the same time, any given bit of land is a lot less valuable to a pipeline or power-line developer than an oil- or gas-rich tract is, so people whose land might be disturbed don't get paid as much for the impact. Add on top of this the fact that a given pipeline or power line can cross half a dozen or more states, each with its own rules and regulators, and you've created quite a mess.

Advocates for renewable energy, of course, argue that the two types of land disturbances are fundamentally different from each other, that there is something innately dissimilar about blowing up mountaintops to extract coal or dotting rural spaces with drilling pads on the one hand and covering desert landscapes with solar collectors or dropping dozens of wind turbines offshore on the other. Daniel Kammen and two colleagues of his at Berkeley have written that "both wind and solar are compatible with many other land uses and neither can be said to spoil the land they sit on in any way analogous to fossil fuel extraction or nuclear waste storage."[77]

There's a lot to the argument. Advocates for clean energy are fond of (correctly) pointing out that that there has never been a wind spill and that no one has ever accused solar power of poisoning aquifer water supply. But the fact that fossil fuels and clean energy pose different environmental challenges doesn't mean local resistance won't remain a common theme. The residents of Meredith, where Israel made her documentary, certainly didn't seem sympathetic to claims that gas drilling was worse than wind development. To them, the sound of the turbines, and the intrusion on their community, made wind development intolerable. Faced with a choice between wind turbines and fracking, their answer was simple: they didn't want either. Whether they are right or wrong is ultimately something that can't be resolved by analysis; it is more spiritual than rational in many ways. What really matters is what people who might stand in the way of development, and be directly affected by it, believe. Many people feel just as intensely about renewable energy development in their own backyard as others do about fracking in theirs. For most people who are passionate about the environment, though, the case for renewable energy development still outweighs most local concerns.

Alternative energy advocates are ultimately right that renewables have made remarkable strides, are on solid ground when defending them against claims that they will destroy massive numbers of jobs, and are correct that natural gas alone can't solve the climate problem. But their opponents are right to be skeptical of overwrought economic promises, and to insist that, most of the time, renewable energy needs help from government to compete with other fuels. For at least a decade or so, natural gas can do a lot of the heavy lifting when it comes to cutting carbon dioxide emissions from U.S. power plants; in fact curbing natural gas would do more to help coal than renewables. But gas can't do the job forever. The primary immediate opportunity in renewable energy is to bring down costs through technology innovation, including by creating bigger markets for alternative power, both things that can be done without radical government intervention in the U.S. economy. Doing this could make it increasingly less expensive for the country to cut its emissions and shift to zero-carbon power. But it is still far from clear whether renewables, nuclear, or coal or gas with CCS will ultimately be able to deliver zero-carbon energy at the scale necessary to truly transform the U.S. energy system. And it is too early to leave fossil fuels behind or designate wind and solar their successors.

WILD CARDS

"Is the world running out of oil?"

The question is chilling: if the answer turns out to be yes, the global economy will be turned upside down, and everything that people think they know about energy will be brought into doubt. Speculation about the prospect skyrocketed after the release of a bombshell book, *Twilight in the Desert: The Coming Saudi Oil Shock and the World Economy.*[1] Published by an energy banker named Matthew Simmons in 2005, the book became a surprise best-seller, waking many Americans up to what Simmons warned was an impending shortage of oil. Simmons pored over scores of technical papers prepared for the Society of Petroleum Engineers, and he concluded that Riyadh was grossly overstating the amount of oil it has left in the ground. Terms like "fuzzy logic" set off alarm bells in Simmons's mind. Oil fields, he discovered, were being beset by falling pressures, making their crude more difficult to produce, and effectively slashing their reserves. It was also safe to assume that others were inflating their numbers too. The combination of rising oil prices and stagnant production, so evident by 2007, seemed to vindicate the arguments from Simmons and his allies. Oil supplies appeared to have hit a wall. The idea of peak oil—that world oil production had maxed out and was now headed downward—was hot.

Then, just as prices peaked and plummeted beginning in the summer of 2008, the talk of peak oil largely disappeared. The pendulum swung toward the bears. Ed Morse, a top Wall Street energy analyst, wrote an essay for the journal *Foreign Affairs* titled "Low and Behold: Making the Most of Cheap Oil." Peak oil, he and others triumphantly declared, had been proven wrong. Instead, with Saudi production climbing and prospects from Canada to Brazil on the rise—an incipient U.S. oil boom was still not on most people's radars—the world was in for a new period of oil market ease.

It was not the first time peak oil fears rose to prominence before being dashed. It was the fourth.[2] The first episode unfolded in the early years of the twentieth century. In 1909, the U.S. Geological Survey reviewed the state of domestic oil resources and came to a deeply pessimistic conclusion: the United States would exhaust its supply of crude by 1935.[3] Soon, World War I led to a surge in U.S. oil demand, sending prices skyward and further reinforcing worries about dwindling supplies. By the 1920s, though, fears subsided. Spurred by high prices, entrepreneurial spirits discovered and developed vast and easily accessible reserves of oil in Texas and Oklahoma; the United States would rest easy for a while.

But peak oil fears returned two decades later in the wake of World War II. Military demand and pessimistic government audits of U.S. resources once again catalyzed fears of impending ruin. Yet surprise production gains, from California and the Rockies to Texas and the Gulf of Mexico, quickly reversed the trend.[4] Combined with the rise of the Middle East as a critical source of oil, fears were again put to rest.

The next peak oil scare would arrive like clockwork a couple of decades later. This time, though, a patina of scientific logic accompanied it. In 1956, M. King Hubbert, a Shell Oil geologist, argued that oil field production should inevitably follow something called a "logistic" curve, rising gradually and then more rapidly, flattening off at a peak, and then falling continuously down the other side. The peak would be reached once half the oil in a field was produced—and the lower forty-eight states were quickly approaching that point. Hubbert himself would turn out to be correct, at least regarding the next half century of U.S. production, but others would appropriate his analysis to make a much bolder claim: not only was U.S. oil output facing an impending peak but so was global output. By the early 1970s, armed with complex models and impenetrable mathematics, the peak oil prophets were predicting impending shortage of oil. Yet once again, when oil prices crashed in the early 1980s, their arguments were crushed too.

Today, peak oil fears persist. Writing in the preeminent scientific journal *Nature* in early 2012, David King, previously the science advisor to British Prime Minister Tony Blair, marshaled a wealth of trends and figures to assert that "oil's tipping point has passed."[5] Others sound similar notes.

But the definitive-sounding arguments for impending peak oil are invariably shaky. The fact that conventional oil production largely flatlined over the first decade of the twenty-first century, a frequent talking point, does not necessarily say anything fundamental about how much oil (or even how much cheap oil) is left in the ground. It is just as likely that politically imposed constraints on production in places such as Saudi Arabia and Russia are holding output back. Nor is there any reason to draw a sharp line between "conventional" and "unconventional" oil, as most peak oil theorists do, in order to focus on the fact that conventional oil production is stagnant, despite rising unconventional production. As the historian Daniel Yergin has observed, what is unconventional today typically becomes conventional tomorrow, making the distinction between the two categories far less meaningful than many assume.[6]

The only thing one can really say with absolute confidence about Middle Eastern oil resources is that it's unclear exactly what is underground within the region. Perhaps there is still a century of oil beneath the desert sands; most informed bets certainly go that way. There is little reason to believe we *know* they are running out. Given how opaque the region is, though, there is also no foundation for complete confidence that the resource is as big as most analysts suppose.

How would we reevaluate the consequences of the two unfolding revolutions in American energy if it turned out that the world was actually facing imminent peak oil? New limits to world oil supplies would imply that big U.S. resources of both oil and gas are even more economically valuable than they otherwise would be. The same would be true for technologies that cut U.S. consumption of crude: scarce oil would mean higher prices and thus greater benefits from using less fuel.

There are two reasonable objections to this conclusion. If we're going to start running out of oil soon, wouldn't it be best for Americans to feel the full brunt of rising prices now, rather than letting those prices be tempered for a while by higher U.S. oil production? Higher prices now would ultimately protect the economy by creating incentives for Americans to start buying more efficient cars and developing alternative fuels right away. Yet the logic in this first objection in turn has two big flaws. The first is the belief that drastically higher prices would spur the investments in efficiency and alternatives that the country needs. If peak oil advocates are right, rapidly rising prices will throw the economy into a tailspin. People won't buy more efficient cars and invest more in alternatives; instead, they will hunker down and wait until they have more money. The second problem is that other strategies can help the country become more resilient at far less cost. High prices have already created strong incentives for energy efficiency and renewable fuels. Government support for development of even better alternatives, and regulations that push higher fuel economy, will be far less painful (and probably cheaper) than letting the economy suffer through ever more expensive crude.

The second objection to the idea that peak oil would make U.S. oil production more valuable comes from people who are convinced that peak oil will at least do away with a big part of the climate problem. In this case, abundant U.S. supplies would undermine an important path to planetary salvation. But this misunderstands the nature of the climate challenge. Scarce oil will do nothing to stop the world from burning enough coal to cook itself many times over. Indeed, dwindling crude supplies might well prompt the United States and others to start converting their coal reserves into liquid fuels for their cars and trucks, leading to higher, not lower, emissions. The consequences of abundant U.S. oil supplies for the climate won't change much if it turns out that the Middle East is running out of oil.

But peak oil is not the only wild card that might fundamentally alter the consequences of the revolutions that are under way in American energy.

❦ ❦ ❦

In 1910, Norman Angell, an English journalist then living in Paris, published a book titled *The Great Illusion.*[7] Europe had become so deeply integrated, he argued, that leaders would be mad to even contemplate war. The British Empire supplied one-fifth of German raw materials and food, and the transactions behind that trade were financed through London.[8] Fully one-third of the rapidly growing foreign investment in Russia came from France.[9] Only a fool would risk a major conflict.

Four years later, the Continent was engulfed in a conflagration. World War I lasted four years and took more than sixteen million lives. It required nearly half a century, and a second world war, for Europe to start a sustained recovery and for the world to begin to move on.

Similar thinking to what prevailed at the turn of the twentieth century pervades modern thinking about the future of international conflict. Many go further to argue that war is not only stupid; it is highly implausible. The United States and China—the leading world power and its chief challenger—are deeply integrated economically. Americans depend on Chinese products to keep consumer prices and industrial production costs under control. Chinese rely on U.S. markets and American technology for economic growth. U.S. firms have staked massive amounts of capital in major investments in China, and Chinese firms are increasingly doing the same in the United States. Moreover, China relies on the United States to provide a stable global system: U.S. control of the world's sea lanes ensures the stable flow of raw materials and finished products to and from China, while American strength deters aggression in Asia and the Middle East. The U.S. Federal Reserve remains the lender of last resort, and even though Beijing sometimes chafes at the preeminent role of the U.S. dollar, the currency remains an essential ingredient to Chinese export-led growth.

The case for optimism appears even stronger than it did amid similar circumstances a century ago. The new factor is the prospect of nuclear war. Atomic weapons, the argument goes, have made war between major powers unthinkable.[10] A century ago, national leaders could at least delude themselves into foreseeing speedy and relatively painless victory against other great powers. But their contemporary counterparts cannot. It is too easy for the losing side in a conflict to launch a dozen or two nuclear bombs against its adversary, delivering a devastating blow even in defeat. This logic of deterrence, theorists argue, is inescapable: it is an automatic consequence of the atomic bomb and, together with economic interdependence, has banished military conflict between great powers for good.

Whether people acknowledge it or not, this optimism undergirds much thinking on all sides of today's battles over the future of American energy. The logic of energy can change dramatically in war—and the shadow of possible future conflict, however remote, can shape thinking in peacetime too.[11] Global energy markets could well collapse, or at least fracture, if two major powers came to blows; this has certainly been the pattern for commodities trade during past wars among major powers. In that world, the geography of energy production would suddenly become far more important. North American self-sufficiency, whether resulting from increased production, constrained oil consumption, or a mix of both, would become far more valuable. This could come into stark contrast with Chinese dependence on imports, all facilitated by sea lanes kept open by U.S. naval power. Chinese dependence on U.S. exports, whether of coal or natural gas, would also redound to the American benefit.

Resurgent fears of great power conflict might also shape current thinking in subtler ways. Climate change might not receive as much attention as it currently does if the United States and China were locked in a second Cold War, though if Cold War experience is any guide, its importance might actually rise as the two parties fought for international reputation. At a minimum, optimism about global cooperation to deal with climate change would surely wane.

So, are Americans and energy analysts correct to be as sanguine as most of them are about the possibility of future conflict with China? Most of the arguments being made today are the same as those made a hundred years ago; for the same reasons, they might turn out to be wrong. Leaders may not want to go to war, but miscalculations and miscommunications could take them down that path anyway.[12] Political scientists have studied the links between economic interdependence and war intensively over the past few decades, and they found that although trade between democracies indeed makes war less likely, economic interdependence among less similar pairs (as the United States and China are) does little or nothing of the sort.[13]

The big difference from 1914 is the advent of nuclear weapons. The prospect of nuclear conflict is good reason to believe that the United States and China will not go to war over each other's territory as the European powers did during the twentieth century. But it is not good reason to entirely dismiss the possibility. Leaders can be guilty of wishful thinking even when nuclear weapons are involved. They may believe that they are taking only limited steps, expecting that their adversary will see things similarly, when in fact the other side feels existentially threatened. The result could be an unintentional escalation to the nuclear level.

Perhaps more important, though, is the prospect of proxy battles in distant lands, much like those that occupied the United States and the Soviet Union for more than four decades of the Cold War. Indeed, the past decade has been rife with warnings that the United States and China will clash over control of energy resources in places from Africa to the Arctic.[14] The thesis is suspect: so long as markets function reasonably well, military confrontation looks awfully unattractive. But just as the United States feared that the Soviet Union would move from Afghanistan to Iran and gain control over world oil resources, it could eventually come to fear similar moves from China. At that point, self-sufficiency in energy, and particularly oil, could change the U.S. calculus, sparing the country harm.

What do these possibilities mean for the future of U.S. energy? Both sides of the fight, as is their wont, will see implications in their own favor. Advocates of greater efficiency and alternative fuels can conclude they would help make the United States independent of global energy systems if need be. Proponents of ramping up domestic oil and gas production will say the same thing. Each side can also find arguments against the other. Partisans of new energy sources can point out that, to borrow a popular phrase from the 1960s, drilling aggressively in the United States might "drain America first" and argue that the country should instead save its resources for a possible future conflict. Partisans of traditional energy sources could emphasize that the United States is likely to depend on China for many of the new energy technologies that people promote, and they may warn that this could become dangerous in a more antagonistic relationship.

What ultimately matters most is the timing of any confrontation. Intense conflict with China, if it materializes, will probably not come out of nowhere but rather emerge over years. That gradual development would create time to adjust. U.S. firms could shift supply chains for electric cars and wind farms back home or toward friendlier partners. U.S. oil and gas producers could ramp up output and put the United States on more solid ground—if they do not deplete U.S. resources beforehand.

It might not take a war, though, for geography to become a far more important force in the energy world. Americans who came of age after World War II have witnessed the tide of globalization go in only one direction. With brief exceptions, U.S. trade with the rest of the world has climbed year after year.[15] In 1960, imports and exports combined totaled $12 billion; by 2011, it had risen to $1.2 trillion. Foreign ownership of U.S. assets rarely exceeded one billion dollars prior to 1967. In 2007, it passed $700 billion.

This economic integration has been matched by the rise of international institutions. In 1946, as the world struggled to emerge from World War II, the United States led the creation of the General Agreement on Tariffs and Trade (GATT), which initially bound twenty-three countries to forty-five thousand tariff reductions affecting "one fifth of the world's total" trade.[16] Further rounds of liberalization steadily expanded trade over the decades that followed. The culmination was the so-called Uruguay Round, concluded in 1994, which gave birth to the World Trade Organization. The WTO set rules and established a remarkably powerful judicial system for resolving disputes and enforcing penalties.

This rise of global trade agreements has been accompanied by a proliferation of even deeper pacts between pairs and groups of countries, from the North American Free Trade Agreement (NAFTA), which slashed barriers to trade and investment among the United States, Canada, and Mexico, to the European Union, which at its heart is an agreement to abolish most barriers to trade, investment, and human mobility among countries within Europe.

This open system of global trade has been remarkably resilient. Even during the 1970s, when the world economy was beset by a toxic mix of economic stagnation, rampant inflation, the collapse of the gold standard, and twin energy crises, open global trade continued its forward march. In the late 1990s, the system weathered another onslaught, this time from those who chafed at what they saw as the antidemocratic workings of the WTO.

Yet a set of strong structural forces has appeared to sustain the system. Helen Milner, a professor of political science at Princeton University, has argued that the newfound political power of multinational corporations explains why the system survived the 1970s.[17] Firms whose operations and markets stretched across borders had powerful reasons to want the global system to remain open. The ability to combine cheap labor in one country with advanced machinery from another and innovative ideas developed in a third became increasingly central to how business was done. The ability to gain economies of scale by selling to customers around the world also became highly important. These forces are arguably only stronger today, as the role of multinationals, something of a novelty in the 1970s, continues to grow. Meanwhile, the success of export-led growth, first among the so-called Asian tigers and later, most impressively, by China, created another set of players with strong incentives to keep the global economic system as open as possible.

But the world has previously seen periods where open trade seemed inevitable just before it collapsed. The 1930s, which saw economic stagnation beget tariff wars, is the most infamous example. Populist forces unleashed by another deep recession could drive U.S. policymakers to erect new barriers to trade. Meanwhile Asian countries—particularly China—that have emerged from poverty on the back of export-led growth are beginning to turn inward to find their future sources of economic growth; in the process, they are becoming more willing to challenge the global trade rules that helped them get to where they are today. This has consequences for multinationals, which depend on an open system for trade and investment but find themselves progressively shut out of lucrative markets, particularly in China. Once easily counted on to defend Chinese aberrations and thus to lobby against any U.S. retaliation, some have started to question whether parts of the deal are doing them more harm than good.[18]

It is not difficult to imagine the global system of relatively open trade in energy—which has emerged so powerfully in the wake of the 1970s energy crises that it seems the only way energy can work—eventually retrenching. There are already signs of moves in this direction, including U.S. debates over whether to bar exports of natural gas, crude oil, gasoline, and diesel, and Chinese flirtation with more rigid approaches to trade in oil. Rules put in place to deal with climate change have also started to fracture the global system for energy trade. Mandates that discriminate among different sources of fuel according to their greenhouse gas emissions, whether applied to Canadian oil sands or Brazilian biofuels, inevitably inject politics into trade rules in ways that oil trade has not been subjected to before.

Indeed, the modern system for trade in energy, and particularly oil, may be an anomaly. Open and flexible global oil markets are a recent invention, dating back to the 1980s (and in some ways to the 1970s) but not much farther than that. Those markets developed in remarkably benign circumstances. Oil prices not only were low for the vast majority of the 1980s and 1990s but also were remarkably stable. At the same time, the United States had no practical option other than to depend on oil from the Middle East. A globally integrated system, anchored in flexible markets, was not just a desirable development; it was one the United States naturally encouraged.

But the conditions in which the present system emerged may be eroding. Oil prices are much higher than they were in the 1980s and 1990s, and, perhaps more important, they are far more volatile. With Saudi Arabia and its partners no longer either able or willing to stabilize markets, prices regularly undergo vicious swings, raising public ire along the way.[19] Meanwhile, with North America coming progressively closer to a state where it produces as much oil as it consumes, an alternative to global energy-market integration is becoming plausible. There is no fundamental reason to assume that integration is forever, particularly when it comes to markets in oil.

That said, it tends to take a lot to knock an established system out of place. In the wake of the 1970s oil crises, it would have been sensible for many oil consumers to move to a market-based system for distributing supplies. Yet the shift didn't truly happen until the mid-1980s, when a massive glut of oil gave producers no choice but to turn to open markets. In turn, the rapid growth of a spot market, in which oil can be bought and sold without long-term contracts, is a central part of what has made true global market integration possible. It might take a similarly pivotal event to shift the global energy system back to a more rigid state. But this is not an impossible eventuality: intense international conflict, or an extended period of extremely volatile oil prices, could drive governments to raise "temporary" barriers to the integration of global markets. Those barriers, though, might persist well after their motivating events subside.

How would a more fractured global trading system affect the consequences of the two energy revolutions under way in America? Self-sufficiency would become much more valuable in a world where the global trading system is far more rigid. Unable to rely as readily on global markets to source energy supplies, having U.S. oil to turn to would become more important. This would boost the value of U.S. fossil-fuel production, increase the benefits of curbing U.S. energy consumption, and raise the payoffs from developing electric vehicles and biofuels.

Like the prospect of armed conflict, the possibility of globalization starting to run in reverse also increases the value of keeping some oil in the ground, in case it becomes more important to have domestic resources in the future. This suggests it would be wise to pair efforts to boost U.S. production with steps to curb U.S. demand, because lower demand would make physical self-sufficiency easier to achieve down the road despite depleted resources. That oil might be worth more in the future also suggests it would be unwise to slash the lease and royalty payments companies make to the U.S. government in exchange for the right to produce oil on federal lands. These charges are a signal that oil in the ground is valuable to the American people; low rates send the opposite (and incorrect) message to the market.

Disintegration of global trade and investment wouldn't lessen the imperative of developing alternative sources of energy, but it would make it more difficult, and fraught, to do. Modern innovation systems rely heavily on combining different capabilities across borders; with a much slower flow of ideas and innovations between countries, the pace of innovation would slow as well, potentially making the adoption of new energy technologies more difficult. Concerns about the limited availability of rare earth metals, lithium, and other critical supplies would take on new urgency, but the same physical reality (availability of ample supplies in the United States or friendly countries) that makes the U.S. predicament relatively benign today would continue.

❖　❖　❖

Alas, one needn't look decades into the future to identify an important economic wild card. On December 1, 2008, the National Bureau of Economic Research certified that the United States had entered a recession the year before.[20] One month later, the Congressional Budget Office (CBO) projected that the economy would return to its full strength by 2015.[21] Unemployment would decline quickly, falling below 7 percent by 2012 and below 6 percent by 2013. But those estimates turned out to be well off the mark. As of July 2012, unemployment remained above 8 percent, a figure that would have been higher but for the fact that many had stopped looking for work.[22] History is littered with cases where a return to full economic strength following a bitter recession took many years. The U.S. economy operated below its potential for a dozen years following the start of the Great Depression, and it recovered in full only with mobilization for World War II. The recession that began with the 1979 oil crisis took nearly a decade to wear off, and within a few years after it had done so, the economy was back in the doldrums.[23] Indeed, the CBO revised its projections in early

2012 to predict a less-than-full-strength economy until 2018.[24] Many analysts are even more pessimistic.

A depressed economy that persists longer that most experts expect could alter the consequences of changes in U.S. energy. In Chapters 2 and 3 I argued that, in the long run, new jobs in oil and gas will merely replace jobs in other sectors. But a persistently weak economy changes what the long run is. If the U.S. economy continues to lag, new jobs in oil and gas, as well as in the sectors that supply them and take advantage of inexpensive fuel, are more likely to be clear-cut gains for workers. Steps helping to facilitate development would thus carry more benefits in this setting, and steps thwarting development would cause more harm.

Efficient vehicles and alternative energy pose trickier analytical challenges. Conventional wisdom usually holds that the types of regulations that are typically needed to spur their growth hurt economic performance (if only slightly when pursued properly). This suggests they would be particularly damaging if the economy were unusually weak.

Reality, however, is slightly more complex. Measures that create demand for new goods and services are precisely what the economy needs when it is operating below its potential. Steps that prompt power companies to buy more wind turbines or car companies to invest in assembly lines for advanced cars and trucks start a chain reaction that ends with more people being hired to deliver those products. It's good news for a sluggish economy.

But there is a big caveat: the same policy measures that prompt more investment in new energy technologies can risk depressing investment and consumption elsewhere in the economy. If a power company spends money on wind turbines that it would otherwise have kept in the bank, that's good news. If the money would have gone instead to natural-gas-fueled power plants and fuel purchases, the shift would probably be close to a wash. If the regulations aimed at spurring the adoption of wind turbines instead prompted the company to invest nothing at all, either in wind power or in natural gas, the consequences would instead be negative.

A similar set of trade-offs could play out with advanced cars and trucks. If regulations prompt consumers to replace purchases of foreign oil with spending on efficient U.S. cars, this boosts the U.S. economy, as automobile manufacturers hire new workers to meet the new demand. But if new regulations aimed at spurring fuel economy raise car prices so much that they deter purchases entirely, it's bad news for an economy running well short of full steam. Without as much demand for new cars, the auto industry would be forced to cut back. In a weak economy, laid-off employees would have a hard time finding other jobs.

The bottom line is straightforward in principle, though difficult to pin down in practice. Expanded oil and gas production is even better economic news in a weak economy than in a strong one. Whether or not a particular development in clean or efficient energy becomes better or worse in a persistently weak economy depends on the forces driving the development.

In May 2010, a group of scientists and policymakers gathered in Monterey, California, to discuss a sensitive question.[25] They were worried about risks that lay well beyond immediate U.S. economic concerns. Climatologists had been watching nervously as signs mounted that the earth might be more sensitive to greenhouse gas emissions than some previously believed. Melting ice in the Arctic might be sparking feedback loops leading to greater warming; so might thawing permafrost in the far north. The group came together to discuss emergency measures that might be taken if climate change soon got out of hand.

Unfortunately it is possible the world will find out that it's in for far more climate change than most models anticipate. This sort of surprise could shake the world just as much as peak oil or a major power conflict could.

The prospect that climate change could turn out to be far worse than anticipated seems to strengthen the case for new energy technologies. If the planet is a lot more sensitive to emissions than most estimates suggest, then the value of cutting those emissions goes up. Yet some contend that if warnings of impending catastrophe are real, the world is in deep trouble regardless of what it does. In this case, they argue, there may be little reason to emphasize emissions cuts in the first place.[26]

Those in this camp often turn to something called geoengineering, which is what the gathering in Monterey was convened to discuss. The basic idea is simple. The temperature of the planet is determined by the balance of heat coming in (from the sun) and heat going out. Greenhouse gas accumulation in the atmosphere cuts the amount of heat leaving, raising average world temperatures. This is why people worrying about climate change typically focus on reducing emissions of greenhouse gases: they want to make sure more heat can escape. Geoengineering advocates aim at the same ultimate objective but focus on the other part of the equation: they look for ways to stop so much heat from getting in.

There are many proposals for geoengineering. Some talk about injecting sulfur particles into the upper atmosphere to slightly block the sun's light, just as the eruption of Mount Pinatubo, a volcano in the Philippines, did in 1991. Others propose schemes that would use custom-made particles instead of sulfur, fleets of aircraft or ships to seed reflective clouds, or constellations of tiny mirrors that are sent up into space to reflect light from the sun.[27]

There is little question that many of these, particularly the simplest ones, would work to cool the planet at fairly low financial cost. There would be side effects: rainfall patterns could shift and new winners and losers could emerge.[28] The sulfur scheme would change the color of sunsets. But faced with the prospect of runaway climate change, geoengineering might become the preferred option. And, unlike slashing global emissions, it could be done by any one country that decided it made sense.[29]

Yet people would be wrong to conclude that a combination of fossil fuels and geoengineering could deliver a safe climate while avoiding any need for cleaner energy technologies. Scientists who study geoengineering consistently come to the same conclusion: the more greenhouse gases the world pumps into the atmosphere, the more geoengineering the world will need, and the more risk of unpleasant side effects the world will incur. Even worse, the simultaneous pursuit of endless fossil-fuel combustion and ever greater geoengineering could create a dangerously brittle system: if geoengineering were ever stopped, the planet's temperature would quickly skyrocket, with potential consequences far worse than what would have occurred had geoengineering not been pursued in the first place.[30] All of this makes slicing emissions almost as valuable even if geoengineering is pursued.

Moreover, no one knows precisely what the climate dangers out there are. There is a genuine chance that efforts to cut emissions will be too late to make a decisive difference, but there is also ample possibility that they will be enough. The point of boosting clean energy, among other things, is to reduce the risks of climate change. There is nothing about the possibility of extreme climate sensitivity that changes the risk calculation.

The prospect of surprisingly high climate sensitivity does, however, add marginally to the downside of boosting fossil-fuel emissions. Yet natural gas, for the time being, is lowering emissions because it's displacing coal. Rising U.S. oil production, meanwhile, will be offset substantially by lower oil production elsewhere, and it remains relatively small in the context of global emissions.

The big wild cards facing the future of U.S. energy—peak oil, major war, deglobalization, a stalled economic recovery, and surprisingly high climate sensitivity—all have something in common: they largely reinforce the benefits of the changes currently sweeping the American energy scene. There are modest exceptions, like somewhat greater climate risks from new oil production if climate sensitivity turns out to be surprisingly large, and bigger economic risks from some new environmental rules meant to foster efficiency and alternatives if economic growth continues to falter. But the broader lesson remains: there are big opportunities to be gained from both of the American energy revolutions that are under way.

THE ENERGY OPPORTUNITY

The United States is in the throes of two unfolding energy revolutions. Yet few are celebrating both. A Gallup poll conducted in March 2012 asked Americans a simple question: Should the United States focus on expanding fossil-fuel supplies, or on developing alternative energy sources?[1] Democrats strongly favored alternatives; Republicans came down decisively on the side of fossil fuels. Only 5 percent offered a third answer: the United States should do both.

Indeed, many scholars, politicians, and ordinary people are convinced that it is incoherent, and perhaps even hypocritical, to support growth of old and new energy sources at the same time. The United States may currently be producing more oil while using less, and boosting natural gas and zero-carbon power at the same time, but many believe one side must prevail over the other very soon. This belief, as we have seen, is wrong. Set aside politics for a moment; we'll return to it soon. The right strategy for the United States would intelligently embrace opportunities in old and new energy alike.

Abundant natural gas is creating jobs today, improving national security by sparing the United States the need to depend on imports, and down the road it might help substantially cut U.S. oil demand. It has also reduced U.S. carbon dioxide emissions and forestalled construction of new coal-fired power plants. But natural gas isn't without flaws: shale gas development, done wrong, entails large environmental risks, and even if done right it could deter deployment of zero-carbon energy in the long run. Yet with solid environmental rules, and policy that steers investment toward zero-carbon energy over the long haul, encouraging natural gas is a clear win.

The benefits from increased oil production are more modest: producing more oil at home can boost U.S. economic fortunes when oil prices are high, creating near-term jobs and long-term wealth while ultimately pushing down oil prices at the margin. But despite some security benefits, it won't deliver the energy independence that many seek. To be sure, producing more oil will also lead to slightly more U.S. oil use, but this won't fatally undermine the benefits of greater oil production; similarly, a boom in U.S. oil production would have surprisingly little impact on the ultimate fate of efforts to avoid dangerous climate change, so long as the oil industry isn't heavily subsidized. The biggest challenge for oil production comes from its impact on the local environment, a tradeoff that will need to be confronted one development at a time.

Meanwhile high oil prices and improvements in car and truck technology have made continuing declines in oil use possible at ever more modest cost. The benefits of adopting ever-more efficient vehicles include a stronger economy, greater resilience in the face of oil market turmoil and hence improved national security, and fewer greenhouse gas emissions. (Efforts to cut demand are a far more powerful weapon against climate change than direct curbs on oil supplies are; if the United States and others slash their oil use, production of costly U.S. oil will fall.) To be certain, the benefits from cutting oil consumption come at a price: more efficient vehicles are more expensive than less efficient ones. But the premium they command is falling, steadily expanding the opportunity for smart moves toward more efficient cars and trucks.

Renewable energy is also gaining extraordinary ground, and over time it has a good shot at being a big part of a zero-carbon energy system. Both sides in the fight over renewable energy have overstated some of their boldest claims: wind and solar, pursued properly, are neither huge economic risks nor world-changing economic opportunities. But there are potentially large environmental payoffs from active efforts to encourage renewable energy innovation as part of a package that promotes zero-carbon energy innovation across the board. To be certain, given current prices, renewable energy is usually not a cost-effective way to cut U.S. emissions. Deploying more of it can help change this by creating opportunities for developers to learn how to cut costs.

All of this points to a strategy that embraces the best of the unfolding opportunities in old and new energy. Big changes in the last decade have greatly expanded the potential to simultaneously pursue gains on multiple fronts. Ten years ago, when oil prices were low and technology less advanced, expanding oil output would have required costly subsidies, opening large and environmentally sensitive tracts of land to development, or both. Growing natural gas use would have entailed high costs and dependence on foreign suppliers had the shale gas boom not happened. Fuel economy goals of the kind being pursued for cars and trucks would have appeared ruinously expensive had oil prices and vehicle technology remained where they were. And if wind and solar were as rare and expensive today as they were then, many now-attractive efforts to encourage their further development, particularly through large-scale deployment, would be far less appealing.

Alas, historic gains for so many energy sources have often reinforced people's prior prejudices about energy. If someone believes that even the smallest gains for their favored technologies are all-important, or that the smallest gains for sources they oppose are intolerable, they will never be able to live with a strategy that pushes forward on multiple fronts. Just as bad, people who are convinced that their favorite energy sources can solve the nation's problems alone will neglect efforts to encourage other sources. If you believe oil production will deliver energy independence for free, why bother trying to cut oil consumption? If you think renewables can solve the climate problem while driving an economic renaissance, why make any sacrifices to help natural gas thrive?

It is precisely these types of attitudes that often drive and polarize thinking in Washington and around the country. Yet no one energy source is a panacea for the economic, security, and environmental challenges the United States faces. (Nor is any source without costs.) At the same time, none of the big gains currently being posted in U.S. energy are disastrous for the economy, national security, or the environment. Each of them, pursued properly, can deliver important benefits that greatly outweigh the attendant costs—and blocking or neglecting any of them could risk big losses. The United States has an important opportunity to strengthen its economy, improve its security, and confront global climate change, all by building on ongoing advances in American energy.

❧ ❧ ❧

Some of these gains will be realized without any action from Washington; indeed, government meddling often does harm. Yet the United States will miss out on much of the opportunity unless Washington plays a wise and active role in taking advantage of it.

Unfortunately, the debate over what government should do is regularly dominated by people who either oppose an active role for government without exception or support a strong government role but too often advocate unwise action. Some who oppose an active role for government contend that the supposed risks associated with energy don't exist. Others insist the free market will confront those dangers effectively on its own. The first seven chapters of this book should put this belief to rest. But there is a subtler and more challenging case for a hands-off approach. The mere existence of problems with markets doesn't mean there are desirable government solutions; intervention has its own set of risks and costs, and in principle they can be greater than the risks and costs of keeping government on the sidelines. But the fact that governments can screw things up shouldn't be taken to an absurd extreme. The risks of government inaction are often large, while keeping the costs of intervention relatively small is often straightforward.

But this doesn't mean government intervention in the energy system always makes sense. Sometimes intervention is simply misguided: efforts to end shale gas development, for example, would deny the United States big benefits without delivering commensurate environmental gains. Other times, government intervention that looks smart today can be undermined by unexpected changes in the world. For instance, fuel economy standards that look like home runs with four dollar a gallon gasoline may turn out to be foolish in a world where gasoline costs only two dollars instead. Moreover, in some cases, government simply lacks the resources and political flexibility to make good decisions; investing large sums of money in individual energy companies in an attempt to spur technology development may be one instance. This problem is exacerbated when top policymakers are asked to make too many energy decisions. Busy leaders who are overwhelmed with overly long lists of decisions to make are unlikely to produce good policy.

The solution is a strategy that increases opportunity while protecting against important risks. Government should expand opportunities to develop new energy supplies of all kinds (old and new) through its approach to permitting and access to land, and by encouraging technology development. Policies constraining supplies should be restricted to those that aim to limit local environmental harm; they should not be wielded in a quixotic effort to solve national economic, security, and climate problems. Those national goals should be tackled by focusing on the demand side of the equation, with government taking steps to deter dangerous activities, be they excessive carbon dioxide emissions or oil consumption—things that markets can't handle alone.

One might call this a most-of-the-above strategy: it embraces a broad set of energy opportunities but is still discriminating. Leaders should follow four rules that flesh this out as they aim to capitalize on the unfolding revolutions in American energy: build a diverse and resilient energy portfolio, focus on big wins, empower energy development, and leverage gains at home to make progress abroad.

Build a Diverse and Resilient Energy Portfolio

Uncertainty is a dominant feature of the American energy landscape. We know many things well: natural gas is far more abundant than most people recently assumed, U.S. oil output has the potential to grow considerably, efficient cars are becoming more affordable every year, and the cost of alternative energy, even though still higher than that of fossil fuels, is on the decline. We also know that high and volatile oil prices hurt the U.S. economy, fossil-fuel emissions increase the likelihood of dangerous climate change, and domestic gas has spared the country some geopolitical risks.

But there is a lot we don't know with anything close to high precision. We can't say with enormous confidence how much oil or gas the United States will produce, how much it will cost to extract, or how welcoming affected communities will be. We can't firmly predict the costs of increasing the efficiency of U.S. cars and trucks, and we certainly don't know when electric vehicles will become a big commercial prospect. We don't know exactly what will happen to the cost of alternative fuels over the next five or ten years. Nor, for that matter, can we predict what will happen with the costs and safety of nuclear power or carbon capture technology.

This uncertainty extends beyond energy sources. After nearly four decades of hard work, economists still can't agree on whether spiking oil prices cause recessions, but they definitely can't rule out the possibility that they do. National security strategists can't agree on whether dependence on natural gas imports would expose the country to big geopolitical risks, but few are anywhere close to dismissing the link. Scientists can't pin down just how bad every ton of greenhouse gas emissions will be for climate change, but most agree that the damages could be very large. Indeed, the unknowns of the energy world are almost always its most troubling elements.

This suggests that a U.S. strategy focused on reducing exposure to big risks rather than on fine-tuning the economy would be wise. Such an approach is alien to many strategists who think about energy, but it is common in other places. Investors regularly face massive uncertainty. They cope in large part by diversifying their financial portfolios. This doesn't mean they invest in every prospect that comes along—some potential investments are clearly destined to be disastrous, and others have little hope of yielding big returns—but it does mean they focus on knowing and reducing their risks. The smart investor also maintains some flexibility, making sure to dispose of bad bets when they materialize and to seize new opportunities as they arise.

There are even parts of the U.S. government that regularly focus on uncertainty. The Department of Defense, at its best, is a great example.

(At its worst, it is as deficient as any other part of government can be.) The investments the Pentagon makes today will be deployed decades from now in a security environment that might look very different. Good planners don't ignore that; instead, they embrace it. They work from a range of contingencies, determining what kind of investments will maximize U.S. advantage and minimize risk. The U.S. government, for example, develops forces that would be needed in a confrontation with China while developing military-to-military ties to reduce the odds of the confrontation arising. It rarely procures a single type of aircraft for a particular task, instead ensuring that multiple platforms are developed, which reduces the risk of single failures having intolerable consequences. Politicians often tag such efforts as waste—after all, do we really need two kinds of advanced fighter jets?—but the logic of uncertainty and risk management often makes it sensible to pursue them.

Strategists who are helping shape the U.S. energy portfolio should also manage risk by pursuing two types of policies. Some should be designed to weed dangerous investments out of the U.S. portfolio, whether by penalizing or regulating greenhouse gas emissions and excessive oil consumption or by shaping strong environmental rules for energy development of all kinds. Others should be aimed at helping to diversify the U.S. energy portfolio, whether by creating conditions in which beneficial oil and gas development can thrive or by supporting innovation in cleaner and more efficient technologies in order to help them become more attractive options.

Focus on Big Wins

Leaders presented with specific proposals for energy-related policies that pursue these two goals should ask two simple questions: Could this lead to big gains for the economy, security, or the environment? And can it be pursued without doing substantial damage on any of those three fronts? They should focus their efforts on those instances where the answers are both yes. This will allow them to pursue necessary intervention without meddling excessively in the economy. It will also help them navigate competing goals.

Some proposals will fail this test because, even if they are pursued, they won't have the potential for much impact, good or bad; they'll simply distract policymakers and create opportunities for missteps. Other proposals should be rejected because they can yield big wins on one front only at the expense of big losses elsewhere. Overly aggressive fuel economy mandates fall in this category: the environmental and security gains come at the expense of excessively large economic costs. (Determining when costs are "excessive," and hence mandates are "overly aggressive," comes down to detailed analysis of the costs and benefits of specific policies; recently implemented mandates generally have benefits that are projected to substantially exceed their costs.) So would efforts to open up protected lands to oil drilling if they went too far; they would deliver gains, but only at the expense of big environmental losses. Policymakers should steer clear of such moves.

The good news is that big advances across the board in American energy have greatly expanded the set of opportunities clearing both bars—opportunities that are both large and, in substantial part because of recent gains in American energy, don't require stark trade-offs. Careful carbon pricing or a clean energy standard can deliver big climate gains without hefty economic or security costs.[2] Strong but sensible fuel economy standards, or a modest oil tax, either of which would have substantial security and environmental benefits, can be implemented without punishing economic costs. Smart government support for innovation in emerging technologies such as advanced cars, renewable energy, and carbon capture, including through direct subsidies or other support for early deployment, can deliver increasingly large returns as markets for those technologies grow. Making room for greater oil production by expanding access to deposits can yield economic gains without developing massive tracts of specially protected land. The same is true for natural gas, which can also deliver big benefits for national security and climate change. Implementing solid environmental regulations for oil and gas development can be done without crushing production from those sources; indeed, by boosting public confidence that energy production is safe, they are actually essential to reliable development over the long run. These are the big, clear wins U.S. leaders should prioritize.

Empower Energy Development

People who envision massive gains in U.S. oil and gas production and people who aspire to build a country dominated by zero-carbon energy have something basic in common: realizing any of their agendas will require a massive amount of energy development. Alas, they all face a social, regulatory, and legal environment in which local concerns and endless litigation have made development ever more difficult. Many want to see this situation fixed, but only for their preferred energy sources. Many environmental advocates who used the current system to block the Keystone XL pipeline in 2011 are also desperate to make it easier to build wind and solar, and the electricity transmission needed to support those energy sources. Backers of oil and gas who seek easier permitting for their projects typically couldn't care less about whether renewable energy developers face similar problems.

Yet the best bet for unlocking the full potential of American energy is across-the-board reform. There are substantial limits to what Washington can do: many of the most powerful policy tools, such as smart zoning to effectively integrate industrial activity near residential areas, will (and should) never end up in federal hands. But the federal government can still take important steps, including imposing minimum standards for safe development of technologies in which public confidence has faltered, facilitating collaboration among regulators in different states, and streamlining permitting for projects of all kinds while retaining smart environmental safeguards.

Leverage Gains at Home to Make Progress Abroad

Extraordinary advances in U.S. energy have created big opportunities to change the American energy system for the better. But most U.S. worries about energy, and many energy-related opportunities, remain anchored in dynamics well beyond the country's shores. The United States remains vulnerable to high and volatile prices borne abroad. Its people worry about climate change because global emissions create ever-larger risks. Many of its economic strategists see value in developing new energy technologies in part because new markets appear to be emerging around the world.

The United States could realize a host of benefits by exporting the technologies that have been developed in recent years. Efforts to spread shale gas technology could yield bigger gas supplies in Eastern Europe, China, and beyond, thereby reducing their reliance on Russia, weakening pressures to become entangled with Middle Eastern exporters, and cutting greenhouse gas emissions. And advances in renewable energy technologies provide an opportunity both to make money through international sales and to cut overseas greenhouse gas emissions, but fully realizing that requires access to foreign markets. Unfortunately, such access has been inconsistent, and particularly difficult to gain in China, which is almost certain to become the world's largest market for alternative fuels. A growing U.S. renewable energy market may provide the United States with more leverage because others may worry about losing access if they fail to become or remain open themselves. The United States should take advantage of those concerns to open up markets abroad.

Big gains in natural gas, energy efficiency, and renewable power, driven by markets and policy, can also strengthen the U.S. hand in pressing others to curb their greenhouse gas emissions. Many countries are concerned about climate change but fear taking strong action in part because they perceive others not to be doing so. Progress on climate within the United States, along with the availability of cheaper emissions-cutting technologies, might help change some of their attitudes. This does not mean the United States should return to a quixotic quest for a climate treaty. American diplomats should focus on adding transparency to all countries' efforts and making it politically costly for them to reverse course. Whether this is done through a treaty or by other means is less important.

At the same time as it exploits international opportunities, the United States should also guard against missteps. Abundant oil and gas supplies have led many to call for bans on exports of both. That would forgo opportunities to shake up global gas markets and strengthen the U.S. economy, all while putting U.S. trade agreements and broader access to foreign markets at risk. The same is true for restrictions on foreign investment in U.S. energy production: the United States should be careful in imposing limits when it is lobbying others to remove theirs.

Policymakers should also be careful to not get carried away in their excitement about the benefits that advances in American energy have delivered. The United States will still depend on global markets, stability in oil-producing regions, and secure sea lanes. If the American navy did not maintain security on the high seas, and if the U.S. Strategic Petroleum Reserves weren't available to help buffer markets during disruptions, oil prices would be higher and more volatile, with far worse consequences for the United States. Those basic tasks need continued attention.

❁　❁　❁

This strategy would embrace advances in old and new energy sources alike to realize large economic, security, and environmental gains, by focusing on big risks and opportunities, unleashing development across the range of energy sources, and leveraging gains at home to make progress abroad. But a basic question remains. Strategy is forged through political battle, not set by dispassionate technocrats coldly weighing costs and benefits. Can a strategy that embraces such disparate developments ever work politically? Partisans on both sides of the battle over the future of American energy are often convinced that the only route to victory for their side is through defeat for the other, a phenomenon exacerbated by the time-tested tendency to use energy issues as proxies for bigger ideological fights.

This instinct is understandable but ultimately wrong. The best hope for big gains in old and new energy is actually through a political deal that can be embraced by both sides.

It is easy to see why advocates of serious action to deal with climate change and curb U.S. oil consumption are skeptical. They have struggled for years against fossil-fuel producers that not only lobby for more support for oil and gas production but have also advocated against constraints on consumption or support for alternatives. For example, the American Petroleum Institute (API), which speaks for oil and gas producers, has long opposed strengthening fuel economy standards for cars and trucks. The U.S. Chamber of Commerce, which has consistently called for expanded access to areas for offshore drilling, has also attacked government efforts to penalize greenhouse gas emissions and to subsidize development of renewable fuels. Even worse, in the eyes of many advocates, are the efforts (far less prominent today than in the past) on the part of some fossil-fuel producers to sow doubt regarding climate change in order to undermine policy that might aim to curb U.S. emissions.[3] So when advocates for serious action on climate change look at the world, they do not want to see their decades-long adversaries become further entrenched.

This is part of what drove many climate activists to shift tactics in 2011 and throw themselves wholeheartedly into the effort aimed at blocking Canadian oil production by killing the Keystone XL pipeline. For nearly a decade, major U.S. environmental groups tried to build broad coalitions aimed at passing legislation that would cut U.S. emissions and boost renewable power. In 2007, the effort yielded its greatest triumph: the creation of the U.S. Climate Action Partnership, known as U.S.-CAP. The partnership brought massive environmental groups such as the Natural Resources Defense Council and the Environmental Defense Fund together with industry heavyweights such as General Electric and Alcoa. Even big oil companies, including BP and Shell, joined the coalition. All pledged support for a strong set of common principles for climate policy. During the 2008 presidential campaign, this broad coalition from business and civil society was matched by agreement from the two candidates for president that the United States ought to adopt an ambitious cap-and-trade program to rein in greenhouse gas emissions.

A year later, the coalition was in tatters. Cap-and-trade was dead, U.S.-CAP was losing members, and any previous semblance of bipartisanship on energy policy was gone. There was no shortage of explanations offered for why the initiative collapsed. Some blamed the financial crisis that began in 2008 and the accompanying recession. Others pointed fingers at poisoned politics, poor political strategy, and what they saw as growing public distaste for climate science.

For a large segment of the environmental community, though, the lesson was starker: compromise was no way to achieve fundamental change. Sure, oil companies signed up for U.S.-CAP, but they did not put their muscle behind any serious legislation; when it came time to fight for change, they did not help. In many cases they seemed to be playing both sides of the issue, remaining members of other groups (like API and the Chamber of Commerce) that were actively lobbying against every climate or oil-saving bill.

Blocking developments such as the Canadian oil sands, or shale gas in the United States, didn't require coalitions with industry and oil supporters or sixty votes within the U.S. Senate. To be certain, they required new alliances, particularly between left-wing greens and right-wing conservationists. But those coalitions could leverage existing law to block development, and they could pressure governments to go slow wherever the law didn't stand firmly in the way.

The problem with this calculus is that, even if all you care about is curbing climate change, cutting oil consumption, and growing clean energy industries, these tactics can't get you very far. Dealing with climate change will require massive additions of new zero-carbon infrastructure to the U.S. energy system. Cutting oil consumption will require mass adoption of ever more advanced vehicles. There is no way to effect these changes just by stopping things. New technologies still require government support, or at least penalties or restraints on other sources, in order to flourish. Creating those incentives ultimately requires serious legislation. (Bits and pieces can be accomplished through regulation under existing law, but progress there is far more vulnerable to political winds, because future regulators can reverse course.) Legislation, in turn, requires broad coalitions, and the only way to build them is by doing things that potential allies can embrace. For people who want to confront climate change and cut oil consumption, this means doing deals with others who want to expand production of oil and gas.

Enthusiasts for oil and gas production, of course, are just as skeptical of the people on the other side of the energy debate. Once again, this is often well founded: many advocates of new and cleaner energy sources have consistently pitted themselves explicitly against all fossil fuels. Some environmental groups have tried to draw natural gas companies (and sometimes nuclear power producers) to their side by pointing out that modest climate policies would help them gain at the expense of coal. Advocates for increasing fuel economy standards sometimes attempt to ally with carmakers that would make money selling efficient cars. But those companies and their supporters are often skeptical. Many of the same people who claim to want to be their friends issue press releases warning of massive risks from shale gas development, describing apocalyptic dangers from nuclear power, and insisting that those companies should pay higher taxes. As far as many oil and gas supporters are concerned, environmental advocates have been prone to exaggerating risks.

Put yourself in the shoes of a shale gas producer confronted by an environmental group that promises gains in demand for natural gas if climate legislation is passed. The group asks for your support, even though your traditional political allies, all longtime supporters of oil and gas, oppose the bill. If you back the legislation, and later come under fire for the local impacts of shale gas production, odds are you will no longer have any friends at all. That is not a gamble many executives or their supporters are willing to make. For most supporters of oil and gas production, then, the best course of action is clear: defend the status quo. Oil and gas production has boomed in recent years without government action. Why ask for anything more?

Alas, such an attitude is shortsighted, at least for many big oil and gas players. Environmental groups and their allies lack the power to pass big new laws alone, but they can cause massive problems for oil and gas developers. Targeted political campaigns that leverage local concerns can do real damage; witness the successful effort to delay the Keystone XL pipeline in 2011. Lawsuits can tie up development for years if not decades even if development is legally allowed. Regulators can impose rules that producers find deeply problematic, and even if future administrations change them, permanent damage may be done in the meantime.

Moreover, although some natural gas developers may do fine absent government efforts to curb climate change or cut oil consumption that also boost demand for natural gas, others that own more marginal resources may not. Many should therefore conclude that the potential benefits of allying with those who seek to confront climate change and cut oil consumption outweigh the risks. Oil and gas producers might also find common cause with supporters of alternative energy in encouraging reforms that make it easier to develop new energy sources, whatever they are.

People on the two sides of the battle for the future of American energy need not coalesce around a common vision of what is good for the country in order to strike a deal. Many people, for example, will never buy into the argument that confronting climate change is worth any serious effort. Many others will never accept that the environmental damages of oil drilling can be outweighed by economic or security gains. Some will always think that green jobs are the only ones that make sense; others will see opportunity only in fossil fuels. Nor is it reasonable to expect that either side will abandon tactical moves that put pressure on their old adversaries. But the two sides ultimately don't need to agree on priorities, or form a consistent common front, in order to support a strategy that pushes forward carefully on multiple agendas. They merely need to both make political judgments that the benefits to their priorities from a broad-based approach will outweigh the concessions they need to make—and decide to treat energy mostly on its own merits instead of as a proxy for far less tractable ideological fights.

Part of this is a matter of building trust, which might be helped along through small deals that benefit both sides. Congress could expand access to areas for oil and gas production while committing the royalties to support clean energy development; it could shift tax breaks for oil producers toward support for carbon capture and sequestration that's used to enhance oil output; it could revamp rules for development in ways that help old and new energy at the same time.

But perhaps the biggest barrier to taking the plunge is suspicion on all sides that accepting much of their opponents' agendas requires fundamentally undermining their own—that even a smart strategy blending old and new energy is incoherent. Fortunately, as we have seen, the suspicion is incorrect.

Only a fool would guarantee that a strategy embracing opportunities in oil, gas, efficiency, and alternatives all at once will become a political hit. But the odds for success with a broad strategy are ultimately far better than those for a narrower and more exclusive effort that focuses on only one part of the American energy opportunity, or that gets so deeply mired in political battles that it does nothing at all. If advocates and politicians continue to fixate on decades-old fights, the United States will lose many of the opportunities it now has to enhance economic prosperity, improve national security, and address climate change. But if the American people and their leaders can embrace a course that exploits both of the unfolding revolutions in American energy, they will realize rewards on every front.

ACKNOWLEDGMENTS

When I first started to spend time studying energy, I despaired over the lack of a book that would help me understand how to think across economic, security, and environmental challenges and opportunities. Eventually, I decided to write one myself, and I quickly discovered why none existed: it's tough. Richard Haass and James Lindsay gave me a wonderful professional home at the Council on Foreign Relations (CFR) where I could think broadly, deeply, and independently about energy and other subjects. They also gave me the time I needed to get this book right.

Lionel Beehner, Jason Bordoff, Gerald Bradley, Megan Bradley, Eileen Claussen, Blake Clayton, Trevor Houser, James Lindsay, Michael O'Hanlon, and Meghan O'Sullivan all read the manuscript and shared their comments and advice. Many others helped me think through the various issues this book wrestles with. I am particularly grateful to those with whom I have collaborated on research closely related to several elements of the analysis in this book: Blake Clayton, Elizabeth Economy, Robert McNally, Shannon O'Neil, and Adam Segal. I have benefited greatly from their wisdom.

I have been privileged to have the assistance of several talented research associates. Monika Adamczyk ably assisted with research while I was developing my initial approach to the book. Charlie Warren joined just as I started to focus intensely on my research and writing. He quickly become indispensible as he researched arcane issues from automobile technology to international pipeline law, found and opened doors to fascinating people and places that I otherwise would never have encountered, and served as a sounding board as I worked through new arguments and ideas. This book would not be the same had he not been part of it. Alexandra Mahler-Haug joined my team as I was wrapping up the manuscript, enthusiastically contributing an eagle eye for fact checking, and helping move the book toward publication.

Geri Thoma, my agent, helped me shape and reshape my book, and was an invaluable and patient counselor along the way. David McBride, my editor at Oxford University Press, was wonderful in helping me craft a manuscript that could speak to a broad audience while remaining solid at the same time. His early enthusiasm for the book did wonders for my moving it forward. Tom Finnegan was the thoughtful and perceptive copyeditor every author hopes for.

Many people whom I had never met before generously welcomed me in California, Colorado, Michigan, New York, Ohio, Pennsylvania, and Vienna as I researched this book. Some of them show up in this book; others do not but taught me just as much. I particularly hope that those who find themselves in these pages feel I have done their perspectives justice.

I owe my greatest debt to Megan Bradley, who read drafts, helped me sift through ideas and arguments, and patiently supported me without fail through the ups and downs that writing a book entails.

This book and the work behind it would not have been possible without the generosity of David M. Rubenstein to the Council on Foreign Relations in support of the endowed chair that bears his name and that I hold. This book has also benefited greatly from the support of the Alfred P. Sloan Foundation for the CFR Project on Energy and National Security. I alone am responsible, of course, for the book's contents.

GLOSSARY

Advanced biofuels	Biofuels not made from materials that compete with food (e.g., corn, soy)
Barrel	A unit of measure for oil that is equivalent to forty-two U.S. gallons
Biofuels	Liquid fuels made from biological materials; substitute for gasoline, diesel, or jet fuel
CAFE standard	Corporate Average Fuel Economy standard, mandating average fuel economy of vehicles sold by each company
Cap and trade	A policy that imposes a limit on greenhouse gas emissions, distributes permits accordingly, and then allows entities to trade those permits among themselves
Carbon capture and sequestration (CCS)	A technology that captures carbon dioxide emissions from industrial facilities (particularly coal- and gas-fired power plants) and deposits them permanently underground
Carbon tax	A policy that levies a fee to entities that emit carbon dioxide, proportional to the amount emitted
Cellulosic ethanol	A gasoline substitute produces from parts of plants that cannot be eaten
Clean energy standard	A policy that mandates a minimum fraction of electricity be generated from clean sources according to a set schedule; "clean" may be defined to include only zero-carbon sources, or may include natural gas (usually with half credit) and/or efficiency
CO_2-EOR	An approach to oil production that injects carbon dioxide into oil wells to increase their productivity

Corporate Average Fuel Economy	The average fuel economy of all the cars and trucks sold by a given company; usually computed as a harmonic average
Enhanced Oil Recovery (EOR)	Any method that increases the amount of oil that can be produced from a given resource; CO_2-EOR is one variation
Ethanol	A gasoline substitute produced from biological materials
Fossil fuels	Oil, natural gas, and coal
Fracking	Colloquial term used to describe either hydraulic fracturing or the entire process of extracting natural gas from shale
Fuel economy standards	See *CAFE standard*
Gas-to-liquids (GTL)	Technology that converts natural gas into gasoline, diesel, jet fuel, or methanol
GDP	Gross Domestic Product; standard measure of national economic output
Gigawatt (GW)	A unit of capacity to produce electricity; a typical nuclear plant has a capacity of one gigawatt
Green jobs	Often ill defined, but generally refers to jobs associated with environmental products and services, including clean energy
Greenhouse gases	Gaseous compounds that block outbound infrared radiation (heat) when they accumulate in the atmosphere
Horizontal drilling	A technology wherein operators drill down before turning their drill bits and then drilling sideways
Hybrid	A type of vehicle that combines a gasoline engine and an electric engine
Hydraulic fracturing	A technology wherein operators inject high-velocity fluids into a well in order to fracture surrounding rock and stimulate the flow of oil or gas
Intermittent sources	Sources of electricity that cannot deliver consistent power, most notably wind and solar
Keystone XL	A proposed pipeline connecting the Canadian oil sands to markets in the United States
kilowatt-hour (kWh)	A measure of electricity use
Levelized cost of electricity	The cost of generating electricity divided by the amount of electricity generated
mpg	miles per gallon; a measure of the efficiency of a vehicle

Natural gas liquids (NGLs)	Liquids that are produced concurrently with natural gas, most prominently ethane, butane, and propane
Oil sands	Oil-bearing sands found primarily in the Canadian province of Alberta; also referred to as tar sands
Oil shale	Rock that can in part be converted to oil through heating
OPEC	Organization of Petroleum Exporting Countries; cartel that attempts to restrain collective oil output and raise prices
Peak oil	The idea that world oil production will soon hit a peak, and then decline, as a result of scarce resources
Rare earth metals	A class of elements in the periodic table, many of which have applications in clean energy technologies
Renewable energy	Energy whose production does not require depletable resources; wind, solar, and geothermal are examples
Renewable Portfolio Standard (RPS)	A policy that mandates a minimum fraction of electricity be generated from renewable sources according to a set schedule
Shale	Dense rock that often bears oil or gas
Shale gas	Natural gas extracted from shale rock
Shale oil	See *tight oil*
Shock	In economics, a sudden change; in this book, most often a change in energy prices
Strategic Petroleum Reserve (SPR)	U.S. government-controlled reserves of already produced oil that can be released in the event of a supply emergency
Tight oil	Oil produced from formations in which oil cannot flow under normal conditions; produced using hydraulic fracturing to enhance mobility
Zero carbon energy	Energy whose production leads to few or no carbon dioxide emissions

NOTES

CHAPTER 1

1. "Bears, Tigers, Lions and Wolves Escape from Ohio Zoo," BBC News, October 19, 2011, http://www.bbc.co.uk/news/world-us-canada-15364027.
2. Tom Davidson, "Farmer Regrets Drilling: Owners Advised to Educate, Protect Selves," *The Herald*, May 31, 2012, http://sharonherald.com/local/x1647290588/Farmer-regrets-drilling.
3. Ohio Department of Natural Resources, "Oil and Natural Gas Well and Shale Development Resources," Division of Oil and Gas Resources Management, July 16, 2012, http://www.ohiodnr.com/portals/11/oil/pdf/utica.pdf; "Chesapeake Energy Corporation Discloses Initial Horizontal Well Drilling Results in Its Utica Shale Discovery and Announces Achievement of Corporate Production Milestones," *Chesapeake News*, September 28, 2012, http://www.chk.com/News/Articles/Pages/1610725.aspx.
4. Mark Williams, "Wind Power in Ohio Enjoys Growth Spurt," *Columbus Dispatch*, April 14, 2012, http://www.dispatch.com/content/stories/business/2012/04/14/wind-power-in-ohio-enjoys-growth-spurt.html; American Wind Energy Association, "Wind Energy Facts: Ohio," January 1, 2012, http://www.awea.org/learnabout/publications/upload/4Q-11-Ohio.pdf.
5. Peter Waldman, "Exxon vs. Obama," *Entrepreneur*, March 30, 2009, http://www.entrepreneur.com/article/200986.
6. David Kreutzer, "Robbing Banks and Subsidizing Green Energy," Foundry Blog, April 11, 2012, http://blog.heritage.org/2012/04/11/robbing-banks-and-subsidizing-green-energy/.
7. John S. Watson, "The Energy Renaissance," October 19, 2011, http://www.chevron.com/chevron/speeches/article/10192011_theenergyrenaissance.news.
8. Ibid.

9. This is the annualized inflation rate for the month of September 1973. Federal Reserve Economic Data, "Consumer Price Index for All Urban Consumers: All Items (CPIAUCSL)," 2012, http://research.stlouisfed.org/fred2/graph/?id=CPIAUCSL.

10. Barbara C. Farhar, Patricia Weis, Charles T. Unseld, and Barbara A. Burns, *Public Opinion about Energy: A Literature Review* (Golden, Colo.: U.S. Department of Energy, 1979), 67–68.

11. Daniel Yergin, *The Prize: The Epic Quest for Oil, Money, and Power* (New York: Simon & Schuster, 1991), 642–643.

12. Michael J. Graetz, *The End of Energy: The Unmaking of America's Environment, Security, and Independence* (Cambridge, Mass.: MIT Press, 2011), 55–56.

13. "Hearings Before the Committee on Commerce, United States Senate, Ninety-third Congress, Second Session," Washington, D.C., November/December 1974.

14. Allen L. Hammond, "The Hard and the Soft Technology of Energy," *New York Times*, August 28, 1977.

15. Tracy Kidder, "Tinkering with Sunshine," *Atlantic Monthly*, October 1977.

16. Amory B. Lovins, "Energy Strategy: The Road Not Taken?" *Foreign Affairs* 55, no. 1 (1976).

17. Mobil, "Display Ad 857," *New York Times*, February 8, 1976.

18. Ray Reece, *The Sun Betrayed: A Report on Corporate Seizure of U.S. Solar Energy Development* (Boston: South End Press, 1979), 102–103.

19. Ibid., 102.

20. Hans H. Landsberg, "Battling on Energy," *New York Times*, October 6, 1980.

21. David Stockman, *The Triumph of Politics: How the Reagan Revolution Failed* (New York: Harper and Row, 1986), 61.

22. Ibid., 38.

23. Ronald Reagan, "Whatever Happened to Free Enterprise?" *Imprimis*, January 1978.

24. Douglas E. Kneeland, "Reagan Charges Carter Misleads U.S. on Threat to Energy Security; Record on Blacks Cited Sees No Energy Shortage," *New York Times*, September 11, 1980.

25. Steven Rattner, "Kennedy Urges Energy Plan Based on Liberal Ideas; Adviser Opposed to Controls Cost on Coal Conversion Based on Driver's Licenses Controls Likely to Continue," *New York Times*, February 3, 1980.

26. Ibid.

27. Ted Kennedy, "'Kennedy for President' 1980 Campaign Brochure," 2011, http://www.4president.org/brochures/1980/tedkennedy1980brochure.htm.

28. Farhar et al., *Public Opinion about Energy*, 111.

29. U.S. Energy Information Administration, "U.S. Crude Oil Imported Acquisition Cost by Refiners (Dollars per Barrel)," 2012, http://www.eia.gov/dnav/pet/hist/LeafHandler.ashx?n=PET&s=R1300____3&f=M. At the time, imported oil and domestic oil were priced differently. The marginal barrel was imported.

30. One consistent policy objective was to end oil-price controls.

31. John S. Herrington, "Market-Oriented Energy Policies Are the Answer to Our Needs," *New York Times*, April 6, 1986.

32. Dennis Frankenberry, "Harbor, Bush-Quayle 1988," 2012, www.living-roomcandidate.org/commercials/1988/harbor.

33. Bill Mintz, "War Hampering Work on New Energy Policy," *Houston Chronicle*, January 21, 1991.

34. For individual wealth, see U.S. Department of Labor, Bureau of Labor Statistics, "Real GDP per Capita in the United States," 2011, http://research.stlouisfed.org/fred2/data/USARGDPC.txt. For energy consumption, see U.S. Energy Information Administration, "Energy Consumption, Expenditures, and Emissions Indicator Estimates, 1949-2010," 2011, http://www.eia.gov/totalenergy/data/annual/showtext.cfm?t=ptb0105.

35. Renewable Fuels Association, "Historic U.S. Fuel Ethanol Production," 2012, http://www.ethanolrfa.org/pages/statistics.

CHAPTER 2

1. U.S. Energy Information Administration, "Henry Hub Gulf Coast Natural Gas Spot Price (Dollars/Mil. BTUs)," 2012, http://www.eia.gov/dnav/ng/hist/rngwhhdm.htm.

2. U.S. Energy Information Administration, "Trends in U.S. Residential Natural Gas Consumption," 2010, ftp://ftp.eia.doe.gov/pub/oil_gas/natural_gas/feature_articles/2010/ngtrendsresidcon/ngtrendsresidcon.pdf.

3. U.S. Energy Information Administration, "U.S. Natural Gas Gross Withdrawals (Million Cubic Feet)," 2012, http://www.eia.gov/dnav/ng/hist/n9010us2a.htm.

4. U.S. Energy Information Administration, *Annual Energy Outlook 2012—Early Release Overview* (Washington, D.C.: U.S. Department of Energy, January 23, 2012).

5. U.S. Energy Information Administration, *Annual Energy Outlook 2011* (Washington, D.C.: U.S. Department of Energy, 2011), 79.

6. Lynn Helms, "Horizontal Drilling," *DMR Newsletter* 35, no. 1 (2008); Tim Carr and Paul Gerlach, "Update on Horizontal Drilling in Kansas Current Status and Case Histories," Kansas Geological Survey, May 10, 2001, http://www.kgs.ku.edu/Class2/horz05092001a/index.htm.

7. Carl T. Montgomery and Michael B. Smith, "Hydraulic Fracturing: History of an Enduring Technology," *Journal of Petroleum Technology* (December 2010).

8. Ibid.

9. U.S. Energy Information Administration, *Annual Energy Outlook 2009* (Washington, D.C.: U.S. Department of Energy, 2009).

10. U.S. Energy Information Administration, *Annual Energy Outlook 2012* (Washington, D.C.: U.S. Department of Energy, June 2012), 62.

11. Vicki Ekstrom, "A Shale Gas Revolution?" MIT News, January 3, 2012, http://web.mit.edu/newsoffice/2012/shale-gas-revolution-report.html.

12. A partial exception can occur if new industries raise overall wages, drawing more people into the labor force; as a result, the number of jobs in the economy can change even if the unemployment rate doesn't. In recent decades, though, economic growth has not translated into higher wages for most, suggesting that one ought to be cautious in expecting this phenomenon to increase the total number of U.S. jobs. The author thanks Trevor Houser for this observation.

13. Mohsen Bonakdarpour et al., "The Economic and Employment Contributions of Shale Gas in the United States," Washington, D.C., IHS Global Insight (USA) Inc., December 2011.

14. Ibid., 20.

15. Ibid.

16. American Chemistry Council, "Shale Gas and New Petrochemicals Investment: Benefits for the Economy, Jobs, and U.S. Manufacturing," Washington, D.C., American Chemistry Council, March 2011, 1.

17. John J. McKetta Jr., *Encyclopedia of Chemical Processing and Design: Volume 1—Abrasives to Acrylonitrile* (New York: Marcel Dekker, 1976), 112; Warren R. True, "Global Ethylene Capacity Continues Advance in 2011," OilandGasJournal.com, July 2, 2012, http://www.ogj.com/articles/print/vol-110/issue-07/special-report-ethylene-report/global-ethylene-capacity.html; IHS Chemical, "Global Ethylene Oxide, Glycol, and Derivatives," March 2011, http://www.ihs.com/ru/ru/Images/EOEG_sample_mar12.pdf. This estimate assumes total production capacity estimated at 141 million tons per year and U.S. contract prices at $1,200 per metric ton.

18. Bonakdarpour et al., "Economic and Employment Contributions of Shale Gas," 39.

19. Ibid., 39–40.

20. In the first few years after the financial crisis, the price of a thousand cubic feet of natural gas was perhaps three dollars or so lower on average than it would have been had the shale boom not occurred. One can infer this by comparing actual prices with projections that preceded recognition of

the shale gas boom, or with prices for LNG imports in the UK. For the latter, see Mohsen Bonakdarpour et al., "The Economic and Employment Contributions of Shale Gas in the United States," Washington, D.C., IHS Global Insight (USA) Inc., December 2011. In the future, if global natural gas prices are high, the gap might open further, perhaps doubling. Americans use about five trillion cubic feet of natural gas in their homes every year; the lower prices thus translate into around fifteen to thirty billion dollars in annual savings. Electric power plants used a bit less than two trillion cubic feet of natural gas to produce power for homes when natural gas prices were high, which adds another five to ten billion dollars or so in savings, though some of that is kept by power producers as profits, rather than passed on to consumers.

21. Andrew Kramer, "Russia Cuts Off Gas Deliveries to Ukraine," *New York Times,* January 1, 2009.

22. "Europeans Shiver as Russia Cuts Gas Shipments," Associated Press, January 7, 2009, http://www.msnbc.msn.com/id/28515983/ns/world_news-europe/t/europeans-shiver-russia-cuts-gas-shipments/#.UBlpMqOIjc8.

23. Mike Sefanov, Anthee Carassava, and Jenny Harrison, "Ukraine, Russia Cut Off Gas to Europe," CNN Money, January 7, 2009, http://money.cnn.com/2009/01/07/news/international/russia_ukraine/index.htm.

24. U.S. Energy Information Administration, *International Energy Outlook 2008* (Washington, D.C.: U.S. Department of Energy, 2008).

25. For background on this perspective, see David G. Victor, Amy M. Jaffe, and Mark H. Hayes, *Natural Gas and Geopolitics* (New York: Cambridge University Press, 2007).

26. U.S. Energy Information Administration, "Annual Energy Outlook 2009—Early Release Reference Case Presentation," December 17, 2008, http://www.sais-jhu.edu/centers/geei/presentations/EIA_AEO_2009.pdf.

27. BP, *BP Statistical Review of World Energy 2009* (June 2009), 30.

28. BP, *BP Statistical Review of World Energy 2012* (June 2012), 28. A small part of the increase compensated for a reduction in Algerian supplies.

29. Jan Hromadko, "E.ON Ups Forecasts after Settling Gazprom Supply Dispute," *Wall Street Journal,* July 3, 2012.

30. U.S. Energy Information Administration, "World Shale Gas Resources: An Initial Assessment of 14 Regions Outside the United States," 2011, http://www.eia.gov/analysis/studies/worldshalegas/pdf/fullreport.pdf.

31. Ibid., 4.

32. Ibid.

33. Michael Warren, "China Looks to Ramp Up Shale Exploration and Production," E&P, May 7, 2012, http://www.epmag.com/Exploration/China-To-Ramp-Shale-Exploration-Production_100059.

34. Ian Urbina, "Hunt for Gas Hits Fragile Soil, and South Africans Fear Risks," *New York Times*, December 1, 2011.

35. Philip K. Verleger, "The Amazing Tale of the U.S. Energy Independence," *International Economy*, Spring 2012.

36. Ibid.

37. Mark Mills, *Unleashing the North American Energy Colossus: Hydrocarbons Can Fuel Growth and Prosperity* (New York: Manhattan Institute, 2012).

38. U.S. Department of Energy (DOE), "LNG Export and Long Term Natural Gas Applications," July 16, 2012, http://www.fossil.energy.gov/programs/gasregulation/authorizations/2012_Long_Term_Applications.html.

39. Michael Levi, *A Strategy for U.S. Natural Gas Exports* (Washington, D.C.: Hamilton Project—Brookings, June 2012).

40. Ibid.

41. U.S. Energy Information Administration, *Annual Energy Outlook 2012* (Washington, D.C.: U.S. Department of Energy, 2012), 208.

42. National Resources Defense Council, "Picking a Clean Energy Plan: NRDC's 'Plug-in Alternative' Is More Efficient Than the Pickens Plan," April 2009, http://www.nrdc.org/energy/files/FINALWEB_CleanEnergyPickensFS_0409_02.pdf.

43. Ernest J. Moniz, Henry D. Jacoby, and Anthony J. M. Meggs, "Chapter 5: Demand," in *The Future of Natural Gas: An Interdisciplinary MIT Study* (Cambridge, Mass.: MIT Energy Initiative, 2011), 120.

44. Ibid.

45. U.S. Census Bureau, "Geographic Distribution—Gasoline Stations: 2007," 2007, http://www.census.gov/econ/industry/geo/g4471.htm.

46. U.S. Department of Energy (DOE), "Alternative Fuels Data Center: Natural Gas Fueling Station Locations Map," 2012, http://www.afdc.energy.gov/fuels/natural_gas_locations.html.

47. Moniz et al., "Chapter 5: Demand," 122.

48. Ibid.

49. Ibid., 122. This estimate assumes thirty miles per gallon and a zero discount rate applied to future savings.

50. For oil prices around $100 a barrel, a gallon of gasoline costs around $2.50, not including marketing, distribution, and taxes, all of which would also need to be added to the sticker price of natural gas. With natural gas prices expected to stay below five dollars per thousand cubic feet for the foreseeable future, this adds up to a savings of close to two dollars per gallon.

51. This estimate assumes a 5 percent discount rate.

52. This estimate assumes an 8 percent discount rate.

53. This assumes a 5 percent discount rate. The figure becomes ten years for a 10 percent discount rate.

54. Moniz et al., "Chapter 5: Demand," 122.

55. These are the author's calculations and are not derived from the MIT study.

56. Shell, "Pearl GTL—An Overview," August 7, 2012, http://www.shell.com/home/content/aboutshell/our_strategy/major_projects_2/pearl/overview/.

57. Paulina Jaramillo, W. Michael Griffin, and H. Scott Matthews, "Comparative Analysis of the Production Costs and Life-Cycle GHG Emissions of FT Liquid Fuels from Coal and Natural Gas," *Environmental Science and Technology* 42, no. 20 (2008): 7563.

58. Arend Hoek, "The Shell GTL Process—Towards a World Scale Project in Qatar: The Pearl Project," October 4, 2006, http://www.dgmk.de/petrochemistry/abstracts_content14/Hoek.pdf.

59. E. P. Robertson, "Options for Gas-to-Liquids Technology in Alaska," Idaho National Engineering and Environmental Laboratory, 1999.

60. Michael Economides, "The Economics of Gas to Liquids Compared to Liquefied Natural Gas," *World Energy* 8, no. 1 (2005).

61. Ian Urbina, "Insiders Sound Alarm Amid a Natural Gas Rush," *New York Times*, June 25, 2011; Ian Urbina, "Behind Veneer, Doubt on Future of Natural Gas," *New York Times*, June 26, 2011.

62. U.S. Energy Information Administration, *Annual Energy Outlook 2011*, 20.

63. Ohio Department of Natural Resources, "Preliminary Report on the Northstar 1 Class II Injection Well and the Seismic Events in the Youngstown, Ohio, Area," Columbus, Ohio Department of Natural Resources, March 2012.

64. Won-Young Kim et al., "Youngstown Earthquake on 24 December 2011 and 31 December 2011," January 2, 2012, http://ohiodnr.com/downloads/northstar/Appendix2-LamontDoherty.pdf.

65. National Research Council, "Induced Seismicity Potential in Energy Technologies," Washington, D.C., National Academies Press, June 15, 2012.

66. Stephen G. Osborn et al., "Methane Contamination of Drinking Water Accompanying Gas-Well Drilling and Hydraulic Fracturing," *Proceedings of the National Academy of Sciences* 108, no. 20 (2011).

67. Ibid.

68. Tom Hayes, "Gas Shale Produced Water, Presentation to the RPSEA/GTI Gas Shales Forum," June 4, 2009, http://www.rpsea.org/attachments/contentmanagers/429/Gas_Shale_Produced_Water_-_Dr._Tom_Hayes_GTI.pdf.

69. Christopher Joyce, "With Gas Boom, Pennsylvania Fears New Toxic Legacy,"NPR,May 14, 2012,http://www.npr.org/2012/05/14/149631363/when-fracking-comes-to-town-it-s-water-water-everywhere; Nicholas Kusnetz, "North Dakota's Oil Boom Brings Damage along with Prosperity," ProPublica, June 13, http://www.propublica.org/article/the-other-fracking-north-dakotas-oil-boom-brings-damage-along-with-prosperi.

70. International Energy Agency (IEA), *Golden Rules for a Golden Age of Gas* (Paris: OECD, 2012).

71. Ibid.

72. Scott Detrow, "Sturla Stands by STD Comment," NPR StateImpact, August 17, 2011, http://stateimpact.npr.org/pennsylvania/2011/08/17/sturla-stands-by-std-comment/.

73. Jim Efstathiou Jr., "Taxpayers Pay as Fracking Trucks Overwhelm Rural Cow Paths," *Bloomberg Businessweek*, May 15, 2012, http://www.businessweek.com/news/2012-05-15/taxpayers-pay-as-fracking-trucks-overwhelm-rural-cow-paths.

74. Sophia Pearson and Mike Lee, "Pennsylvania High Court Takes Appeal on Marcellus Shale Rights," *Bloomberg*, April 5, 2012, http://www.bloomberg.com/news/2012-04-05/pennsylvania-high-court-takes-appeal-on-marcellus-shale-rights.html.

75. Erika Staaf, *Risky Business: An Analysis of Marcellus Shale Gas Drilling Violations in Pennsylvania 2008-2011* (Philadelphia: PennEnvironment Research and Policy Center, February 2012).

76. Erich Schwartzel, "Color Me Fracked: Energy Industry Produces Coloring Book to Make Case for Gas Drilling to Kids," *Pittsburgh Post Gazette*, June 19, 2011.

CHAPTER 3

1. Howard Jonas, "A Letter from Our CEO," American Shale Oil LLC, June 2010, http://amso.net/wp-content/uploads/2013/01/df3154f7-b520-470b-b1c7-d6544c01067c.pdf.

2. Rich Miller, Asjylyn Loder, and Jim Polson, "Americans Gaining Energy Independence with U.S. as Top Producer," *Bloomberg*, February 6, 2012.

3. U.S. Energy Information Administration, "Table 4.6: Crude Oil and Natural Gas Exploratory Wells, Selected Years, 1949-2010," in *Annual Energy Review 2010* (Washington, D.C., 2011).

4. "U.S. Field Production of Crude Oil," July 30, 2012, http://www.eia.gov/dnav/pet/hist/LeafHandler.ashx?n=pet&s=mcrfpus1&f=a.

5. "Alaska North Slope Crude Oil Production," July 30, 2012, http://www.eia.gov/dnav/pet/hist/LeafHandler.ashx?n=pet&s=manfpak1&f=a.

6. "Cushing, OK WTI Spot Price FOB," July 18, 2012, http://www.eia.gov/dnav/pet/hist/LeafHandler.ashx?n=PET&s=RWTC&f=A. Adjusted for inflation.

7. Steven G. Grape, *Technology-Based Oil and Natural Gas Plays: Shale Shock! Could There Be Billions in the Bakken?* (Washington, D.C.: U.S. Energy Information Administration, November 2006).

8. U.S. Energy Information Administration, *The Availability and Price of Petroleum and Petroleum Products Produced in Countries Other Than Iran* (Washington, D.C.: U.S. Department of Energy, June 2012).

9. North Dakota Industrial Commission, "North Dakota Annual Oil Production," Department of Mineral Resources, Oil and Gas Division, 2011, https://www.dmr.nd.gov/oilgas/stats/annualprod.pdf.

10. Railroad Commission of Texas, "Texas Eagle Ford Shale Oil Production, 2004 through April 2012," July 19, 2012, http://www.rrc.state.tx.us/eagleford/EagleFordOilProduction.pdf.

11. Edward L. Morse, Eric G. Lee, Daniel P. Ahn, Aakash Doshi, Seth M. Kleinman, and Anthony Yuen, *Energy 2020: North America, the New Middle East?* (New York: CitiGroup, 2012), http://fa.smithbarney.com/public/projectfiles/ce1d2d99-c133-4343-8ad0-43aa1da63cc2.pdf.

12. "U.S. Monthly Crude Production Reaches Highest Level Since 1998," U.S. Energy Information Administration, December 4, 2012. Accessed at http://www.eia.gov/todayinenergy/detail.cfm?id=9030.

13. James Gilluly, Aaron C. Waters, A. O. Woodford, and Robert R. Compton, *Principles of Geology* (San Francisco: W. H. Fremmil, 1958), 602.

14. Ibid.

15. U.S. Energy Information Administration, "Crude Oil Production," June 28, 2012, http://www.eia.gov/dnav/pet/pet_crd_crpdn_adc_mbblpd_a.htm.

16. Morse et al., *Energy 2020*.

17. John M. Broder, "Obama Oil Drilling Plan Draws Critics," *New York Times,* March 31, 2010.

18. Bettina Boxall and Richard Simon, "Obama Administration Withdraws Offshore Drilling Plan," *Los Angeles Times,* December 2, 2010.

19. National Petroleum Council, "Prudent Development: Realizing the Potential of North America's Abundant Natural Gas and Oil Resources," Washington, D.C., September 15, 2011, 67.

20. National Commission on the BP Deepwater Horizon Oil Spill and Offshore Drilling, "Deep Water: The Gulf Oil Spill and the Future of Offshore Drilling," Washington, D.C., January 2011.

21. For a discussion of steps taken, see Strategic Energy Policy Initiative, *America's Energy Resurgence: Sustaining Successes, Confronting Challenges* (Washington, D.C.: Bipartisan Policy Center, 2013).

22. U.S. Energy Information Administration, "Potential Oil Production from the Coastal Plain of the Arctic National Wildlife Refuge: Updated Assessment," Washington, D.C., May 2000; *Annual Energy Outlook 2009* (Washington, D.C., 2009), 201.

23. Natural Resource Defense Council, "Arctic Wildlife Refuge: Why Trash an American Treasure for a Tiny Percentage of Our Oil Needs?" December 19, 2011, http://www.nrdc.org/land/wilderness/arctic.asp; The IUCN Red List of Threatened Species, "Ovibos moschatus," August 1, 2012, http://www.iucnredlist.org/details/29684/0.

24. U.S. Senate Legislation and Records, "Roll Call Votes 109th Congress 1st Session: On the Amendment (Durbin Amdt. No. 902) to H.R. 6 (Energy Policy Act of 2005)," Washington, D.C., June 23, 2005; "Roll Call Votes 109th Congress 1st Session: On the Amendment (Cantwell Amdt. No. 168) to S.Con.Res. 18," Washington, D.C., March 16, 2005.

25. National Petroleum Council, "Working Document of the National Petroleum Council North American Resource Development Study: Arctic Oil and Gas," Resource and Supply Task Group Arctic Subgroup, September 15, 2011.

26. Natural Resources Defense Council, "Reducing Imported Oil with Comprehensive Climate and Energy Legislation," March 2010, http://www.nrdc.org/energy/files/reducingimportedoil.pdf.

27. Vello A. Kuuskraa, Tyler Van Leeuwen, and Matt Wallace, "Improving Domestic Energy Security and Lowering CO_2 Emissions with 'Next Generation' CO_2-Enhanced Oil Recovery (CO_2-EOR)," National Energy Technology Laboratory, Washington, D.C., June 20, 2011.

28. Energy Information Administration, "Energy Market and Economic Impacts of the American Power Act of 2010," Office of Integrated Analysis and Forecasting Washington, D.C., July 2010.

29. Natural Resources Defense Council, "Reducing Imported Oil."

30. Kuuskraa et al., "Improving Domestic Energy Security."

31. James T. Bartis, Tom LaTourrette, Lloyd Dixon, D. J. Peterson, and Gary Cecchine, *Oil Shale Development in the United States: Prospects and Policy Issues* (Santa Monica, Calif.: RAND Corporation, 2005). Figures were converted from 2005 dollars to 2012 dollars by using CPI.

32. James T. Bartis, Frank Camm, and David S. Ortiz, *Producing Liquid Fuels from Coal: Prospects and Policy Issues* (Santa Monica, Calif.: RAND Corporation, 2008). Figures were converted from 2007 dollars to 2012 dollars by using CPI.

33. Bartis et al., *Oil Shale Development in the United States*.

34. Ibid.

35. Quoted in David Ignatius, "An Economic Boom Ahead?" *Washington Post*, May 4, 2012.

36. Jocelyn Fong, "20 Experts Who Say Drilling Won't Lower Gas Prices," Media Matters for America, March 22, 2012, http://mediamatters.org/blog/2012/03/22/20-experts-who-say-drilling-wont-lower-gas-pric/184040.

37. Energy Security Leadership Council, "The New American Oil Boom: Implications for Energy Security," Washington, D.C., 2012.

38. International Monetary Fund, *World Economic Outlook: Tensions from the Two-Speed Recovery*, Washington, D.C. (April 2011). Author's calculations.

39. James D. Hamilton, "Historical Oil Shocks," in *The Handbook of Major Events in Economic History*, ed. Randall E. Parker and Robert M. Whaples (New York: Taylor & Francis, 2013).

40. The economy also suffers from sudden obsolescence of a part of its oil-using capital stock, but this cannot account for the bulk of the historical relationship between oil-price spikes and economic losses. In any case, this dynamic is not significantly affected by growth in U.S. oil production.

41. International Monetary Fund, *World Economic Outlook*. Author's calculations.

42. Mat McDermott, "Oil and Gas Industry Jobs Overstated Four Times by American Petroleum Institute," Treehugger.com, September 26, 2011, http://www.treehugger.com/fossil-fuels/oil-gas-industry-jobs-overstated-four-times-by-american-petroleum-institute.html.

43. Bureau of Economic Analysis, "Full-Time and Part-Time Employees by Industry," December 13, 2011.

44. As noted in Chapter 2, a partial exception can occur if new industries raise overall wages, drawing more people into the labor force; as a result, the number of jobs in the economy can change even if the unemployment rate doesn't. In recent decades, though, economic growth has not translated into higher wages for most, suggesting that one ought to be cautious in expecting this phenomenon to increase the total number of U.S. jobs.

45. Alex Kowalski, "Trade Deficit of U.S. Unexpectedly Surges on Increase in Crude-Oil Imports," *Bloomberg*, July 12, 2011, http://www.bloomberg.com/news/2011-07-12/trade-deficit-of-u-s-unexpectedly-surges-on-increase-in-crude-oil-imports.html.

46. Carmen M. Reinhart and Kenneth S. Rogoff, *This Time Is Different: Eight Centuries of Financial Folly* (Princeton, N.J.: Princeton University Press, 2009).

47. Daniel Yergin, *The Prize: The Epic Quest for Oil, Money, and Power* (New York: Simon & Schuster, 1991), 613.

48. Clifford Krauss and Eric Lipton, "U.S. Inches Toward Goal of Energy Independence," *New York Times*, March 22, 2012.

49. Blake Clayton and Michael Levi, "The Surprising Sources of Oil's Influence," *Survival*, January/February 2013.

50. Steve Coll, *Private Empire: ExxonMobil and American Power* (New York: Penguin Press, 2012).

CHAPTER 4

1. Chris Tackett, "It Begins. 70 Arrested at White House on Day 1 of Tar Sands Action," Treehugger.com, August 20, 2011, http://www.treehugger. com/corporate-responsibility/it-begins-70-arrested-at-white-house-on-day-1-of-tar-sands-action-updated.html.
2. Brad Johnson, "Keystone XL Tar Sands Action Day Four: Montanans Sit In," Climate Progress, August 23, 2011, http://thinkprogress.org/climate/2011/08/23/301862/keystone-xl-tar-sands-action-day-four-montanans-sit-in/.
3. Ibid.
4. Canadian Association of Petroleum Producers, "Crude Oil: Forecast, Markets and Pipelines," Calgary, Alberta, June 2011.
5. James Hansen, "Silence Is Deadly," June 3, 2011, http://www.columbia. edu/~jeh1/mailings/2011/20110603_SilenceIsDeadly.pdf.
6. DemocracyNow, "Over 160 Arrested in Ongoing Civil Disobedience against Keystone XL Tar Sands Oil Pipeline," August 23, 2011, http://www.democracynow.org/2011/8/23/over_160_arrested_in_ongoing_civil#transcript.
7. Neil C. Swart and Andrew J. Weaver, "Commentary: The Alberta Oil Sands and Climate," *Nature Climate Change* 2 (March 2012).
8. The Alpine-Treeline Warming Experiment, "Overview," 2011, https:// alpine.ucmerced.edu/pub/htdocs/project_details.html.
9. British Columbia Government, "A History of the Battle against the Mountain Pine Beetle, 2000–2012," Ministry of Forests, Lands and Natural Resource Operations, May 23, 2012, http://www.for.gov.bc.ca/hfp/mountain_pine_beetle/Pine%20Beetle%20Response%20Brief%20History%20May%2023%202012.pdf.
10. U.S. Forest Service, *Review of the Forest Service Response: The Bark Beetle Outbreak in Northern Colorado and Southern Wyoming* (Washington, D.C.: U.S. Department of Agriculture, September 2011).
11. Tom Yulsman, "In the Curve: How We Know CO_2 in the Atmosphere Is Increasing—and It's Our Bad," Center for Environmental Journalism: CE Journal, March 1, 2011, http://www.cejournal.net/?p=4997.
12. National Oceanic and Atmospheric Administration, "Atmospheric CO_2 at Mauna Loa Observatory," Global Monitoring Division, August 2012, http://www.esrl.noaa.gov/gmd/webdata/ccgg/trends/co2_data_mlo. pdf.
13. Richard S. Lindzen, "Global Warming: How to Approach the Science," Campaign to Repeal the Climate Change Act Seminar, http://impactofcc.

blogspot.com/2012/02/richard-s-lindzen-reconsidering-climate.html, 4. This was an audiovisual presentation at the UK House of Commons on February 22, 2012.

14. Intergovernmental Panel on Climate Change, "Box 10.2, Figure 1," in *Climate Change 2007: The Physical Science Basis. Contribution of Working Group I to the Fourth Assessment Report*, ed. S. Solomon et al. (Cambridge, UK: Cambridge University Press, 2007).

15. David Chandler, "Revised MIT Climate Model Sounds Alarm," MIT TechTalk 53, May 20, 2009, http://web.mit.edu/newsoffice/2009/tech-talk53-26.pdf.

16. More precisely, if the atmospheric concentration of carbon dioxide is raised by 1 ppm, it takes about a hundred years for that to decay to 0.37 ppm (i.e., by a factor of e).

17. Department of Energy, "Energy Conservation Program: Energy Conservation Standards for Small Electric Motors, Final Rule," *Federal Register* 75, no. 45 (March 9, 2010).

18. Richard S. J. Tol, "The Economic Effects of Climate Change," *Journal of Economic Perspectives* 23, no. 2 (2009).

19. Basic economics says that the value added to the economy from a barrel of oil production is equal to the difference between what it costs to produce the oil and the value of the oil to its consumer (which is bounded below by the price of oil), minus any externalities. The full impact of a given barrel stays positive so long as this difference is greater than the resulting climate damage.

20. James Hansen et al., "Target Atmospheric CO_2: Where Should Humanity Aim?" *The Open Atmospheric Science Journal* 2 (2008).

21. Intergovernmental Panel on Climate Change, *IPCC Third Assessment Report: Climate Change 2001 Synthesis Report*, ed. Robert T. Watson (Cambridge, UK: Cambridge University Press, 2002).

22. James Hansen, "Game Over for the Climate," *New York Times*, May 9, 2012. Hansen notes that the oil sands contain enough carbon to increase concentrations by 120 ppm, but he does not note that only about half of CO_2 emissions end up in the atmosphere; the rest end up in oceans and land. This estimate corrects for that.

23. U.S. Energy Information Administration, "U.S. Field Production of Crude Oil," July 30, 2012, http://www.eia.gov/dnav/pet/hist/LeafHandler.ashx?n=PET&s=MCRFPUS2&f=A.

24. Government of Canada, "Oil Sands: A Strategic Resource for Canada, North America and the Global Market," 2011, http://www.canadainternational.gc.ca/eu-ue/assets/pdfs/Oilsands-sables_petroliferes_2011-eng.pdf.

25. Many mainstream estimates actually assume a considerably greater offset, which leads to even lower climate damages. See, for example, estimates in

U.S. Energy Information Administration, "International Liquids Supply and Disposition Summary, Reference and High Oil Price Cases," 2012, http://www.eia.gov/oiaf/aeo/tablebrowser/#release=AEO2012&subject=0-AEO2012&table=19-AEO2012&region=0-0&cases=hp2012-d022112a,ref2012-d020112c.

26. The World Bank, "Oil Rents (% of GDP)," 2012, http://data.worldbank.org/indicator/NY.GDP.PETR.RT.ZS.

27. The author thanks Trevor Houser for this observation.

28. Michael Levi, "Separating Fact from Fiction on Keystone XL," *Energy, Security, and Climate,* September 1, 2011, http://blogs.cfr.org/levi/2011/09/01/separating-fact-from-fiction-on-keystone-xl/.

29. Ibid.

30. U.S. Energy Information Administration, "Table 1.1. Net Generation by Energy Source: Total (All Sectors), 2002-May 2012," *Electric Power Monthly,* July 26, 2012, http://www.eia.gov/electricity/monthly/epm_table_grapher.cfm?t=epmt_1_1.

31. Gas-fired generation rose from 342 terawatt-hours between January and May 2010 to 479 terawatt-hours between January and May 2012.

32. Author's calculations are based on figures taken from International Energy Agency, *World Energy Outlook 2011* (Paris: OECD, 2011).

33. The author thanks Paul Joskow for this observation.

34. Intergovernmental Panel on Climate Change, *Climate Change 2007.*

35. Michael A. Levi, "Climatic Consequences of Natural Gas as a Bridge Fuel," *Climatic Change,* January 2013.

36. Daniel P. Schrag, "Is Shale Gas Good for Climate Change?" *Daedalus* 141, no. 2 (Spring 2012).

37. Tom Zeller Jr., "Studies Say Natural Gas Has Its Own Environmental Problems," *New York Times,* April 11, 2011.

38. Piers Forster et al., "2007: Changes in Atmospheric Constituents and in Radiative Forcing," in *Climate Change 2007:The Physical Science Basis. Contribution of Working Group I to the Fourth Assessment Report of the Intergovernmental Panel on Climate Change,* Susan Solomon et al., eds. (Cambridge, UK: Cambridge University Press, 2007).

39. Robert W. Howarth, Renee Santoro, and Anthony Ingraffea, "Methane and the Greenhouse-Gas Footprint of Natural Gas from Shale Formations: A Letter," *Climatic Change Letters* 106, no. 4 (2011).

40. Gabrielle Pétron et al., "Hydrocarbon Emissions Characterization in the Colorado Front Range: A Pilot Study," *Journal of Geophysical Research* 117, no. D04304 (2012).

41. Lawrence Cathles III, Larry Brown, Milton Taam, and Andrew Hunter, "A Commentary on 'The Greenhouse-Gas Footprint of Natural Gas in Shale Formations' by R. W. Howarth, R. Santoro, and Anthony Ingraffea," *Climatic Change* 113, no. 2 (2012).

42. U.S. Energy Information Administration, "Monthly Energy Review," July 2012.

43. Michael A. Levi, "Comment on 'Hydrocarbon Emissions Characterization in the Colorado Front Range: A Pilot Study' by Gabrielle Pétron et al.", *Journal of Geophysical Research* 117, no. D21203, doi:10.1029/2012JD017686.

44. Michael A. Levi, "Comment on 'Hydrocarbon Emissions Characterization in the Colorado Front Range—A Pilot Study,'" *Journal of Geophysical Research* 117, no. D21203 (2012).

45. "Editorial: Dismal Outcome at Copenhagen Fiasco," *Financial Times,* December 20, 2009.

46. All figures from the International Energy Agency, *World Energy Outlook 2010* (Paris: OECD, 2010).

47. Michael Levi, "Beyond Copenhagen," *Foreign Affairs* online, February 22, 2010. Accessed at http://www.foreignaffairs.com/articles/65985/michael-levi/beyond-copenhagen.

48. David G. Victor, *Global Warming Gridlock: Creating More Effective Strategies for Protecting the Planet* (Cambridge, UK: Cambridge University Press, 2011).

49. David G. Victor, Kal Raustiala, and Eugene B. Skolnikoff, *The Implementation and Effectiveness of International Environmental Commitments: Theory and Practice* (Cambridge, Mass.: MIT Press, 1998).

50. Ibid.

CHAPTER 5

1. "2006 Hummer H2 SUV Features and Specs," Edmunds.com, http://www.edmunds.com/hummer/h2/2006/features-specs.html?sub=suv.

2. General Motors, Hummer Division, "Hummer Sustains Steady, Upward Sales Trend in North America and Overseas," October 10, 2006, http://www.autospectator.com/cars/general-motors-corporate/0022653-hummer-sustains-steady-upward-sales-trend-north-america-and-oversea.

3. Nick Bunkley, "G.M. to Close Hummer after Sale Fails," *New York Times,* February 24, 2010.

4. John D. Stoll and Alex P. Kellogg, "Detroit Reels as Auto Sales Skid," *Wall Street Journal*, February 4, 2009.

5. U.S. Energy Information Administration, "Fuel Economy Standards Have Affected Vehicle Efficiency," 2012, http://www.eia.gov/todayinenergy/detail.cfm?id=7390#.

6. U.S. Alternative Fuels Data Center, "U.S. HEV Sales by Model, 1999-2011," 2012, http://www.afdc.energy.gov/data/tab/vehicles/data_set/10301; U.S. Energy Information Administration, "Light-Duty Vehicle Sales by Technology Type, United States (Thousands)," 2012, http://www.eia.gov/oiaf/aeo/tablebrowser/#release=AEO2012&subj

ect=15-AEO2012&table=48-AEO2012&region=1-0&cases=cafey-d03
2112a,ref2012-d020112c; U.S. Alternative Fuels Data Center,
"Light-Duty Vehicles Sold in the U.S.," http://www.afdc.energy.gov/
data/tab/vehicles/data_set/10314.

7. U.S. Energy Information Administration, "U.S. Product Supplied of Distillate Fuel Oil, 1945-2012," 2012, http://www.eia.gov/dnav/pet/hist/LeafHandler.ashx?n=PET&s=MDIUPUS1&f=M.

8. U.S. Energy Information Administration, "Crude Oil Production, Monthly Thousand Barrels," 2012, http://www.eia.gov/dnav/pet/pet_crd_crpdn_adc_mbbl_m.htm; U.S. Energy Information Administration, "Product Supplied, 1945-2012," 2012, http://www.eia.gov/dnav/pet/pet_cons_psup_dc_nus_mbbl_m.htm.

9. Edward L Morse et al., *Energy 2020: North America, the New Middle East?* (New York: CitiGroup, 2012), 32; Philip K. Verleger, "The Amazing Tale of U.S. Energy Independence," *International Economy* (Spring 2012): 62.

10. Based on U.S. Energy Information Administration, *Annual Energy Outlook 2000* (Washington, D.C.: U.S. Department of Energy, December 1999), 122. The figures are converted from MMBtu to gallons and from 1998 to 2012 dollars by using the Consumer Price Index. The figures include state and federal taxes.

11. Experian, "Number of Older Vehicles on the Road in the United States Increased by More Than 17 Million since 2009, According to Experian Automotive's Q1 2012 Vehicles in Operation Analysis," June 27, 2012, http://press.experian.com/United-States/Press-Release/number-of-older-vehicles-on-the-road-in-the-united-states-increased-by-more-than-17.aspx.

12. For example, see Meghan R. Busse, Christopher R. Knittel, and Florian Zettelmeyer, "Pain at the Pump: The Differential Effect of Gasoline Prices on New and Used Automobile Markets," *NBER Working Paper No. 15590* (2009); Thomas Klier and Joshua Linn, "The Price of Gasoline and New Vehicle Fuel Economy: Evidence from Monthly Sales Data," *American Economic Journal: Economic Policy* 2, no. 3 (2010).

13. Jessica Frohman Lubetsky, "History of Fuel Economy: One Decade of Innovation, Two Decades of Inaction," Pew Environment Group, April 2011, http://www.pewenvironment.org/uploadedFiles/PEG/Publications/Fact_Sheet/History%20of%20Fuel%20Economy%20Clean%20Energy%20Factsheet.pdf, 171–172; Robert W. Crandall, "Policy Watch: Corporate Average Fuel Economy Standards," *Journal of Economic Perspectives* 6, no. 2 (1992).

14. U.S. Energy Information Administration, *Annual Energy Outlook 2012* (Washington, D.C.: U.S. Department of Energy, June 2012).

15. Ibid.

16. U.S. Environmental Protection Agency, "EPA Finalizes Regulations for the National Renewable Fuel Standard Program for 2010 and Beyond," February 2010, http://www.epa.gov/oms/renewablefuels/420f10007.pdf.

17. Robert Lutz, *Car Guys vs. Bean Counters: The Battle for the Soul of American Business* (New York: Portfolio/Penguin, 2011).

18. W. M. Carriere, W. F. Hamilton, and L. M. Morecraft, *Synthetic Fuels for Transportation: The Future Potential of Electric and Hybrid Vehicles* (Washington, D.C., U.S. Office of Technology Assessment, 1982), 64.

19. Ibid.

20. Ibid.

21. Ibid., 67–70.

22. U.S. Office of Technology Assessment, *Replacing Gasoline: Alternative Fuels for Light-Duty Vehicles* (Washington, D.C., U.S. Office of Technology Asssessment, 1990), 122.

23. Victor Wouk, "Interview with Victor Wouk," interviewed by Judith R. Goodstein, Oral History Project, California Institute of Technology Archives, May 24, 2004, http://resolver.caltech.edu/CaltechOH:OH_Wouk_V, 57.

24. Ibid.

25. Carriere et al., *Synthetic Fuels for Transportation*, 64.

26. Wouk, "Interview with Victor Wouk," 57.

27. Carriere et al., *Synthetic Fuels for Transportation*, 73–74.

28. Ibid.

29. Ibid., 72–73.

30. U.S. Office of Technology Assessment, *Increased Automobile Fuel Efficiency and Synthetic Fuels: Alternatives for Reducing Oil Imports* (Washington, D.C., U.S. Government Printing Office, September 1982), 128.

31. Standing Committee to Review the Research Program of the Partnership for a New Generation of Vehicles, *Review of the Research Program of the Partnership for a New Generation of Vehicles: Sixth Report* (Washington, D.C.: National Academies Press, 2000), 13.

32. Matthew L. Wald, "Hoping Not to Repeat the Mistakes of the Past," *New York Times*, November 21, 2008.

33. David Hermance and Shoichi Sasaki, "Hybrid Electric Vehicles Take to the Streets," *IEEE Spectrum* (November 1998).

34. Alan Ohnsman and Yuki Hagiwara, "Toyota Prius Escapes Niche to Surge into Global Top Three," *Bloomberg*, May 29, 2012, www.bloomberg.com/news/2012-05-29/toyota-prius-escapes-niche-to-surge-into-global-top-three.html.

35. Bay Partners, "Active Portfolio and Greatest Hits," August 14, 2012, http://www.baypartners.com/portfolio/.

36. Enphase Energy, "Enphase Energy Secures $22.5 Million in Financing: Company to Expand Manufacturing, Sales and Development to Meet Surging Demand," May 18, 2009, http://enphase.com/wp-uploads/enphase.com/2010/12/Enphase_Press_Release_22M_Funding.pdf; Camille Ricketts, "Envia Raises $3.2M for Lithium Ion Batteries," October 23, 2008, http://venturebeat.com/2008/10/23/envia-raises-32-million-for-lithium-ion-batteries/.

37. U.S. Energy Information Administration, "Light-Duty Vehicle Miles per Gallon by Technology Type (Miles per Gallon Gasoline Equivalent)," 2012, http://www.eia.gov/oiaf/aeo/tablebrowser/#release=AEO2012&subject=15-AEO2012&table=50-AEO2012&region=0-0&cases=cafey-d032112a,ref2012-d020112c.

38. Ibid.

39. National Highway Traffic Safety Administration, "Preliminary Regulatory Impact Analysis: Corporate Average Fuel Economy for MY 2017-MY 2025 Passenger Cars and Light Trucks," Washington, D.C., U.S. Department of Transportation, November 2011, 156, 165.

40. Ibid., 361, 363.

41. U.S. Energy Information Administration, *Annual Energy Outlook 2012*, 164; Office of Transportation and Air Quality U.S. Department of Energy, "Find and Compare Cars," 2012, www.fueleconomy.gov.

42. Stan Cox, "Drive 1,000 Miles or Feed a Person for a Year? The Biofuels Dilemma," AlterNet, May 8, 2008, http://www.alternet.org/story/84628/drive_1%2C000_miles_or_feed_a_person_for_a_year_the_biofuels_dilemma.

43. "A Texas Time-Out on Biofuels," *Wall Street Journal*, May 24, 2008.

44. Donald Mitchel, "A Note on Rising Food Prices," Washington, D.C., World Bank, July 2008, 2.

45. Ibid., 3.

46. Ibid., 4.

47. James Sallee, "The Taxation of Fuel Economy," *NBER Working Paper No. 16466* (2010). Cited in Mitchel, "A Note on Rising Food Prices," 4.

48. This calculation is based on the assumption that gasoline has one and a half times the energy density of ethanol.

49. U.S. Environmental Protection Agency, "EPA Finalizes Regulations."

50. Committee on Economic, Environmental Impacts of Increasing Biofuels Production, and National Research Council, *Renewable Fuel Standards: Potential Economic and Environmental Effects of U.S. Biofuel Policy* (Washington, D.C.: National Academies Press, 2011), 2.

51. The U.S. government uses a complex set of accounting rules to calculate effective fleet efficiency. They do not compare directly to on-road experience. See National Highway and Transportation Safety Administration,

"2017-25 CAFE Fact Sheet," 2010, http://www.nhtsa.gov/staticfiles/rulemaking/pdf/cafe/2017-25_CAFE_NPRM_Factsheet.pdf.

52. Mike Antich, "Proposed 2025 CAFE Standards to Be the Catalyst for the Hybridization of Fleets," Green Fleet, August 17, 2011, http://www.green-fleetmagazine.com/article/50545/proposed-2025-cafe-standards-to-be-the-catalyst-for-the-hybridization-of-fleets.

53. Office of Transportation and Air Quality and U.S. Department of Energy, "Find and Compare Cars."

54. Ibid.

55. Sallee, "The Taxation of Fuel Economy"; Ian W. H. Parry and Kenneth A. Small, "Does Britain or the United States Have the Right Gasoline Tax?" American Economic Review 95, no. 4 (2005).

56. National Highway Traffic Safety Administration, "Preliminary Regulatory Impact Analysis."

57. Ibid., 731.

58. U.S. Department of Commerce Bureau of Economic Analysis, "National Data,"2011,http://www.bea.gov/iTable/iTable.cfm?ReqID=12&step=1, 477; 520–521. A new light truck would see its price rise by about $1,300.

59. Carl Pasurka, "Perspectives on Pollution Abatement and Competitiveness: Theory, Data, and Analyses," Review of Environmental Economics and Policy 2, no. 2 (2008).

60. National Highway and Transportation Safety Administration, "2017–25 CAFE Fact Sheet."

61. Paul N. Leiby, "Estimating the Energy Security Benefits of Reduced U.S. Oil Imports," Oak Ridge National Laboratory, Department of Energy, February 28, 2007.

62. Ibid., cited in National Highway Traffic Safety Administration, "Preliminary Regulatory Impact Analysis," 644.

63. One can prove this contradiction. Assume that U.S. production rises, oil prices fall, and U.S. oil demand increases so much that net imports actually go up. But rising imports mean more demand on oil supplies beyond the United States—and more demand means higher prices. We've just painted a logically incoherent picture: oil prices are both higher and lower at the same time. The only possible conclusion is that our initial assumption—that oil imports would increase—was wrong.

64. Leiby, "Estimating the Energy Security Benefits of Reduced U.S. Oil Imports," 31.

65. If U.S. demand for imports were to rise as a result of falling production, world oil prices would need to rise too in order to stimulate additional supplies (or reduce others' consumption). But then U.S. oil prices would also rise, implying that U.S. oil output could not have fallen in the first place.

66. Federal Highway Administration, "Average Annual Miles per Driver by Age Group," April 4, 2011, http://www.fhwa.dot.gov/ohim/onh00/bar8.htm.

67. Research and Innovation Technology Administration, Bureau of Transportation Statistics, and U.S. Department of Transportation, "Table 4-23: Average Fuel Efficiency of U.S. Light Duty Vehicles," National Transportation Statistics 2012, January 2012, http://www.bts.gov/publications/national_transportation_statistics/html/table_04_23.html.

68. This assumes a fifteen-year lifetime and a 3 percent discount rate. A 6 percent discount rate would reduce the savings to just over $4,000, a qualitatively similar result.

69. This accounts for a 10 percent rebound effect. A complete cost-benefit calculation would go well beyond this, including costs from additional congestion and savings from reductions in local pollution. The numbers given, though, should be similar to those from a more complete analysis.

70. U.S. Department of Energy, "Compare Side-by-Side, 2008 Chevrolet Cobalt and 2008 Chevrolet Aveo," 2012, http://www.fueleconomy.gov/feg/Find.do?action=sbs&id=25078&id=24287. U.S. government data on fuel efficiency rankings differ depending on the model specifications, including engine size and type.

71. Paul Edelstein and Lutz Kilian, "How Sensitive Are Consumer Expenditures to Retail Energy Prices?" *Journal of Monetary Economics* 56, no. 6 (2009).

72. Ibid., 774.

73. Ibid., 776.

74. Olivier J. Blanchard and Jordi Gali, " The Macroeconomic Effects of Oil Shocks: Why Are the 2000s So Different from the 1970s?" *NBER Working Paper No. 13368* (2007).

75. Justin McCurry, "Japan-China Row Escalates over Fishing Boat Collision," *Guardian*, September 9, 2010.

76. Erica Strecker Downs and Phillip C. Saunders, "Legitimacy and the Limits of Nationalism: China and the Diaoyu Islands," *International Security* 23, no. 3 (1998).

77. Ibid.; Zhong Yan, "China's Claim to Diaoyo Island Chain Indisputable," *Beijing Review*, no. 45 (1996).

78. Keith Bradsher, "Amid Tension, China Blocks Crucial Exports to Japan," *New York Times*, September 23, 2010.

79. U.S. Department of Energy, *Critical Materials Strategy* (Washington, D.C.: U.S. Department of Energy, 2011), 65.

80. Keith Bradsher, "China Restarts Rare Earth Shipments to Japan," *New York Times*, November 19, 2010.

81. BP, *BP Statistical Review of World Energy 2012* (London: BP, June 2012).

82. Daniel J. Cordier, "Mineral Commodity Summaries, U.S. Geological Survey (USGS)," January 2012, minerals.usgs.gov/minerals/pubs/commodity/rare_earths/mcs-2012-raree.pdf.

83. For information regarding Canada, see Cordier, "Mineral Commodity Summaries."

84. Marc Humphries, "Rare Earth Elements: The Global Supply Chain," Washington, D.C., Congressional Research Service, June 8, 2012.

85. Michael Allan McCrae, "Substitution Hurts Rare Earth Demand," October 2, 2011, http://www.mining.com/substition-hurts-rare-earth-demand/.

86. Lee Levkowitz and Nathan Beauchamp-Mustafaga, "China's Rare Earths Industry and Its Role in the International Market," Washington, D.C., U.S.-China Economic and Security Review Commission, November 3, 2010, 7.

87. Brian W. Jaskula, "Lithium," Mineral Commodity Summaries, U.S. Geological Survey, http://minerals.usgs.gov/minerals/pubs/commodity/lithium/mcs-2011-lithi.pdf.

88. Ibid.

89. Linda Gaines and Paul Nelson, "Lithium-Ion Batteries: Examining Material Demand and Recycling Issues," Argonne National Laboratory, Argonne, Ill., 2009.

90. Ibid.

91. Lithium Americas, "Lithium Carbonite Prices, 1960-2009," 2012, http://www.lithiumamericas.com/about-us/lithium-info/.

92. Gaines and Nelson, "Lithium-Ion Batteries."

93. U.S. Environmental Protection Agency, "Emission Facts: Average Annual Emissions and Fuel Consumption for Passenger Cars and Light Trucks," Washington, D.C., Office of Transportation and Air Quality, April 2000.

94. John Deutch and Ernest J. Moniz, The Future of Coal: Summary Report (Cambridge, Mass.: Massachusetts Institute of Technology, 2007), ix. This MIT study reports three million tons of CO_2 per year for a typical 500-megawatt coal plant.

95. W. S. Jevons, The Coal Question: An Enquiry Concerning the Progress of the Nation, and the Probable Exhaustion of Our Coal-mines (London: Macmillan, 1865).

96. Kenneth P. Green, "The Paradox of Efficiency," AEI Ideas Blog, March 11, 2011, http://www.aei-ideas.org/2011/03/the-paradox-of-efficiency/.

97. The new car would save you one dollar in gasoline costs on every trip. But if, as a result, you were to drive twice as much, each extra trip would suck up ten dollars more of your time, a terrible trade.

98. Qing Su, "A Quantile Regression Analysis of the Rebound Effect: Evidence from the 2009 National Household Transportation Survey in the United States," Energy Policy 45, pp. 368–377 (2012); Kent M. Hymel, Kenneth

A. Small, and Kurt Van Dender, "Induced Demand and Rebound Effects in Road Transport," *Transportation Research Part B: Methodological* 44, no. 10 (2010).

99. Tad W. Patzek, "Thermodynamics of the Corn-Ethanol Biofuel Cycle," *Critical Reviews in Plant Sciences* 23, no. 6 (2004); David Pimentel and Tad W. Patzek, "Ethanol Production Using Corn, Switchgrass, and Wood; Biodiesel Production Using Soybean and Sunflower," *Natural Resources Research* 14, no. 1 (2005); Yang Yi et al., "Replacing Gasoline with Corn Ethanol Results in Significant Environmental Problem-Shifting," *Environmental Science and Technology* 46, no. 7 (2012).

100. Michael Wang, Wu May, and Huo Hong, "Life-Cycle Energy and Greenhouse Gas Emission Impacts of Different Corn Ethanol Plant Types," *Environmental Research Letters* 2, no. 2 (2007).

101. David M. Lapola et al., "Indirect Land-Use Changes Can Overcome Carbon Savings from Biofuels in Brazil," *Proceedings of the National Academy of Sciences* 107, no. 8 (2010).

102. Michael Williams, *Americans and Their Forests: A Historical Geography* (New York: Cambridge University Press, 1992).

103. Timothy Searchinger et al., "Use of U.S. Croplands for Biofuels Increases Greenhouse Gases through Emissions from Land-Use Change," *Science* 319, no. 5867 (2008).

104. Michael Wang and Zia Haq, "Ethanol's Effects on Greenhouse Gas Emissions—A Response to Searchinger et al. 2008," *Science* (2008); Steven A. Kolmes, "Food, Land Use Changes, and Biofuels—Response to Searchinger et al. 2008," *Science* (2008); Timothy Searchinger, "Response to M. Wang and Z. Haq's E-Letter," *Science* (2008).

105. Chris Rhodes, "Why Electric Cars Are Really Coal Cars," OilPrice.com, April 5, 2011, http://oilprice.com/Energy/Energy-General/Why-Electric-Cars-Are-Really-Coal-Cars.html.

106. Green Car Congress, "Ford Focus Electric EPA-Certified at 105 MPGe Combined; 110 MPGe City, 99MPGe Highway," March 2, 2012, http://www.greencarcongress.com/2012/03/focus-20120302.html.

107. U.S. Environmental Protection Agency, "How Clean Is the Electricity I Use? Power Profiler," 2012, http://www.epa.gov/cleanenergy/energy-and-you/how-clean.html.

108. Alternative Fuels Data Center, U.S. Department of Energy, "Comparing Well-to-Wheel Greenhouse Gas Emissions: Emissions and Fuel Cost for a 100 Mile Trip," 2012, http://www.afdc.energy.gov/vehicles/electric_emissions.php. This calculation is adjusted for the Prius (50 mpg) rather than 42 mpg as assumed. See U.S. Department of Energy, "2012 Most and Least Efficient Vehicles," 2012, http://www.fueleconomy.gov/feg/best-worst.shtml.

109. Don Anair and Amine Mahmassani, "State of Charge: Electric Vehicles' Global Warming Emissions and Fuel-Cost Savings across the United States," Cambridge, Mass., Union of Concerned Scientists, 2012.

CHAPTER 6

1. Wunderground.com, "History for Midland, TX—Wednesday, June 8, 2011," June 8, 2011, http://www.wunderground.com/history/airport/ KMAF/2011/6/8/DailyHistory.html.
2. Ibid.
3. National Weather Service Weather Forecast Office, "Top Ten Consecutive # Days 100 F 1930-2011, Midland, Texas," 2012, http://www.srh. noaa.gov/maf/?n=cli_maf_temp_100fconsecutive_topten.
4. Electric Reliability Council of Texas, "Historical RTM Load Zone and Hub Prices, June 2011," June 2011, http://mis.ercot.com/misapp/GetReports. do?reportTypeId=13061&reportTitle=Historical%20RTM%20Load%20 Zone%20and%20Hub%20Prices&showHTMLView=&mimicKey.
5. U.S. Energy Information Administration, "Electricity: Detailed State Data," November 9, 2011, www.eia.gov/electricity/data/state/.
6. Trip Doggett, "ERCOT's Challenges and Opportunities," May 17, 2012, http://www.ercot.com/content/news/presentations/2012/ Doggett-AECT%20May%2017%202012.pdf, 14.
7. The Eagle.com, "Midland, TX on Wednesday, June 8, 2011, NWS Daily Summary," June 8, 2011, http://weather.theeagle.com/auto/theeagle/ history/airport/KMAF/2011/6/8/DailyHistory.html?req_ city=NA&req_state=NA&req_statename=NA;%20http://weather-spark.com/averages/30843/Midland-Texas-United-States.The National Weather Service data include wind-speed distribution.
8. Ernst & Young, *Global E&P Benchmark Study* (London: Ernst & Young, 2011), reports $76 billion in exploration and production spending. Bloomberg New Energy Finance, "Solar Surge Drives Record Clean Energy Investment in 2011," January 12, 2012, http://bnef.com/Press-Releases/view/180, reports $55.9 billion invested in alternative energy sources (e.g., biofuels, solar, and wind). Spending on energy efficiency is far more difficult to estimate. I estimate an additional $5 billion in hybrid vehicle sales, based on sales volumes from U.S. Alternative Fuels Data Center, "U.S. HEV Sales by Model, 1999-2011," 2012, http://www.afdc. energy.gov/data/tab/vehicles/data_set/10301, and an assumed cost of at least $20,000 for each vehicle. I also conservatively (and very crudely) estimate another $5 billion spent on fuel efficiency in conventional cars, on the basis of sales of at least ten million new cars and at least $500 of the cost of each new car going toward efficiency measures.

9. U.S. Energy Information Administration, *Annual Energy Outlook 2001* (Washington, D.C.: U.S. Department of Energy, December 2000).

10. U.S. Energy Information Administration, "Renewable Energy Generating Capacity and Generation, Reference Case," 2013, http://www.eia.gov/oiaf/aeo/tablebrowser/#release=AEO2013ER&subject=6-AEO2013ER&table=16-AEO2013ER&region=0-0&cases=early2013-d102312a.

11. Based on total generation; U.S. Energy Information Administration, *Annual Energy Outlook 2012—Early Release Overview* (Washington, D.C.: U.S. Department of Energy, January 23, 2012).

12. U.S. Energy Information Administration, *Annual Energy Outlook 2012* (Washington, D.C.: U.S. Department of Energy, 2012).

13. U.S. Energy Information Administration, "State-Level Energy-Related Carbon Dioxide Emissions, 2000-2009," January 2012, http://www.eia.gov/environment/emissions/state/analysis/pdf/stateanalysis.pdf.

14. "Al Gore's Speech on Renewable Energy," NPR.org, July 17, 2008, http://www.npr.org/templates/story/story.php?storyId=92638501.

15. John M. Broder, "Gore Urges Change to Dodge an Energy Crisis," *New York Times*, July 18, 2008.

16. Ibid.

17. David Louie, "Solyndra Files for Bankruptcy, Lays Off 1,100 Workers," ABC 7 San Francisco, August 31, 2011, http://abclocal.go.com/kgo/story?section=news/business&id=8336915.

18. American Bankruptcy Insitute, "Annual Business and Non-business Filings by Year (1980-2011)," 2012, http://www.abiworld.org/AM/AMTemplate.cfm?Section=Home&TEMPLATE=/CM/ContentDisplay.cfm&CONTENTID=65139.

19. Chris Gentilviso, "President Obama Visits Green Energy Start-Up Solyndra," Time.com, May 26, 2010, http://newsfeed.time.com/2010/05/26/president-obama-visits-green-energy-start-up-solyndra/.

20. Seema Mehta, "Romney Accuses Obama of 'Crony Capitalism' in Solyndra Trip," *Los Angeles Times*, May 31, 2012.

21. Clean Energy Ministerial, "Energy Ministers Announce Achievements and Actions for a Clean Energy Future at CEM3," 2012, http://www.cleanenergyministerial.org/MediaPublications/Newsletters/Summer2012/TopStory1.aspx.

22. Krister Aanesen, Stefan Heck, and Dickon Pinner, *Solar Power: Darkest before Dawn* (New York: McKinsey and Company, May 2012).

23. Ramez Naam, "Smaller, Cheaper, Faster: Does Moore's Law Apply to Solar Cells?" *Scientific American Guest Blogs*, March 16, 2012, http://blogs.scientificamerican.com/guest-blog/2011/03/16/smaller-cheaper-faster-does-moores-law-apply-to-solar-cells/.

24. Duncan Clark, "Price of Solar Panels to Drop to $1 by 2013, Report Forecasts," *Guardian*, June 20, 2011.
25. More precisely, this refers to grid parity.
26. Bloomberg New Energy Finance, "Onshore Wind Energy to Reach Parity with Fossil-Fuel Electricity by 2016," November 10, 2011, http://bnef. com/PressReleases/view/172.
27. This figure is based on a reported value of 5 eurocents, converted at a rate of €1.40 to $1.00.
28. U.S. Energy Information Administration, "Renewable Energy Generating Capacity."
29. International Energy Agency, *World Energy Outlook 2011* (Paris: OECD), 558–559.
30. Ibid., 622.
31. Ibid., 557–558.
32. Paul Schwabe, Sander Lensink, and Maureen Hand, *Multi-National Case Study of the Financial Cost of Wind Energy* (Golden, Colo.: National Renewable Energy Laboratory, 2011), 15.
33. Ibid.
34. Annette Evans, Vladimir Strezov, and Tim J. Evans, "Assessment of Sustainability Indicators for Renewable Energy Technologies," *Renewable and Sustainable Energy Reviews* 13, no. 5 (2009); David S. Ginley, Reuben Collins, and David Cahen, "Direct Solar Energy Conversion with Photovoltaic Devices," in *Fundamentals of Materials for Energy and Environmental Sustainability*, ed. D. S. Ginley and D. Cahen (New York: Cambridge University Press, 2011).
35. Paul L. Joskow, "Comparing the Costs of Intermittent and Dispatchable Electricity Generating Technologies," *American Economic Review* 101, no. 3 (May 2011).
36. In this example, I assume that each power plant is rated at five hundred megawatts.
37. People would also cut back on electricity use as prices rose.
38. U.S. Department of Energy analysis, though far from infallible, bears this intuition out. To simulate the impact of high ($10/MMBtu) natural gas compared to lower ($5/MMBtu) natural gas, I use a Department of Energy simulation of the impacts of high and rapid natural gas exports and low U.S. natural gas supplies, since this produces similarly high natural gas prices. (Energy Information Administration, *Effect of Increased Natural Gas Exports on Domestic Energy Markets*, U.S. Department of Energy, January 2012; these simulations assume that all energy subsidies, including for wind power, expire as scheduled as of early 2012.) I then compare that to the reference case, which features the lower prices. The higher natural gas prices, in 2020, prompt coal power to rise by nearly ten times as much as

wind power does. (Solar power is not affected, but this conclusion should be treated skeptically.)

39. Jenna Goodward and Mariana Gonzalez, *Renewable Energy Tax Credits,* (Washington, D.C.: World Resources Institute, October 2010).

40. Ibid.

41. The 500-megawatt Hidden Hills solar project is reported to entail $2.7 billion in capital costs. Scott DiSavino, "California to Hold Workshop on Giant Solar Power Plant," Reuters, May 4, 2012, http://uk.reuters.com/article/2012/05/04/utilities-brightsource-hiddenhills-idUKL1E8G43 H720120504. Thirty percent of that is roughly $800 million.

42. U.S. Department of Energy, Interstate Renewable Energy Council, and North Carolina Solar Center, "Database of State Incentives for Renewables and Efficiency," 2012, http://www.dsireusa.org/searchby/index.cfm?ee=1&re=1.

43. David Victor and Kassia Yanosek, "The Crisis in Clean Energy," *Foreign Affairs* 90, no. 4 (2011).

44. Jeffrey Leonard, "Get the Energy Sector Off the Dole," *Washington Monthly,* January/February 2011.

45. Author's calculations based on data in National Energy Technology Laboratory, "Natural Gas Combined-Cycle Plant," Fossil Energy Power Plant Desk Reference, Washington, D.C., U.S. Department of Energy, May 2007.

46. "MiaSolé Awarded $100m in U.S. Tax Credits to Ramp Up CIGS PV Manufacturing," January 16, http://indiumsamplesblog.com/2010/01/16/miasole-awarded-100m-in-us-tax-credits-to-ramp-up-cigs-pv-manufacturing/.

47. Daron Acemoglu et al., "The Environment and Directed Technical Change," *American Economic Review* 102, no. 1 (2012).

48. U.S. National Energy Technology Laboratory, "Natural Gas Combined-Cycle Plants With and Without Carbon Capture and Sequestration," Washington, D.C., U.S. Department of Energy, 2007.

49. U.S. National Energy Technology Laboratory, "GE Energy IGCC Plant," 2007, http://www.netl.doe.gov/KMD/cds/disk50/IGCC%20Plant%20Case_GEE_051507.pdf; U.S. National Energy Technology Laboratory, "Natural Gas Combined-Cycle Plants."

50. U.S. Energy Information Administration, *Annual Energy Outlook 2012.*

51. The combination of particularly aggressive regulation of air pollution with lower-than-expected natural gas prices could boost retirements to twice that level, but this would be because gas knocked coal aside, not because emerging energy technologies stepped in.

52. Susan Helper and Timothy Krueger, "Locating American Manufacturing: Trends in Geography and Production—Pittsburgh, PA Metro Area," May 9, 2012, http://www.brookings.edu/~/media/Research/Files/Reports/2012/5/09%20locating%20american%20manufacturing%20wialh/pdf/Pittsburgh.pdf.

53. Chuck Biedka, "Closing of Brackenridge's FLABEG Will Put 100 Out of Work," TribLive, November 19, 2011, http://triblive.com/x/valleynewsdispatch/s_768171.html.

54. FLABEG, "Parabolic Mirrors for Concentrating Solar Power," February 5, 2009, http://www.docstoc.com/docs/20106528/Parabolic-Mirrors-for-Concentrating-Solar-Power-%28CSP%29#.

55. Allegheny Conference on Community Development, "Press Release on FLABEG's New Solar Mirror Facility," October 30, 2009, http://www.eprenergynews.com/2009/10/30/flabeg-solar-us-corp-opens-new-solar-mirror-plant/.

56. Thomas Friedman, *Hot, Flat, and Crowded: Why We Need a Green Revolution—and How It Can Renew America* (New York: Farrar, Straus and Giroux, 2008).

57. Mark Muro, Jonathan Rothwell, and Devashree Saha, *Sizing the Clean Economy: A National and Regional Green Jobs Assessment,* (Washington, D.C.: Brookings Institution, July 13, 2011), 20, 22.

58. Leigh Hendrix, Nitzan Goldberger, and Sarah Ladislaw, *Understanding "Green Jobs"* (Washington, D.C.: Center for Strategic and International Studies, March 2010).

59. Trevor Houser, Shashank Mohan, and Ian Hoffman, *Assessing the American Power Act: The Economic, Employment, Energy Security, and Environmental Impact of Senator Kerry and Senator Lieberman's Discussion Draft* (Washington, D.C.: Peterson Institute for International Economics, May 2010).

60. International Energy Agency, *World Energy Outlook 2010* (Paris: OECD), 401.

61. OECD, "Share of ICT Manufacturing and ICT Services Value Added, 2006," OECD Factbook 2010, 2010, http://www.oecd-ilibrary.org/sites/factbook-2010-en/07/02/01/07-02-01-g1.html?contentType=&itemId=/content/chapter/factbook-2010-57-en&containerItemId=/content/serial/18147364&accessItemIds=&mimeType=text/html.

62. Michael Levi, Elizabeth Economy, Shannon O'Neil, and Adam Segal, "Globalizing the Clean Energy Revolution," *Foreign Affairs*, November/December 2010.

63. See examples of differing views in Paul Krugman, ed., *Strategic Trade Policy and the New International Economics* (Cambridge, Mass.: MIT

Press, 1986). Considerable progress has been made in the last twenty years, but disagreements remain.

64. Kate Sheppard, "America's Paltry Energy R&D Spending," *Mother Jones*, October 15, 2010, http://www.motherjones.com/blue-marble/2010/10/energy-research-development-CAP-report.

65. American Association for the Advancement of Science, "Historical Table 1. Total R&D by Agency, FY 1976-2009," March 2008, http://www.aaas.org/spp/rd/hist09p.pdf.

66. Vernon W. Ruttan, *Is War Necessary for Economic Growth? Military Procurement and Technology Development* (New York: Oxford University Press, 2006).

67. Kurt Zenz House, Justin Dawe, and Charles Brankman, "An Open Letter from the Founders," C12 Energy, http://c12energy.com/the-letter/.

68. Edward S. Rubin and Haibo Zhai, "The Cost of Carbon Capture and Storage for Natural Gas Combined-Cycle Power Plants," *Environmental Science and Technology* 46, no. 6 (2012).

69. Mohammed Al-Juaied and Adam Whitmore, "Realistic Costs of Carbon Capture," Discussion Paper 2009–08, Energy Technology Innovation Research Group, Belfer Center for Science and International Affairs, Harvard Kennedy School, July 2009.

70. World Nuclear Association, "Nuclear Power in France," July 2012, http://www.world-nuclear.org/info/inf40.html.

71. Justin McCurry, "Japan Marks First Anniversary of Earthquake and Tsunami," *Guardian*, March 11, 2012, http://www.guardian.co.uk/world/2012/mar/11/japan-earthquake-disaster-tsunami-anniversary.

72. U.S. Energy Information Administration, "Electricity Generating Capacity (Gigawatts), Reference Case," 2012, http://www.eia.gov/oiaf/aeo/tablebrowser/#release=AEO2012&subject=0-AEO2012&table=9-AEO2012&region=0-0&cases=co2fee25-d031312a,ref2012-d020112c. This calculation is based on the $25 per ton of CO_2 tax case.

73. Nicole Sperling, "Matt Damon and John Krasinski's Zigzag Path to 'Promised Land'," *Los Angeles Times*, December 13, 2012.

74. Mark Z. Jacobson, "Review of Solutions to Global Warming, Air Pollution, and Energy Security," *Energy and Environmental Science* 2, no. 2 (2009).

75. Sarah M. Jordaan, David W. Keith, and Brad Stelfox, "Land and Water Impacts of Oil Sands Production in Alberta," *Environmental Science and Technology* 46, no. 7 (2012).

76. I infer 30 W/m^2 for oil sands mining from the calculations above.

77. Daniel Kammen, Sam Borgeson, and Kevin Fingerman, "Honest Assessments of Our Energy Future," RMI Outlet Blog, June 29, 2011, http://blog.rmi.org/HonestAssessmentsOurEnergyFuture.

CHAPTER 7

1. Matthew Simmons, *Twilight in the Desert: The Coming Saudi Oil Shock and the World Economy* (Hoboken, NJ: Wiley, 2005).
2. Blake Clayton, *The End of the Oil Age: A Century of Panics, Crises, and Crashes in the World Oil Market* (New York: Oxford University Press, forthcoming).
3. Diana Davids Olien and Roger M. Olien, "Running Out of Oil: Discourse and Public Policy, 1909-1929," *Business and Economic History* 22, no. 2 (Winter 1993).
4. James D. Hamilton, "Oil Prices, Exhaustible Resources, and Economic Growth," in *Handbook of Energy and Climate Change*, ed. Roger Fouqet (Cheltenham, UK: Elgar, 2013).
5. James Murray and David King, "Climate Policy: Oil's Tipping Point Has Passed," *Nature* 481, no. 7382 (2012).
6. Daniel Yergin, *The Quest: Energy, Security, and the Remaking of the Modern World* (New York: Penguin, 2011), 262.
7. Norman Angell, *The Great Illusion: A Study of the Relation of Military Power to National Advantage* (New York: Putnam, 1913).
8. Paul A. Papayoanou, *Power Ties: Economic Interdependence, Balancing, and War* (Ann Arbor: University of Michigan Press, 1999), 63.
9. Ibid., 65.
10. Scott D. Sagan and Kenneth N. Waltz, *The Spread of Nuclear Weapons: A Debate*, 2nd ed. (New York: Norton, 2002).
11. Rosemary Kelanic, "Black Gold and Blackmail: The Politics of International Oil Coercion," PhD dissertation, University of Chicago, 2012.
12. Marc Trachtenberg, "Waltzing to Armageddon?" *National Interest* (Fall 2002).
13. Dale C. Copeland, "Economic Interdependence and War: A Theory of Trade Expectation," *International Security* 20, no. 4 (Spring 1996).
14. For example, see Michael T. Klare, *Blood and Oil: The Dangers and Consequences of America's Growing Dependency on Imported Petroleum* (New York: Holt, 2005).
15. Federal Reserve Economic Data, "Exports of Goods and Services," Federal Reserve Bank of St. Louis, June 14, 2012, http://research. stlouisfed.org/fred2/series/BOPXGS?cid=16; Federal Reserve Economic Data, "Imports of Goods and Services," Federal Reserve Bank of St. Louis, June 14, 2012, http://research.stlouisfed.org/fred2/series/ BOPMGS?cid=17.
16. World Trade Organization, "Understanding the WTO: Basics," July 2011, http://www.wto.org/English/thewto_e/whatis_e/tif_e/utw_chap1_e. pdf, 15.

17. Helen Milner, "Resisting the Protectionist Temptation: Industry and the Making of Trade Policy in France and the United States during the 1970s," *International Organization* 41, no. 4 (1987).

18. Guy Dinmore and Geoff Dyer, "Immelt Hits Out at China and Obama," *Financial Times,* July 1, 2010.

19. Robert McNally and Michael Levi, "A Crude Predicament: The Era of Volatile Oil Prices," *Foreign Affairs* 90, no. 4 (July/August 2011).

20. National Bureau of Economic Research, "Business Cycle Dating Committee, National Bureau of Economic Research," December 11, 2008, http://www.nber.org/cycles/dec2008.html.

21. Congressional Budget Office, "The Budget and Economic Outlook: Fiscal Years 2009 to 2019," Washington, D.C., January 2009.

22. U.S. Bureau of Labor Statistics, "The Employment Situation: July 2012," U.S. Department of Labor, Washington, D.C., August 3, 2012.

23. Congressional Budget Office, "The Budget and Economic Outlook: Fiscal Years 2009 to 2019."

24. Congressional Budget Office, "The Budget and Economic Outlook: Fiscal Years 2012 to 2022," Washington, D.C., January 2012.

25. Gretchen Weber, "Concerns Abound as Geoengineering Conference Opens," Climate Watch, March 21, 2010, http://blogs.kqed.org/climatewatch/2010/03/21/concerns-abound-as-geoengineering-conference-opens/.

26. Bjorn Lomborg, *Cool It: The Skeptical Environmentalist's Guide to Global Warming* (New York: Knopf Doubleday, 2008).

27. For a summary, see Jay Michaelson, "Geoengineering: A Climate Change Manhattan Project," *Stanford Environmental Law Journal* 17, no. 1 (1998); Alan Robock, "20 Reasons Why Geoengineering May Be a Bad Idea," *Bulletin of the Atomic Scientists* 64, no. 2 (2008).

28. Juan B. Moreno-Cruz, Katharine L. Ricke, and David W. Keith, "A Simple Model to Account for Regional Inequalities in the Effectiveness of Solar Radiation Management," *Climatic Change* 110, no. 3 (February 2012).

29. David G. Victor et al., "The Geoengineering Option: A Last Resort against Global Warming?" *Foreign Affairs* 88, no. 2 (March/April 2009).

30. H. Damon Matthews and Ken Caldeira, "Transient Climate–Carbon Simulations of Planetary Geoengineering," *Proceedings of the National Academy of Sciences of the United States of America* 104, no. 24 (2007).

CHAPTER 8

1. Jeffrey M. Jones, "Americans Split on Energy vs. Environment Trade-Off," March 23, 2012, http://www.gallup.com/poll/153404/Americans-Split-Energy-Environment-Trade-Off.aspx. The same poll asked whether the

United States should focus on fossil-fuel production or energy conservation, and it elicited similarly polarized responses.

2. See, for example, Energy Information Administration, *Energy Market and Economic Impacts of the American Power Act of 2010*, Department of Energy, Washington, D.C., July 2010.

3. Naomi Oreskes and Erik M. Conway, *Merchants of Doubt: How a Handful of Scientists Obscured the Truth on Issues from Tobacco Smoke to Global Warming* (New York: Bloomsbury, 2010).

INDEX

A123 (battery company), 117
Advanced Resources International, 60
Ahn, Daniel, 74–75
Alaska
    climate change and, 84
    North Slope of, 8, 53
    oil production in, 8, 14, 53, 56,
        58–59, 61, 82, 93
    Ronald Reagan's projections
        regarding, 12
    Trans-Alaskan Pipeline and, 8
    Alaska National Wildlife Refuge
        (ANWR) and, 58–59
Alcoa, 206
alternative energy. See renewable
    energy
AltraBiofuels, 5–6
Amazon rainforest, 91
American Chemistry Council, 28
American Petroleum Institute
    (API), 73, 205, 207
American Shale Oil (AMSO), 51,
    63–64

American Soda, 63
Angell, Norman, 183
Antarctica, 92
Arab-Israeli War (1973), 7, 76.
    See also Oil Shock (1973)
Argentina, 32–33, 37
Athens County (Ohio), 20–22, 174
automobiles. See also individual
    companies
    battery technology and, 114,
        116–118, 134
    biofuels for, 110–111, 120
    cooled exhaust gas recirculation
        and, 119–120
    cost of, 124–125
    electric cars, 5, 114, 116, 118–119,
        132, 135, 141–142, 200
    fuel cells for, 114
    fuel efficiency of, 6, 8–9, 13, 15,
        17–18, 59, 110, 112–113, 118–120,
        122–125, 127–131, 138, 142,
        191–192, 196–197, 199–200, 202,
        205, 207–208

automobiles (*Cont.*)
  hybrid vehicles, 110, 114–116, 119,
    132, 135
  Japanese manufacturers of, 18, 97,
    114, 116, 122, 132, 135, 141
  natural gas use in, 7, 35–41, 116,
    128–129
  safety standards and, 119, 123–124
  stoichiometric gasoline direct
    injection and, 119
  U.S. manufacturers of, 5, 18,
    109–110, 113–116, 118–119,
    122–123, 129–130, 136

Baker, Bob, 157, 167
Bakken oil field, 54–55
Bartis, Jim, 62–63
battery technology, 114, 116–118,
  134
Bay Partners, 116–117
biofuels
  automobiles and, 110–111, 120
  cellulosic materials for, 121, 139, 141
  climate change and, 111, 138–139
  corn-based, 120–121, 138–140
  cost of, 120, 122, 126, 138–139
  ethanol, 5, 17, 110, 120–121, 126,
    138–139, 175
  government support for, 113,
    120–122
  impact on food prices, 111, 120–121,
    140–141
  land use consequences, 140–141,
    175
  natural gas requirements for, 139
  soybean-based, 121
  sugarcane-based, 140
Bolivia, 134
Boulder (Colorado), 83, 87–88
BP
  Deepwater Horizon oil spill and,
    56–58

  U.S. Climate Action Partnership
    and, 206
Brackenridge (Pennsylvania), 161
Bradford County (Pennsylvania),
  48–49
Brazil, 67, 69, 140, 180, 188
Briggs and Stratton Corporation, 115
BTU tax, 15
Burnham, Alan, 62
Bush, George H. W., 14, 53
Bush, George W., 122
butane, 27, 56

C12 (carbon capture company),
  170–172
California
  carbon emissions in, 116, 146
  oil production in, 56, 180
  Santa Barbara Oil Spill and, 10
  Silicon Valley, 5, 36–37, 116–118,
    157–159, 166–167
  solar energy in, 154, 157–159,
    166–167
  wind energy in, 175
Calzada, Gabriel, 163–164
Canada
  NAFTA and, 187
  natural gas and, 30, 33, 48
  oil production in, 18, 67, 69, 79, 180
  oil sands in, 52, 54, 81–83, 93–94,
    96–97, 175, 188, 206–207
  rare-earth metals and, 134
cap-and-trade, 97, 101, 155, 171, 206
Cape Wind project, 175
carbon capture and sequestration
  (CCS), 61, 100–101, 170–172, 173,
  200, 202, 209
carbon dioxide emissions. *See under*
  climate change
carbon dioxide enhanced oil
  recovery (CO$_2$-EOR), 60–61,
  170–172

carbon tax, 101, 155, 202
Carrollton (Ohio), 1–3, 73
cars. *See* automobiles
Carter, Jimmy, 11–12, 51
Chavez, Hugo, 78
Chesapeake Energy, 2–3, 47
China
  climate change and, 105–106
  coal and, 96
  economic development in, 17, 96,
    130, 187–188
  energy consumption by, 68, 75,
    105–106, 130, 184
  globalization and, 187–188
  natural gas and, 32–33, 204
  nuclear energy and, 173
  oil production in, 69
  rare-earth metals and,
    132–134
  solar energy and, 149–150, 157,
    166–167
  South China Sea conflict and,
    132–134
  U.S. relations with, 78, 183–186,
    201
Chrysler, 109, 116
Clayton, Blake, 78
clean energy. *See* renewable energy;
  solar energy; wind energy
Clean Energy Ministerial (CEM)
  summit, 148
climate change
  Arctic ice and, 84, 86, 91
  biofuels and, 111, 138–139
  cap-and-trade and, 97, 101, 155, 171,
    206
  carbon dioxide emissions and, 85,
    87, 89–100, 102–103, 136, 139
  carbon tax and, 101, 155, 202
  clean energy standard (CES) and,
    101, 155, 202
  coal and, 97–101, 170, 182, 194

  Copenhagen climate summit and,
    104–106
  deforestation and, 85, 91, 105, 140
  geoengineering and, 193–194
  globalization and, 188
  international treaties and,
    104–107, 204
  introduction to the science of,
    84–88
  methane and, 102
  mountain pine beetles and, 83–84,
    87–88
  natural gas and, 97–103, 107, 155,
    177, 200, 204, 208
  nuclear energy and, 97–99, 101,
    173, 175
  oil and, 80, 83, 85–86, 88–90,
    93–97, 101, 107–108, 110, 136–137,
    182, 194, 196, 200
  renewable energy and, 170, 178,
    194, 196–197
  social cost of carbon, 89–90
Clinton (Pennsylvania), 161–162
Clinton, Bill, 15, 116
coal
  carbon capture and sequestration
    and, 100, 158, 172
  China and, 96
  climate change and, 97–101, 170,
    182, 194
  land use and, 22, 175–176
  power plants and, 3, 17, 88, 98–100,
    103, 107, 141, 153, 158, 160–161,
    168, 170, 196
Coal Question, The (Jevons), 137
cobalt, 133
Colbert, Stephen, 48
Cold War, 10, 16, 64, 169, 185
Colorado
  climate change in, 83–85, 87–88
  mountain pine beetles in, 83–84,
    87–88

Colorado (*Cont.*)
  natural gas production in, 102–104
  tight oil in, 51, 56, 61, 80, 93–94
Columbus (Ohio), antifracking
    protest in, 3–4, 22, 92
compressed natural gas (CNG),
    37–39
Congo, 133
Copenhagen climate summit,
    104–106

Dawe, Justin, 170–172
Day, Roger, 62
Dearing, Becky, 26
Deepwater Horizon oil spill, 52,
    56–58
defense spending, innovation and,
    169, 201
deglobalization, 189–190, 194
Delaware, 56
Department of Defense, 169,
    200–201
Department of Energy, 15, 115, 146
Detroit automakers, 5, 18, 109–110,
    113–116, 118–119, 122–123,
    129–130, 136
Deutch, John, 24
Diaoyu Islands, 132
Dix, Bill, 20–22, 25, 46, 48
Dukakis, Michael, 14

E.ON, 32
Eagle Ford shale (Texas), 55
Earth Summit (1993), 15
earthquakes, natural gas production
    and, 44–45, 47
economic development
  natural gas and, 27–29, 47, 49, 192
  oil and, 74–75, 127, 192
  renewable energy and, 147,
    162–163, 166, 191–192
Economides, Michael, 41

Edelstein, Paul, 129–130
EGL Oil Shale company, 51, 62
el-Badri, Abdallah Salem, 69
electric cars, 5, 114, 116, 118–119, 132,
    135, 141–142, 200
electricity. *See also* power plants
  dynamics of demand for, 151–153
  levelized cost of electricity
    (LCOE) and, 151–152
  price for, 143
  renewable energy sources and,
    145–146, 148–150
  storage of, 160
  U.S. consumption of, 143–144, 151
Elm Coulee Field (Montana), 54
Energy Crisis. *See* Oil Shock (1973)
energy independence, 3, 8, 51–52, 70,
    79–80, 82, 196
Energy Information Administration,
    54, 112, 149, 173
Energy Policy Act (1992), 14
energy security
  Great Recession and, 16
  market-based approaches to, 14
  natural gas and, 25, 35, 49, 200
  oil and, 3, 16, 64–65, 72, 76–79, 111,
    125, 127, 131–132, 136–137, 142,
    185, 196, 209
  rare-earth metals and, 111,
    132–134, 136
  renewable energy and, 9, 110–111,
    125, 161, 163
  sea lanes and, 78, 183–184, 205
  September 11, 2001 terrorist
    attacks and, 15–16
  United States and, 7, 13–14, 18–19,
    163, 197–198, 200, 210
Energy Security Leadership
    Council, 65
Enphase Energy, 117
Envia Systems, 36, 117, 133
Environmental Defense Fund, 206

environmentalists
   Alaska National Wildlife Refuge
      (ANWR) and, 59
   energy companies and, 207–208
   natural gas production and, 3–4,
      29, 43–44, 48, 92, 98, 208
   pollution and, 14
estimated ultimate recovery (EUR),
   41–43
ethane, 27–28, 35, 56
ethanol. *See under* biofuels
ethylene, 27–28
Europe. *See also individual countries*
   natural gas and, 30–35
   natural gas vehicles in, 38–39
Exxon, 10
Exxon Valdez disaster, 15, 52

Federal Reserve, 131, 183
Ferrenberg, Scott, 83–84, 87–88
FLABEG, 161–162, 167–168
food prices, biofuels impact on,
   120–121, 140–141
Ford Motor Company
   Congressional testimony by, 9
   Focus Electric model and, 114, 116,
      118, 141
   Mustang model and, 118–119
   research and development at, 5,
      114–116, 118–119, 122–123, 136
Ford, Gerald, 51
Ford, Henry, 17
Foulkes, John, 62
Fox, Josh, 4
fracking
   natural gas production and, 2–3,
      24, 35, 44–47, 98
   oil production and, 54
   opposition to, 3–4, 22, 35, 92,
      98, 177
France, 24, 33, 172
Frederick, Jamie, 4–5

Friedman, Tom, 163
Friendly Frackasaurus, 48
fuel cells, 114
fuel efficiency. *See under* automobiles
fuel taxes, 123, 202
Fukushima (Japan) earthquake and
   tsunami, 172–173

Gaines, Linda, 134–135
gas-to-liquids (GTL), 40–41, 129
Gasland (Fox), 4, 174
Gazprom, 32
General Agreement on Tariffs and
   Trade (GATT), 186
General Electric, 206
General Motors
   bankruptcy of, 109
   Chevrolet Cobalt model, 129
   Chevy Impala model and, 119
   Hummer and, 97, 109
   Lordstown Assembly Complex, 129
   research and development at, 116
geoengineering, 193–194
geopolitics. *See also* energy security;
      national security
   Arab-Israeli War (1973), 7, 76
   Cold War, 10, 16, 64, 169, 185
   globalization and, 35, 186–190, 194,
      204–205
   Gulf War (1991), 13–14, 76, 112
   Organization of Petroleum
      Exporting Countries (OPEC),
      7, 13, 66–69, 90, 95–96
   sea lanes and, 78, 183–184, 205
   South China Sea conflict, 132–134
Germany, 156, 173, 183
global warming. *See* climate change
globalization
   Asian tiger economies and, 187
   China and, 187–188
   climate change regulation and,
      188

globalization (*Cont.*)
  deglobalization, 189–190, 194
  energy trade and, 35, 188–190,
    204–205
  Great Depression and, 187
  multinational corporations and,
    187–188
  trade agreements and, 186–187
  United States and, 186
Gore, Al, 96–97, 146
Grant County (Kansas), 24
Grape, Steven, 54
Great Depression, 187, 190
Great Illusion, The (Angell), 183
Great Recession
  climate change initiatives and,
    206
  Congressional Budget Office
    projections and, 190–191
  natural gas production and, 23,
    25–26, 28
  oil consumption and, 110
  oil prices and, 16
  renewable energy and, 145–146,
    191
  unemployment and, 190–191
Gulf of Mexico
  Deepwater Horizon oil spill, 52,
    56–58
  oil production in, 3, 56–57, 180
Gulf War (1991), 13–14, 76, 112

Halliburton, 4, 24
Hamilton, Jim, 70
Hammond, Allen, 9
Hanergy, 167
Hansen, James, 82, 92
Hart, Gary, 10
Herrington, John S., 14
Honda GX, 38
Horizon Wind, 170
horizontal drilling, 23–24, 47, 52, 54

Hot, Flat, and Crowded (Friedman),
  163
House, Kurt Zenz, 170–172
Howarth, Robert, 101–104
Hubbert, M. King, 180–181
Hugoton field (Kansas), 24
Hummer, 97, 109
Hurricane Katrina, 16, 125
Hurricane Sandy, 84
Hussein, Saddam, 14, 76, 78
Hybrid Test Vehicle (HTV-1), 115
hybrid vehicles and, 110, 114–116, 119,
  132, 135
hydroelectric power, 144,
  149–150

IDT, 50–51
IHS Global Insight, 26–27
India, 35, 68, 105, 130, 167–168
information and communications
    technology (ICT) revolution,
    167
Ingraffea, Anthony, 101–104
innovation
  automobiles, 113–120
  limits of, 159–161, 168–189
  oil and gas, 23–24
  policy tools to support, 156–159
  renewable energy, 148–151
Iran
  Cold War and, 185
  natural gas and, 33
  oil and, 78, 95, 133–134
  revolution and hostage crisis in,
    13, 68, 76, 112
Iraq
  Gulf War (1991) and, 14, 76, 112
  oil production in, 69, 78, 95
  oil reserves in, 133–134
Ishigaki Island, 132
Israel, 7, 76, 167
Israel, Laura, 174–175, 177

Jackson Dome (Mississippi), 60
Japan
  auto companies in, 97, 114, 116,
    122, 134–135, 141
  Fukushima disaster and, 172–173
  natural gas and, 34–35
  South China Sea conflict and,
    132–134
Jevons, William Stanley, 137–138
jobs
  natural gas and, 3, 25–28, 191
  oil and, 73–74, 82, 191, 196
  renewable energy and, 6, 147,
    161–165, 168, 177
Jonas, Howard, 50–52, 61–63, 80
Jordaan, Sarah, 175
Joskow, Paul, 152

Kaiser, Jennifer, 73
Kammen, Daniel, 176
Kansas, 24
Kapadia, Atul, 36–37, 39, 116–117, 133
Karoo region (South Africa), 33
Kashagan oil field (Kazakhstan), 62
Kennedy, Ted, 12
Keystone XL pipeline, 81–82, 176,
    203, 206, 208
Killian, Lutz, 129–130
King, David, 181
Kissinger, Henry, 76
Kivalina (Alaska), 84
Koehler, Torsten, 162
Korea, Republic of, 34
Kreutzer, David, 6
Kuwait
  Gulf War (1991) and, 14, 76, 112
  oil and, 78, 95, 134
Kyoto Protocol, 15

LaBarge gas plant (Wyoming), 60
Landsberg, Hans, 11
Layden, Kevin, 114, 117–118

levelized cost of electricity (LCOE),
    151–152
Libya, 76–77
Limits to Growth, The, 10–11
Lindzen, Richard, 85
liquefied natural gas (LNG), 30–31,
    33–34, 39
lithium, 134–136, 190
Lordstown Assembly Complex
    (Ohio), 129
Louisiana
  Deepwater Horizon oil spill, 52,
    56–58
  Hurricane Katrina and, 16, 125
  shale gas in, 42
Lovins, Amory, 9–10
"Low and Behold: Making the Most
    of Cheap Oil" (Morse), 180
Lutz, Bob, 113

Marcellus shale, 20–21
McCain, John, 97, 146, 206
McKibben, Bill, 81–82, 92
McKinsey & Company, 148–149
Media Matters, 64–65
Meredith (New York), 177
Merkel, Angela, 173
methane
  climate change and, 102
  coalbed methane, 23
  leakage of in natural gas
    production, 45–46, 102–104
  Siberian permafrost and, 92
  water contamination and,
    45–46
methanol, 40
Mexico, 18, 30, 32, 187
MiaSolé, 157–159, 166–167
Midland (Texas), 143–144
Mills, Mark, 33
Milner, Helen, 187
Mississippi, 60

Mitchell, George, 24
Mitton, Jeff, 83–84, 87–88
Mobil, 10
Montana, 54
Morse, Ed, 180
Mount Pinatubo (Philippines), 193
mountain pine beetles, 83–84,
    87–88

nahcolite, 62
naphtha, 27, 56
National Commission on the BP
    Deepwater Horizon Oil Spill
    and Offshore Drilling, 58
National Oceanic and Atmospheric
    Administration (NOAA),
    102–104
National Petroleum Council, 59
national security. *See also* energy
    security; geopolitics
  China–U.S. relations and, 78,
      183–186, 201
  Department of Defense, 169,
      200–201
  energy trade and, 35, 188–190,
      204–205
  natural gas and, 25, 35, 49, 200
  nuclear weapons, 106, 183–185
  oil and, 16, 64–65, 72, 76–79, 111,
      125, 127, 131–132, 136–137, 142,
      185, 196, 209
  rare-earth metals and, 111, 132–134,
      136
  renewable energy and, 9, 110–111,
      125, 161, 163
  sea lanes and, 78, 183–184, 205
  September 11, 2001 terrorist
      attacks and, 15–16
National Review, 164
natural gas
  automobiles and, 7, 35–41, 116,
      128–129
  carbon capture and sequestration
      and, 100–101, 172, 173
  climate change and, 97–103, 107,
      155, 177, 200, 204, 208
  coalbed methane and, 23
  community impacts of
      production, 21, 25, 46–47, 49
  compressed natural gas (CNG)
      and, 37–39
  earthquakes and, 44–45, 47
  economic development and,
      27–29, 47, 49, 192
  energy security and, 25, 35, 49, 200
  environmental concerns
      regarding, 25, 35, 44–46, 83, 86,
      97, 196, 202, 208
  estimated ultimate recovery
      (EUR) and, 41–43
  ethane and, 27
  European market and, 29–32, 204
  fracking and, 2–3, 24, 35, 45–47, 98
  gas-to-liquids (GTL), 40–41, 129
  gasoline produced from, 39–40
  government incentives and, 39, 41
  Great Recession and, 23, 25–26, 28
  greenhouse gas emissions and,
      194, 196
  horizontal drilling, 23–24, 47, 52
  jobs and, 3, 25–28, 191
  liquefied natural gas (LNG) and,
      30–31, 33–34, 39
  natural gas liquids (NGLs), 27, 56
  power plants and, 3, 35–36, 88,
      98–99, 102–103, 141, 152–153, 155,
      160, 172, 177, 196
  price of, 22–24, 28–29, 31, 34, 40,
      42–43, 172
  shale gas boom and, 23–32, 41–44,
      49, 73, 83, 97–98, 107, 145, 147,
      153, 197–198, 208
  tight gas and, 23
  water pollution and, 4, 45–46

natural gas liquids (NGLs), 27, 56
Natural Resources Defense Council
     (NRDC), 37, 60–61, 206
Nebraska, 82
Nelson, Paul, 134–135
New Mexico, 60
New Orleans (Louisiana), 16, 125
New York, 174–175, 177
Niwot Ridge (Colorado), 83–85
Nixon, Richard, 7–8, 51
North American Free Trade
     Agreement (NAFTA), 187
North Dakota, 54–56, 58
Northstar 1 well (Ohio), 44
Norway, 69
nuclear energy
     carbon emissions and, 97–99, 101,
          173, 175
     Fukushima disaster and, 172–173
     opposition to, 15, 208
     power plants and, 133, 153
     United States and, 9, 12, 15, 17,
          171, 173
nuclear weapons, 106, 183–185

Oak Ridge National Laboratory, 126,
     128
Obama, Barack
     climate change and, 97, 206
     fuel efficiency standards and, 122
     offshore oil drilling and, 56–58
     renewable energy and, 146–147,
          164
     shale gas industry jobs and, 27
offshore drilling. *See under* oil
Ohio
     earthquakes related to fracking in,
          44–45, 47
     fracking opposition in, 3–4, 22, 92
     General Motors plant in, 129
     natural gas and fracking in, 1–3,
          20–22, 26, 44–47

renewable energy in, 5–6
     tight oil in, 73
oil
     carbon dioxide enhanced oil
          recovery (CO_2-EOR) and, 60,
          170–172
     climate change and, 80, 83, 85–86,
          88–90, 93–97, 101, 107–108, 110,
          136–137, 182, 194, 196, 200
     developing world's demand for,
          68–69
     economic development and, 74–75,
          127, 192
     global market dynamics of, 31,
          65–70, 72, 77, 95, 126, 137,
          188–190
     jobs and, 73–74, 82, 191, 196
     land use and, 175–177, 202
     national security and, 16, 64–65,
          72, 76–79, 111, 125, 127, 131–132,
          136–137, 142, 185, 196, 209
     offshore drilling and, 15, 52–53,
          56–58, 61, 205–206
     peak oil hypothesis and, 179–182,
          194
     price of, 13–14, 31, 38–39, 53, 57–59,
          62–68, 70–73, 75–79, 82, 95–96,
          112–113, 115–117, 123, 125–127,
          129–131, 136–137, 142, 181–182,
          188, 196, 199–200
     tight oil and, 51, 54–56, 61–63, 73,
          80, 82–83, 93–94, 96–97
oil sands, 52, 54, 81–83, 93–94,
     96–97, 175, 188, 207
oil shale, 61–64
Oil Shock (1973), 7–8, 50–51, 64, 112, 131
Oklahoma, 180
Organization of Petroleum
     Exporting Countries (OPEC),
     7, 13, 66–69, 90, 95–96
outer continental shelf of the United
     States (OCS), 57, 82

Pavilion (Wyoming), 45
peak oil hypothesis, 179–182, 194
Pearl project (Qatar), 39–41
Pennsylvania
    manufacturing in, 161–162
    shale gas drilling in, 20–21, 42,
        46–49
Permian Basin (Texas), 55
Perry, Rick, 120
Pickens, T. Boone, 37
PNGV (Partnership for a New
    Generation of Vehicles)
    program, 116
Poland, 29, 32
policy recommendations, 198–205
power plants
    air pollution and, 100
    carbon dioxide emissions and,
        60–61
    coal and, 3, 17, 88, 98–100, 103, 107,
        141, 153, 158, 160–161, 168, 170,
        196
    natural gas and, 3, 35–36, 88,
        98–99, 102–103, 141, 152–153, 155,
        160, 172, 177, 196
    regulation of, 156, 160–161
    renewable energy sources and,
        152, 160, 168
Promised Land, 174–175
propane, 56
Prudhoe Bay (Alaska), 8

Qatar, 28, 31–32, 39–41

RAND Corporation shale oil study,
    62–63
rare-earth metals, 111, 132–135, 190
Reagan, Ronald, 11–13
Reilly, William, 14
renewable energy
    Bloomberg New Energy Finance
        report on, 149

Clean Energy Ministerial (CEM)
    summit and, 148
climate change and, 97–98, 170,
    178, 194, 196–197
cost of, 6, 150, 151, 153, 155–156, 161,
    165, 197, 199–200
defense spending comparison
    and, 169, 201
economic development and, 147,
    162–163, 166, 191–192
electricity grid integration
    and, 151
energy security and, 9, 110–111,
    125, 161, 163
environmental opposition to,
    174–175
exports and, 166–168, 204
government support for, 6, 13, 14,
    17, 146–147, 150, 153–154, 156,
    158–159, 161, 164–165, 168, 177,
    182, 191, 202, 207, 209
greenhouse gas emissions and,
    147
jobs and, 6, 147, 161–165,
    168, 177
land use and, 175–176
McKinsey & Company report on,
    148–149
natural gas and, 153
power plants and, 152, 160, 168
renewable energy standard (RES)
    and, 155–156
renewable portfolio standards
    and, 154
research and development (R&D)
    of, 156–157
Solyndra and, 146–147
"Spanish study" on, 163–165
technological advances in
    (expand), 159–161, 177
venture capital and, 158–159
Rifle (Colorado), 61–62

Russia
  natural gas and, 29–35, 204
  oil and, 78, 95, 181
  Siberian permafrost and, 91–92

Salazar, Ken, 57
Sammarone, Chuck, 44, 47
Santa Barbara (California) Oil Spill
    (1969), 10
Santoro, Renee, 101–104
Saudi Arabia. *See also* Organization
    of Petroleum Exporting
    Countries (OPEC)
  ethelyne and, 28
  Gulf War and, 14, 76
  oil production in, 53, 66, 78, 95,
    180–181, 188
  oil reserves in, 12, 51, 61, 133–134, 179
  September 11, 2001 terrorist
    attacks and, 16
  United States and, 78
Savitz, Jacqueline, 56
Schroeder, Gerhard, 32
Schulz, Mark, 116, 118
Senkaku Islands, 132
September 11, 2001 terrorist attacks,
    15–16, 125
shale gas. *See under* natural gas
shale oil. *See* tight oil
Shell Oil, 27, 39–41, 63, 206
Siberian permafrost, 91–92
Sichuan Tengzhong Heavy
    Industrial Machinery
    Company, 109
Sieminski, Adam, 52
Sierra Club, 83
Silicon Valley (California), 5, 36–37,
    116–118, 157–159, 166–167
Simmons, Matthew, 179
  social cost of carbon, 89–90
solar energy. *See also* renewable
    energy

California and, 154, 157–159,
    166–167
China and, 149–150, 157,
    166–167
  climate change and, 97, 196–197
  cost of, 148–149, 151–153
  India and, 167–168
  land use and, 175–177
  manufacturing requirements for,
    157–158, 162
  technological advances in, 145,
    148, 150–151, 157, 162
Solyndra, 146–147, 159
South Africa, 32–33
South China Sea conflict, 132–134
Soviet Union
  Cold War and, 10, 16, 169, 185
  natural gas production in, 103
Spain, 163–165
Stanolind Oil, 24
Stockman, David, 11
stoichiometric gasoline direct
    injection, 119
Strategic Petroleum Reserve,
    18, 205
sugarcane. *See under* biofuels

Talisman Energy, 48
Talisman Terry, the Friendly
    Frackasaurus, 48
Taylor, Warren, 20–22, 43–44, 46
Tesla Motors, 118
Texas
  carbon emissions in, 146
  electricity usage in, 143–144, 151
  ethanol and, 120
  oil production in, 52, 180
  shale gas in, 42
  tight oil in, 55–56
  wind power in, 144, 146, 154
Three Mile Island (Pennsylvania), 15
tight gas. *See under* natural gas

tight oil
  carbon dioxide emissions and, 93,
    96–97
  geology of, 55
  production process and, 54–55, 63
  United States and, 51, 54–56,
    61–63, 73, 80, 82–83, 93–94
TOTAL (French oil company),
  51, 62
Toyota Motor Company
  battery technology and, 134
  Prius model and, 97, 114, 116, 122,
    135, 141
Trans-Alaskan Pipeline, 8
trucks. *See* automobiles
Twilight in the Desert (Simmons), 179

U.S. Chamber of Commerce,
  205–207
U.S. Climate Action Partnership
  (U.S.-CAP), 206–207
Ukraine, 29
United Arab Emirates, 95
United Kingdom, 69, 137, 183
Uruguay Round (trade
  negotiations), 186
Utica shale, 2, 21, 73

V&M, 44
Venezuela, 69, 78, 133–134
Victor, David, 154
Viera, John, 119, 122–123
Vietnam War, 7, 10
Volkswagen Passat, 39

water pollution. *See under* natural gas
West Antarctic Ice Sheet, 92

West Virginia, 48–49
wind energy. *See also* renewable
    energy
  climate change and, 98, 196–197
  community relations and,
    174–175, 177
  cost of, 149–151, 153
  dynamics of demand for, 152
  electricity production and, 145
  land use and, 175–177
  projections regarding, 144–145,
    149–150
  rare-earth metals and, 132
  technological advances in, 148, 150
  Texas and, 144, 146, 154
Windfall (Israel), 174–175
World Trade Organization (WTO),
    186–187
World War I, 180, 183
World War II, 180, 190
Wouk, Victor, 115
Wyoming, 45, 56, 60, 83

Yanosek, Kassia, 154
Yergin, Daniel, 181
Youngstown (Ohio), 3, 26, 44, 129

zero-carbon energy
  carbon capture and sequestration
    (CCS), 61, 100–101, 170–172,
    173, 200, 202, 209
  nuclear energy, 9, 12, 15, 17, 97–99,
    101, 133, 153, 172–173, 175
  renewable energy, 6, 9, 13, 14, 17,
    97–98, 110–111, 125, 146–170,
    174–178, 182, 191–192, 194,
    196–202, 204, 207, 209